WAR
CRIMES

Highly civilized human beings are flying overhead, trying to kill me . . . Most of them, I have no doubt, are kindly, law-abiding men who would never dream of committing murder in private life.

George Orwell

WAR CRIMES

*Underworld Britain
in the Second World War*

M J Trow

Pen & Sword
MILITARY

First published in Great Britain in 2008 by
Pen & Sword Military
an imprint of
Pen & Sword Books Ltd
47 Church Street
Barnsley
South Yorkshire
S70 2AS

Copyright © M J Trow, 2008

ISBN 978 1 84415 728 0

A CIP catalogue record for this book is
available from the British Library.

Typeset in Sabon by
Phoenix Typesetting, Auldgirth, Dumfriesshire

Printed and bound in England by
Biddles Ltd, King's Lynn

Pen & Sword Books Ltd incorporates the imprints of Pen & Sword
Aviation, Pen & Sword Maritime, Pen & Sword Military, Wharncliffe
Local History, Pen & Sword Select, Pen & Sword Military Classics and
Leo Cooper.

For a complete list of Pen & Sword titles please contact
PEN & SWORD BOOKS LIMITED
47 Church Street, Barnsley, South Yorkshire, S70 2AS, England
E-mail: enquiries@pen-and-sword.co.uk
Website: www.pen-and-sword.co.uk

Contents

List of Illustrations

This book is about the thousands of people who did not
behave themselves during the Second World War.
It is dedicated to the millions who did.

CHAPTER ONE

'Don't You Know There's a War On?'

'The day war broke out, my missus said to me . . .' became the comforting, tireless catchphrase of Rob Wilton, one of the Second World War's favourite comedians. As long as Rob and his missus could reminisce about that day – and do it with humour – everything would be all right, wouldn't it?

On the day itself, an altogether grimmer broadcast was delivered to the nation, by a man not really known for his one-liners. A querulous, out of touch voice coming out of everybody's valve wireless on Sunday, 3 September 1939:

> I am speaking to you from the Cabinet Room at 10 Downing Street. This morning the British Ambassador in Berlin handed the German Government a final note stating that, unless we heard from them by eleven o'clock that they were prepared at once to withdraw their troops from Poland, a state of war would exist between us. I have to tell you now that no such undertaking has been received and that consequently this country is at war with Germany.

This was to be the People's War: a unique experience in which everybody, it seemed, was thrust into uniform, was watched, whispered about, expected to 'do their bit' in a hundred different ways.

It promised – and delivered – horror on an unprecedented scale. Spain had seen it already. On 27 April 1937, the Condor Legion, comprising Heinkel 111s, Dornier 17s and Junkers 52s, complete with fighter escort, snarled south of the Pyrenees and gave the world in general – and the town of Guernica in particular – its first taste of Blitzkrieg – lightning war.[1] A reporter who was there wrote:

> I saw a priest in one group. I stopped the car and went up to him. His face was blackened, his clothes in tatters. He couldn't talk. He just pointed to the flames, still about four miles away, then whispered, 'Aviones . . . bombas . . . mucho, mucho.' In the city, soldiers were collecting charred bodies. They were sobbing like children. There were flames and smoke and grit and the smell of burning human flesh was nauseating . . . The shocked survivors all had the same story to tell: aeroplanes, bullets, fire.[2]

We had it all to come.

But some believed the war had started already. It was Friday, 25 August 1939 – the day on which the British government signed an alliance treaty with Poland – and Broadgate, in the thriving Midlands city of Coventry, was crowded with shoppers. Nobody noticed the bike parked on the kerb outside John Astley and Sons paint merchants, nor the anonymous package in the basket on its handlebars. But everybody noticed at 2.32 p.m. when all hell broke loose. Glass flew everywhere as twenty-five shop windows exploded.

Coventry was the home of the motor car and several cars were hurled into the air by the explosion of the blast. When the debris landed and the screaming stopped, the place looked like a battlefield – a grim foretaste of what would follow fourteen months later when Coventry's experiences of the Blitz would create a new verb – 'to coventrate'. And in that battlefield, 21-year-old Elsie Ansell lay dead. She had been shopping for her wedding, due in two weeks time. So did fifty-year-old Gwilym Rowland, who worked for the Corporation. And pensioner James Clay, eighty-one. And thirty-year-old clerk, Rex Gentle. And the shop assistant in his first job after leaving school, John Corbett, fifteen . . .

In analyzing the murder count of the Second World War, the Broadgate bombing does not fit the pattern. Bombs of this type, planted by the IRA as part of their on-going war of attrition, but in terms of international politics, timed to perfection, are indiscriminate. That is their purpose. Other murders can be classified by motive, links between killer and victim; bombings cannot. In the event, two men hanged for this crime. Peter Barnes and James Richards died at the experienced hands of Thomas Pierrepoint – 'Uncle Tom' – and his assistants at Birmingham gaol on Wednesday, 7 February 1940. Richards had made a short speech at his trial before Mister Justice Singleton on 14 December, ending with the defiant words 'God Bless Ireland'. But all that was to come.

Even before Chamberlain's message to the nation, Britons were on the move, either to mobilization centres or safety. Even so, the curiously nosey Mass Observation Unit reported that only one person in five expected war. And they must have been astonished when the BBC's infant television station, broadcasting from Alexandra Palace, was suddenly closed down in the middle of a Mickey Mouse cartoon. The football matches planned for Saturday, 2 September were largely cancelled because of a shortage of players. Most of the West Ham team, for example, found themselves in the itchy, unfriendly khaki battledress of the Essex Regiment's searchlight section by lunchtime.

That night, as the newly created Air Raid Wardens turned instantly into 'Little Hitlers' by setting up blackout instructions, an edgy and belligerent House of Commons, lights still blazing, demanded that the Prime Minister, Neville Chamberlain, take on Hitler's bullying Third Reich once and for all. 'Speak for England, Arthur,' roared Leo Amery across the House to Arthur Greenwood, the deputy Labour leader. And consensus politics forced Chamberlain into action. It must have been heartbreaking to Amery that six years later, his feckless son John, already a gun-runner for the Fascists in war-torn Spain, was hanged for treason. He offered his services to Hitler in 1942, made Nazi propaganda speeches on the wireless and even formed a military unit, the rather grandly named Legion of St George, to fight the Russians on the Eastern Front. Arthur Greenwood may have spoken for England, but John Amery did not.

That day, Sunday, 3 September, the ghastly wail of the air raid sirens was heard for the first – but by no means the last – time over London. It was 11.27 a.m. People on the streets found themselves herded by men in tin hats with the letters ARP stencilled on them into the Underground stations. Worshippers in St Paul's were led by vergers into the crypt. In fact, it was a false alarm. A lone French fighter had come, unannounced, into British airspace. And in an example of what today we call friendly fire, the usually efficient early warning Radar system had developed a technical fault and two units of fighters found themselves firing on each other in the skies over a disbelieving London. Two planes went down and a pilot died – the first of many whom Winston Churchill would christen 'The Few'.

What followed was even more odd. The lull before the storm, certainly, but it went on for so long that people began to wonder whether there would be a storm at all. Those who remembered the start of the last world war – the one that would end all wars – recalled flags and bands and lines of soldier-boys, smiling and waving to their loved ones, everyone confident that it would all be over by Christmas. But this was the 'Phoney War', when nothing military seemed to be happening at all. The French and the Germans felt the same – it was *drôle de guerre* (the funny war) and *Sitzkrieg* (the armchair war).

But in fact a lot was happening. Under a hitherto unknown mass movement code-named 'Yellow' and 'Black', over 3½ million people were shunted around the country in six weeks. Some of this was official. The BBC, its toe in the waters of television removed 'for the duration', decamped to Bristol and Evesham. The Bank of England scurried out of Threadneedle Street to Overton in Hampshire. The cultural heritage of the country, as displayed in the National Gallery, was wrapped up carefully in a cave in a slate quarry in North Wales.

Shortly before dawn on the last day of August, huge numbers of children – shivering with excitement and incomprehension – appeared in 'crocodiles' marshalled by teachers and tearful parents. As if some terrible Piper were luring them into the mountains for a better life, the 'townies', clutching toothbrushes, sandwiches, a favourite toy, comb, handkerchief and the already ubiquitous – and pointless – gas mask in a cardboard box, were herded into waiting trains. No one in those early days could have imagined that within less than two years, and all over Europe trainloads of Jews would be departing for an altogether different destination.

The children had gone to the schools as embarkation points and were then conveyed by buses to the nearest station. In London, seventy-two Underground stations served a similar function. The figures are staggering, if only because an official exodus like this had never been seen before in Britain. There were 827,000 children, 524 mothers with children under school-age. Thirteen thousand mothers were pregnant; 7,000 children were blind or handicapped and there were 103,000 teachers.

Not surprisingly, there were hiccups. Journeys took hours and with no corridor-trains, carriages soon began to smell. Hotels and country schools ready to take dozens, received nobody; tiny country cottages were awash with children who did not know what a cow was or had any idea of the seasons. The evacuation experience, though nostalgically captured in fiction by Michelle Magorian in *Goodnight, Mister Tom* was not a success. The kids began to drift back. And criminal psychologists, writing in the years ahead, believed with considerable justification that this evacuee generation was the most criminal the country had ever known.

But a considerable amount of evacuation was not official (i.e. organized by a well meaning, if woefully inexperienced, government): those wealthy enough, fearing a Guernica on their own doorstep, fled the cities, especially London, to their country cottages or to stay with rural relatives. J B Priestley, a regular contributor to the new and widely read *Picture Post*, wrote of Bournemouth in July 1941 that the place was enjoying a peacetime summer, with hotels, dinner dances, tea parties, theatres, cinemas and orchestras. It was all part of a mythology, which continued while the war lasted, that the rich were less affected than the poor, culminating in the famous line from the Queen after the bombing of Buckingham Palace, that she could at last 'look the East End in the face'. But if the 'them and us' notion was largely a myth, it bred resentment and it led directly to crime. Even the Ministry that imposed rationing had to admit that the system was 'inequitable'.

On the day before the IRA's bombing of Coventry, Chamberlain's Cabinet put before both Houses the Emergency Powers (Defence) Bill. Passed by 457 votes to 11, the regulations that came into play as a result gave the government more power than any in modern history. The aim was laudable enough – to secure 'public safety, the defence of the Realm, the maintenance of public order and the efficient prosecution of any war in which his Majesty may be engaged'.[3] Most people welcomed this as a necessary evil, but the scale of the evil was hardly recognized. The more astute would have noted the irony that across the Channel within a few months, such regulations would exist everywhere the Nazis held sway. And we were supposed to be fighting for freedom.

Four days later, regulations came into force regarding the ownership of cameras and what kind of photographs could be taken with them. Owners of racing pigeons had to have special permits and were watched closely lest their feathered friends were acting as go-betweens for *Herr* Hitler. Most disturbing of all, in its paranoia to find and destroy a supposed Fifth Column operating in our midst, the new regulations could override Parliamentary sovereignty, ignore *habeas corpus* and invert the centuries-old dictum that a man was innocent until proven guilty. There were those who grumbled uneasily that democracy was dead in Chamberlain's England. And if anybody heard them, they could be sent to prison. E S Turner wrote of the Emergency Powers (Defence) Bill, which became law nearly two weeks before war was declared: 'One day sufficed to turn Britain into a totalitarian state.'[4]

Income tax – that 'evil' introduced by William Pitt's government as a temporary measure to beat Revolutionary France – rocketed to 7s 6d in the pound (37.5 per cent). The government also ordered the manufacture, more ominously, of 100,000 cardboard coffins in readiness for the aerial bombardment that was bound to come – eventually.

A bombardment of a different kind came out of the newly created Ministry of Information: leaflet upon leaflet telling people what to do 'if the invader comes'. Southampton was typical; its local Invasion Committee published information so that everyone in the area would know it was working hard for public safety:

During the present period the Committee is engaged in making preparations to deal with the local problems which will arise in invasion such as:

Organization of civilian labour to assist the military in preparing defence works, digging trenches, clearing roads etc.

Care of wounded.

Housing and sheltering the homeless.

Emergency cooking and feeding.

Emergency water supplies.

Messenger services.

And car owners got the message too:

Immobilization of vehicles in the event of invasion . . . It is important that owners of vehicles should satisfy themselves that they can carry out the order at any time without delay.

The most famous leaflet was a full-blown booklet called *If the Invader Comes*, published in June 1940:

Do not give any German anything. Do not tell him anything. Hide your food and your bicycles. Hide your maps . . . Think always of your country before you think of yourself.

Meanwhile – at least before the bombs started and privations bit deep – there was a real sense of community. People who had never spoken to each other cracked jokes (usually at Hitler's expense) and worked together to cope with the blackout, evacuation and the novelty of a government that was, however well-meaning, almost arbitrary in its style and attitude.

To enforce the regulations, an army of 'Little Hitlers' sprang up, blowing whistles and barking orders. 'Put that light out!' became the best-known catchphrase of 1940. Photographs of the time show pompous little men in glasses and Hitlerian moustaches with polished tin hats, gas masks in canvas bags and (almost always) a cup of tea. One definition of the meaning of ARP (Air Raid Precaution) painted on those tin hats was Angling Round Pubs.

Luckily for everybody, the ARP wardens could laugh at themselves as well:

> Big-helmet Wilkie they call me,
> Big-helmet Wilkie, that's me:
> Now that they've made me a warden
> I get my torch batteries free![5]

A blackout was rigidly enforced. Silly stories circulated widely that Dorniers and Heinkels bombing at 15,000 feet could see cigarette lighters and matches glowing in the dark, so all lights had to be extinguished. Thick curtains were *de rigueur*. Cardboard shields were fitted over car headlights, making driving at night a seriously dangerous business. On 8 December 1941, a high-speed car chase took place in the centre of Glasgow, when a police car followed a lorry involved in a robbery for 140 miles, sending pedestrians – including point duty policemen – leaping for their lives. The chase was carried out in total darkness with neither vehicle using headlights. It ended with the lorry crashing and both its occupants charged with burglary.[6]

Once rationing had been imposed, petrol was so difficult to obtain that casual car usage became a thing of the past anyway. The army of officials kept up the bombardment, asking everybody if their journey was really necessary? One man who put his car into cold storage for the duration was Albert Pierrepoint, the public executioner. When called upon to do his grim duty by the Home Office, he always travelled by train. Those who had to travel relied on white-painted kerbs to keep them on the straight and narrow, and in towns, men walked around for safety at night with their shirt-tails hanging out.

Even so, at a time of fewer cars than usual, the accident rate on the roads rocketed. A cartoon of 1941 shows two sketches 'before and after' wartime restrictions. In the first, a rather aggrieved trio of car-users are stopped by a uniformed constable, who asks to see the driver's licence. In the second, a brainwashed, defeated trio are handing over a sheaf of papers to the constable, who is now saying 'May I see your driving licence please and your petrol permit and your insurance certificate and your identity cards and your authority for employment of a mechanical vehicle and your area passes and your registration book and the name of your employer and documents setting forth nature of employment and reason for which journey undertaken?' It was not so very far from the truth.

Huge billboards were the outward sign of a country on the verge of hysteria. The Ministry of Information warned people of an active Fifth Column of spies operating in their midst. Censorship became a way of life. At first, even good news was suppressed by newspapers and radio alike. When the *Daily Mirror* questioned what Churchill's government was doing in the summer of 1940, the new Prime Minister held talks with key members of his War Cabinet about the real possibility of closing the paper down. When an American journalist asked a censor the text of a message dropped in thousands by the RAF over Germany, he was told, 'We are not allowed to disclose information which may be of value to the enemy.'[7]

The newly instituted and highly influential *Picture Post* ran a series of articles on this topic, with blacked-out rectangles where photographs should have been. A spoof signpost read:

Keep out! This is a private war. The War Office, the Admiralty, the Air Ministry and the Ministry of Information are engaged in a war against the Nazis. They are on no account to be disturbed. Nothing is to be photographed. No one is to come near.

'Is this war?' the *Picture Post* asked in its caption. 'Is this democracy? Is this common sense?' And, with its tongue firmly in its cheek, it produced a photograph of Lord Raglan and two colleagues at the Picture Censorship Department with the caption: 'Without their co-operation and far-seeing initiative we could never have presented these exciting pictures of Britain at war.'[8]

In full paranoia however, the Ministry of Information swept on with its now famous posters – 'Careless Talk Costs Lives' – in which the cartoonist Fougasse portrayed casual conversation overheard by Hitler, Goebbels and Goering. 'Keep It Under Your Hat' the hoardings said, 'Tittle-Tattle Lost The Battle', 'Be Like Dad – Keep Mum'.

On a more positive note, thousands were encouraged to buy War Bonds and to Dig For Victory. Flower beds became allotments; carrots and parsnips replaced petunias and Michaelmas daisies. Everyone was encouraged to 'do their bit'.

Everyone, that is, except aliens. In London, in one month of 1939, 6,000 aliens were rounded up by the CID operating from Scotland Yard. Anyone with a German – and later, Italian – surname was suspect. Ice cream parlours virtually vanished overnight. The irony was that some of these internees were actually evacuees from Nazi-occupied Europe, just as dedicated to fighting the German threat as any Briton. Nevertheless, as the *Daily Mail* (in particular) demanded that we 'Intern the Lot!' in its banner headlines, various categories of aliens were classified according to the potential threat they offered. It was not until 1942 that this sort of hysteria died down.

Rationing came next. From December 1939, butter and bacon; four months later, meat. Ersatz substitutes appeared, like powdered egg and the indescribable 'snoek' (tinned fish) and rich, sickly whale meat. The coupons in the ration books dictated that one egg a fort-night was allowed. 'Dried egg,' said Lord Woolton, Minister of Food, 'is not a substitute at all.' Most people took his words liter-ally. Recipe books of the time, such as that produced by Freddie Grisewood and Mabel Constanduros, entitled *The Kitchen Front*, based on wireless broadcasts, advocated producing vast quantities of spaghetti, noodles, gnocchi or risotto. Unfortunately, the vast majority of the British public had never heard of these, still less tried them, so the exhortation was largely wasted. Everyone, especially the mothers, went hungry.

Clothing coupons arrived in June 1940, by which time, the 'miracle' of Dunkirk had happened, Churchill had replaced Chamberlain at Number Ten and 'Fortress Britain' was a reality. Everything became 'Utility' – wide lapels and turn-ups disappeared from men's jackets and trousers; pleats from women's skirts and frills from their knickers. For the patriotic, however, an advertise-ment in the *Birmingham Post* in December 1939 was still able to offer:

These slick little panties, beautifully embroidered with the 'Washing on the Siegfried line' and the slogan 'England Expects' might come in the category of 'improperganda' but as a gift for any lingerie drawer, they're certain of a rapturous welcome.

There was no lipstick and no stockings and queuing for anything became almost a national pastime. A common joke in the forties was that housewives would automatically tag on to the end of any line of people as a knee-jerk reaction. An estimated one million of them waited patiently for hours every day, often with their own newspaper for wrapping, because paper itself was in short supply. By the end of the queue, they would discover whether anything was left for them and how many coupons it would cost. And the most common initials heard throughout the war came from the housewives' whisper to the shopkeeper – 'AUC?' ('Anything under the counter?').

The wireless became the mainstay of peoples' lives. The BBC – still staffed by rather stuffy individuals who broadcast in evening wear – pumped out from Alexandra Palace and its Home Service all sorts of propaganda, conscious, unconscious, black and white. Newsreaders, at a time when whole families listened avidly, became household names – 'Here is the nine o'clock news and this is Alvar Liddell reading it.'

'Are the little ones used to seeing you in YOUR [gas] mask?' a children's programme asked in the first winter of the war, 'make a game of it, calling it "Mummy's Funny Face".'[9] In fact, by January 1940, most people had stopped carrying gas masks; the things were just too inconvenient and would not readily fit into a handbag.

It was via the radio that the propaganda war was being waged in earnest. While German broadcasts in October 1940 claimed that 'London is facing riots, the authorities prove to be helpless and everywhere there is wildest confusion', Churchill's voice double[10] was able to be more accurate:

I see the damage done by the enemy attacks; but I also see, side by side with the devastation and amid the ruins, quiet, confident, bright and smiling eyes, beaming with a consciousness of being associated with a cause far higher and wider than any human or personal issue. I can see the spirit of an unconquerable people.

For radio escapism, Uncle Mac said 'Hello children, everywhere!' to the younger listeners, while the older ones fell about at the antics of Tommy Handley and co. in *ITMA* [*It's That Man Again*], which put the war in perspective and laughed at the unthinkable. As self-appointed Minister of Aggravation and Mysteries, Handley announced on 12 December 1939:

> It is my duty tonight on the umpteenth day of the war against Depression to explain to you that I have seven hundred further restrictions to impose upon you . . . some of the most irritating regulations you have ever heard of.

At the same time, he was able to 'quote' from various 'German newspapers', including '*Der Diplomatsche-damgibberische unt Politischedamrubbische mit Sauerkraut unt Saussiche stuffed mit Garbische*' with such authority that many found him nearly as entertaining as the traitor William Joyce ('Lord Haw Haw'), broadcasting from Berlin. So popular was *ITMA* that wags said if Hitler chose to invade on a Thursday night between half past eight and nine o'clock, he'd meet no resistance at all.

From February 1940, the Forces Programme provided twelve hours each day of light entertainment, the big band sound of Henry Hall and the oily smooth singing voice of Hutch. By far the BBC's biggest property however, was Vera Lynn, the Forces' Sweetheart and everybody looked forward to bluebirds flying over the white cliffs of Dover, rather than the Hurricanes and Spitfires that routinely patrolled there.

But the biggest form of escapism was the cinema. Between 25 million and 30 million tickets were sold each week and queues formed – again – outside Gaumonts and Majestics and Regals all over the country, not just to watch the newsreels and propaganda 'shorts' but to get away from it all, to watch Clark Gable not giving a damn about Vivien Leigh in *Gone With The Wind* and Nöel Coward being undeniably fine in *In Which We Serve*. No doubt cinema-goers rolled in the aisle in 1942 when an amazingly cock-sure Errol Flynn, in *Desperate Journey*, said 'Now for Australia and a crack at those Japs!'

In January 1940, 2 million men between the ages of nineteen and forty-one were called up. They left behind wives, sweethearts, parents, and above all children – who began to run wild. Not every teacher could claim to be – like the miners and munitions workers – in a reserved occupation, nor did they want to be, and they were rushed, with all other conscripts, into training camps on their way to combat zones. Whether they found themselves in Catterick, Crete or North Africa, they were not in their schools – and neither were many of their charges. When the bombing started, schools in inner cities were hit and children, many of them evacuees who had returned under their own volition, were left to their own devices. Bomb-scarred Britain was one vast adventure playground for this generation and it carried untold hazards. Two of them, whose names would become household words briefly in the early 1950s, were Derek Bentley and Christopher Craig. Two others, whose notoriety came later, were the East End twins, Ronnie and Reggie Kray.

If the Dunkirk experience and the Battle of Britain dominated the first year of the war, what made it the People's War was the arrival of the Blitz – saturation bombing of major cities, which left London with 2,000 casualties after the first night. Buckingham Palace was scratched; the East End flattened. Between 7 September 1940 and the end of the year, 13,339 Londoners were killed and 17,937 badly injured. On the single night of 10 May 1941 – the night Hitler's deputy Rudolf Hess flew to Scotland – 1,436 people were killed and 1,752 seriously hurt. 'London could take it' – but only just.

Plymouth, Coventry and Hull bore the brunt of Goering's Luftwaffe attacks beyond the capital:

'You laid the dead of London at our doors,' the poet Archibald Macleish wrote to Ed Morrow, the American journalist whose Blitz broadcasts reached America, 'and we knew the dead were our dead – were all men's dead – were mankind's dead . . . [11]

[13]

Anderson shelters, built furiously in the opening weeks of the war, now, at last, came into their own. Everyone was *supposed* to carry a gas mask and practise wearing it every day. ARP wardens gave lectures on aircraft recognition. Classes were held to help people recognize unexploded bombs and differentiate between various types of poison gas.[12] Tom Harrisson, one of the founders of the historically invaluable Mass Observation Unit in the late thirties, wrote a description of an East End shelter for the *New Statesman* in September 1940:

When you get over the shock of seeing so many sprawling people, you are overcome with the smell of humanity and dirt. Dirt abounds everywhere. The floors are never swept and are filthy. People are sleeping on piles of rubbish. The passages are loaded with dirt. There is no escaping it. The arches are dark and grim.

There they sit in darkness, head of one against the feet of the next. There is no room to move, hardly any room to stretch.[13]

Some people preferred the bombs to the smell and took their chances above ground. In London, the Underground platforms, escalators and in places, even the track, became camping grounds for a populace bloodied but unbowed.

By the spring of 1941, the Ministry of Labour's figures made grim reading. The average British family (if there could actually be such a thing in the People's War) was living on less than £5 a week. Rent was 10s 6d, clothes 9s 6d, light and fuel 6s 5d, food £1 14s 1d. Ernest Bevin, the Minister of Labour, urged women to do their bit: 'I cannot offer them a delightful life,' he warned. He could not even offer them the carrot of the vote, which had been dangled before women on the eve of the First World War. That had been obtained for all women by 1928. It did offer freedom, however. Mass Observation reports of the time are full of the greater horizons and hope that women experienced. By April, all women between the ages of twenty and twenty-one had been registered and were working in some capacity. They wore the brown corduroy jodhpurs of the Land Army or the blue serge of munitions workers. They drove buses, trams and trains. Still others were in uniform, working behind the scenes with the Armed Forces, flying Spitfires from factories to airfields, plotting ship movements on Admiralty tables, connecting the fighting world via telephone and typing millions of letters. This was all so different from the American experience that when the 'Yanks' arrived they were warned that some officers were female and they were to be taken seriously – 'she didn't get her medals for knitting'.

And the strain began to tell. Molly Lefebure was a 22-year-old secretary in 1941, when she went to work for the Home Office pathologist Dr Keith Simpson, sitting alongside him, making notes while he carried out post-mortems on murder victims and suicides. She spoke of war-weariness:

> It was a real illness . . . and as the war went on, almost everybody fell victim to it . . . Some it made drink a lot. Others took to bed – with others – a lot. Some became hideously gay, brave and hearty. Others became sardonic and bored. Some seriously depressed. The Cockneys sharpened their celebrated wit until it had an edge which cut as painfully and bitterly as grass. A few took to prayer . . . [14]

The Canadians had already arrived in their thousands, as part of the British Empire contingent, but it took Japan's attack on the naval base at Pearl Harbor on 7 December 1941 to bring America in. The first troops came ashore in Northern Ireland a month later. They were 'overpaid, oversexed and over here', although most of them denied the first two. They brought candy, nylons, gum and vast temptation – especially for young women. The jokes were legion: 'Have you heard about the new Utility knickers? One Yank and they're off!' Meanwhile, President Roosevelt's government issued stern warnings to its troops:

> Don't make fun of the British speech or accents. *Never* criticize the King or Queen . . . Stop and think before you sound off about lukewarm beer and cold, boiled potatoes . . . [15]

And towards the end, when the Americans and the Canadians and the Poles and the free French had gone, via the beaches of Normandy into the dazzling morning that was D-Day, pushing on in a crusade of liberation to Berlin itself, came the Doodlebugs, the last deadly gasp of Hitler's promised thousand year Reich – V1 and V2 rockets that brought the second Blitz and new terror to the cities.

Crime – however we read the statistics – rocketed too: though not as much as it might have done. In 1939 over 300,000 crimes of all types were reported in England and Wales.[16] By the end of the war, the figure was 475,000 – an increase of well over 60 per cent. Keith Simpson, at the sharp and usually unpleasant end of some of this crime, had his own theories of the cause:

> Emergency regulations, uniforms, drafting, service orders and a life of discipline cramp the freedom of many young men and during the long periods of wartime training and waiting, not a few of them got bored – 'browned-off' was the common term. Some missed their wives or girlfriends and got into trouble with local girls and camp followers . . . urged on by long periods of sex starvation. So . . . there was a steady flow of rapes (some with strangling and other violence), of assaults (some fatal), of abortions and infanticides, of breaking into 'deserted' houses (sometimes with violence), all arising from the changes in life that were thrust by service conditions on ordinary people.[17]

Because he was the Home Office pathologist, murder was the crime that filled Simpson's life, but it was not the only game in town. Read this opening chapter again, this time from the point of view of opportunities for crime. There were the thoughtless criminals, never quite able to come to terms with the reality of war or the government's sweeping powers. They left their curtains open in the blackout, failed to put tape over their glass – both punishable offences by 1940. They talked down Britain's war effort, moaning about Chamberlain's lack of action, Churchill's warmongering; for that, they could serve time at His Majesty's pleasure. They chatted too casually in pubs; as one Canadian poster had it – the soldier told his sweetheart (all about the troop train); the sweetheart told her father; the father talked at his club (where a spy overheard); the spy instructed the saboteur; the saboteur wrecked the train. There were the political criminals – people whose instincts pre-war had been to admire Adolf Hitler and Benito Mussolini – they were now classed as traitors. Just for having a foreign name people were rounded up and imprisoned in 1940, as were the conscientious objectors whose fathers had suffered a similar fate in the last war.

There were the selfish criminals, not prepared to 'tighten their belts' and 'make do and mend' like everyone else. Some of these were professionals, men who had made a living from crime before the war and now saw a way of even greater gain once it had started. They became Black Marketeers, thieves and receivers of stolen goods, who could find their way around the restrictions of the rationing system. There were the pilferers, who stole goods in short supply from docks and railway stations or from their own workplaces. The thousands of Americans, Canadians, Poles and Free French stationed here, because of the boredom Simpson alludes to, got into scrapes with each other and the locals. In the case of the Americans in particular, they brought their racial tensions and their gun culture to a country that had little experience of either. They had sex with underage girls, lured, Pied Piper-like, to the big cities. Some, like the Canadian Cree August Sangret, killed them.

The combination of rationed goods, shattered shops and the darkness of the blackout proved too much of a temptation for many people. There was the bomb lark, of claiming compensation for a house that was undamaged; the billeting lark, which claimed compensation for housing troops who had already moved on. The downside of the extraordinary heroism that was Coventry was the rate of looting that routinely happened after air raids. The penalty for this, in theory, was death by hanging – or at best life imprisonment – but in reality, it was fourteen years 'inside'.

The bottom line was that life became cheap. The majority of Britons behaved themselves, followed instructions, obeyed orders, got on with a grim life because it was in their nature to do so. To buckle and to surrender, as the Germans hoped, was unthinkable. But that did not mean that all was well. Tom Harrisson might have been concerned with the grime in air raid shelters, but a London magistrate in November 1940 had other worries:

> The things that are going on now in these public shelters are very dreadful. For a young girl to go into a . . . shelter now without her father and mother is simply asking for trouble.[18]

The West End firm of Marshall and Snelgrove might sell gleaming white coats for the dogs of the well-to-do, so they would be safe in the blackout, but *Reynolds News* reported that

> West End solicitors, who before the war netted five figure incomes for divorce cases, have been heavily hit by the blackout. In the winter months at any rate, private enquiry agents are helpless. Adultery cannot be proved because identification is impossible in the pitch-dark.[19]

And the country was horrified to discover that Nöel Coward, playing Louis Mountbatten in *In Which We Serve* – 'One of the screen's proudest achievements at any time and in any country', as *Newsweek* put it – had defrauded the government by not handing in dollars to the Treasury he had earned as unofficial ambassador to the States. He was fined £200. The aging actor George Arliss, as well known in the States as in this country, was fined a third of his assets at the Mansion House court in London, for failing to declare his holding of American and Canadian securities when the war began. And Ivor Novello, musical impresario and actor, served four weeks in prison over shady dealings involving continued use of his Rolls Royce, despite the embargo on petrol and unnecessary journeys.

The 'live for today' mentality produced a new situation in the country that has never quite gone away. Leading Aircraftsman Arthur Heys strangled WAAF Winnie Evans in an aircraft hangar in Suffolk. Samuel Morgan killed fifteen-year-old Mary Hagan in a Liverpool blockhouse. Gunner Harold Hill strangled and stabbed two little girls in a field in Buckinghamshire. Officer Cadet Gordon Cummins killed and mutilated four women in blacked-out London.

And although their killing sprees were not to end until long after the war, John Reginald Halliday Christie, War Reserve Constable, was making good use of his back garden at 10 Rillington Place, while John George Haigh, ex-choirboy, was experimenting with drums of sulphuric acid.

Winston Churchill said of the British people of the years 1939 to 1945, 'this was their finest hour'. Well, not quite everybody's. This book is about the darker moments of that hour.

CHAPTER TWO

The Fifth Column

As the Spanish Civil War rumbled through the Iberian peninsula in the years before Hitler's invasion of Poland, a new phrase entered the English language.

'Now there is no time to waste,' wrote the Falangist leader, General Francisco Franco. 'Madrid's plans of resistance make me smile. We shall get there as fast as we can march, crushing whatever ridiculous resistance is attempted.'

In fact, his four column advance was held up by a stubborn republican defence, but Franco's second-in-command, General Emilio Mola, dismissed this hiccup by explaining that a Fifth Column was working on the insurgents' behalf, inside Madrid itself, spreading fear and despondency and carrying out timely acts of sabotage. Three years later, as the German war machine, delivering its terrible payload of blitzkreig tore West, similar anti-government groups were believed to be at work in most, if not all, targeted countries. Why did the Netherlands capitulate after only five days? Denmark after one? Clearly, for them the war was lost before it had begun. And much of that was laid at the door of the Fifth Column.

The *Kensington Gazette* reported a case in March 1942 in which a man had been caught importuning in North End Road, Fulham, wearing a silk petticoat, knickers and a bra filled with 'inflatable balloons'. Laying aside the fact that prostitution and homosexual acts were illegal in this country, the defendant was also guilty of wasting precious silk that should have been used for parachutes. The story he told in court was a tragic one. Partially paralyzed and half-blinded at Dunkirk, in that straightforward defeat that Churchill's propaganda managed to turn into a victory, the accused had been discharged from the Army, but 'had been reading a lot about Fifth Columnists dressed in women's clothing'. He decided to try it for himself and 'walked three miles before being detected'. The bizarre explanation was not accepted by the magistrate, but it illustrates two vital points about crime in wartime Britain: it affected people in different ways and the Fifth Column was considered a reality.

The military situation by 1940 meant that Britain was a fortress. Every European country was either overrun by Germany or allies of the Third Reich. And the next victim for Hitler, by the summer of that year, was us. The Fifth Column was real and it must be shut down at all costs. It operated at various levels and it had to be fought on all of them.

First came the operations of the Intelligence Services. At the beginning of the war, there were two principal agencies of the secret services, MI5 and MI6. Careless talk cost lives in 1939–45; so did careless action and sometimes, no action at all. MI5, working in close co-operation with the Metropolitan Police's Special Branch, was the 'home' service, monitoring with extraordinary zeal the various 'un-British' interests who might pose problems. The unit had perhaps seventy-five staff working out of their headquarters at Millbank and this was patently not enough for the job in hand. There were 71,600 registered aliens in Britain by the end of 1939 and countless others who were not registered. While the government trawled the City and the established universities for new blood, the existing cohort moved into the relative security of Wormwood Scrubs. Even though officially this was simply a War Department move, its actual purpose was common knowledge. A joke of the time said that the conductor of the No. 72 bus that ran past the prison gates would call out 'All change for the Scrubs and MI5!'

Latchmere House, in a quiet residential area near Ham Common was utilized as Camp 020, the Roman numerals XX for twenty giving rise to the term 'double-cross'. Here, agents were to be 'turned', apparently operating for the Reich, but actually working undercover for MI5. Many of the cases of espionage that came to light were tried here by the notorious 'Hanging Committee', without consideration of *habeas corpus*, jury or even defence counsel. Not for the last time in this book, we meet the irony of all this. In an all-out war against the forces of tyranny, we became tyrants ourselves.

The first to be executed for spying were, in fact, tried at the Old Bailey on 22 November 1940. Jose Waldeburg, a German; Carl Meier and Charles Van Dem Kieboorn, Dutchmen, landed on British soil disguised as refugees fleeing from Nazi-controlled Europe. They carried English currency and radio transmitters and their job was to feed back any military information they could, as a possible prelude to invasion. By the time of their trial, this threat was actually over, but the attacks on southern airfields that culminated in the Battle of Britain, had switched to the Blitzing of cities and this still looked and felt uncomfortably like a 'softening up' exercise that would prefigure a landing. The men's cover stories were flimsy and Stanley Cross hanged Waldeburg and Meier at Pentonville on 10 December, postponing Van Dem Kieboorn's execution for a week, pending his (untrue) claim that he had been forced into this mission by threats against his family.

More worrying than the arrival of badly briefed and poorly disguised foreigners was the case of George Armstrong, an engineer serving with the Merchant Navy at the outbreak of war. Though British born, Armstrong offered his services to Hitler's Reich by contacting the German embassy in Washington. He was quickly caught in this country, tried at the Bailey and hanged by Thomas Pierrepoint at Wandsworth on Wednesday 9 July 1941.

But still the agents kept coming, bringing with them a sense of pantomime not out of place in *Dad's Army*. Karl Drucke and Werner Walti were landed by seaplane in a rubber dinghy on the coast of Scotland on a cloudless night in July. Splitting up, they were making for England via railway stations when one of them was spotted. Walti was noticed studying railway timetables (always incomprehensible in a foreign country) at Porgordon station in Banff. His suitcase contained large amounts of cash, a pistol and, the giveaway that probably hanged him, a length of *knockwurst* sausage. Identical equipment and rations were found on Drucke in Edinburgh some days later and Thomas Pierrepoint despatched them both at Wandsworth on 6 August.

Josef Jakobs was also carrying a sausage when arrested by the Home Guard after only twelve hours on British soil. A former NCO in the German Army, working for the Meteorological Office, he parachuted into England and dumped his flying suit before he ran into a detachment of the Local Defence Volunteers. Tried at the Duke of York's Headquarters in London, Jakobs faced military court martial on account of his rank. He was the only victim of a firing squad in the war, shot beneath the White Tower on 14 August.

Four months later, it was Albert Pierrepoint who hanged Karel Richter. The 29-year-old had parachuted into sleeping Hertfordshire on the night of Tuesday, 13 May and camped out in the woods around London Colney before moving on. It was only fifteen minutes before he was accosted by the local constable, Alec Scott, who was unhappy with Richter's answers and accent. There was no sausage in his belongings this time, but there were maps and a compass. His parachute and Swastika-emblazoned helmet were found where he had half-buried them.

Two men who died on the same day were José Kay and Alphonse Timmerman, but they worked independently of each other. Kay, a British subject by virtue of his Gibraltan birth, had been passing information on Royal Naval movements via 'neutral' Spain for months. He was sent to England for trial. Timmerman, as a Belgian ship's steward before the war, was familiar with British ports. Posing as a refugee, he no doubt hoped that his nationality would help. Invisible ink ingredients and large quantities of cash sealed his fate and led to his appointment with Albert Pierrepoint on 7 July 1942.

Mr Justice Birkett presided over the case of Duncan Scott-Ford three months later. Another Merchant seaman, Scott-Ford was lured with cash into espionage in Lisbon. Today, the offer of £18 seems derisory and it is likely that British, as opposed to foreign, agents had their own personal agenda for risking their lives. In fact, to make matters worse, Scott-Ford was double-crossed. His *Abwehr*

(German Secret Service) paymasters withheld payment and black-mailed him into further work, picking up unconsidered trifles in bars up and down the coast and feeding them back. Pierrepoint stopped all that on 3 November.

He was busy again, with the well-rehearsed ritual at Wandsworth on the last day of December. Johannes Dronkers was a Dutch Nazi who worked for the Post Office before the war. His role as spy was to report on British troop movements in this country, especially as, by this time, the Americans were arriving. In fact, he was suspected even before he set foot on British soil. When his yacht was picked up by a British trawler in the Channel, Dronkers expressed delight, claiming he was a refugee on the run from the Nazis. He soon dropped the subterfuge and was found guilty of spying at the Old Bailey on 17 November.

Three weeks later, the same court, under Mr Justice Humphreys, saw the case for spying against forty-year-old Franciscus Winter, who arrived in Britain at the end of July. Posing not only as a refugee, but a concentration camp escapee, Winter was yet another seaman attempting to feed back information on naval convoys. Under questioning, he admitted his involvement with the *Abwehr* and was hanged just days after his fortieth birthday in January 1943.

By the time the next spy trial opened, again at the Bailey, thousands of British, American and Free French troops were being moved into the south of England for the, as yet unspecified, purpose that would become D-Day. At fifty-eight, Oswald Job was the oldest man executed for spying in wartime England. Specifically, the French collaborator's task was to report the damage inflicted by German bombing and the information was to be fed back by writing coded letters to prisoners-of-war at the St Denis internment camp, which would then be intercepted. Job's defence was that he was actually offering his services as a double agent (there were several of these already operating successfully by 1943) but no one was buying that and Job hanged at Pentonville in March.

In the summer two spies were executed in the same prison within three weeks of each other. Pierre Neukermans was a career soldier in the Belgian Army before the war and had been working for the *Abwehr* since 1940. He arrived in Britain on 16 July and escaped during questioning, but was still plausible enough to work in the Free Belgian Office in London. It was over a year before his cover was blown and by then he had smuggled information on Belgian troop movements via two accomplices. He faced the very busy and highly proficient Albert Pierrepoint on 23 June 1944, by which time, Operation OVERLORD was a reality and Allied troops were pushing actively across France towards Cherbourg.

Eleven days before Colonel von Stauffenberg's bomb would be set to blow the Führer to smithereens, Joseph Van Hove died at the end of Pierrepoint's rope. A Dutch Black Marketeer caught by the Germans in Antwerp, he offered his espionage services in exchange for immunity. In complicated moves, he arrived in England in February 1943, his mission to report on troop build-up, but his story was disbelieved.

What characterizes all these cases is the incompetence of the agents concerned. In general terms, the *Abwehr*'s sophistication seems limited by comparison with their equivalent in MI6. Everybody, especially in the war's early stages – from government officials in sandbagged Whitehall to housewives on lonely farm-steads – was very alert to strangers. Anyone with a foreign accent was a suspect, as a Dane and a Swede discovered in Liverpool in June 1940 when they were randomly arrested 'on account of their foreign appearance' and fined £15 each! What was of more concern was the next level down. Spies, after all, were largely foreign and doing a basic job; in a sense 'their bit' as everyone else was encour-aged to do. The worry and paranoia of whom they may be collaborating with is well expressed by E G Robey, prosecuting a case of illegal photography of an aircraft in Luton:

> 'Motive did not matter,' he told the court with a fine disregard for the rules of evidence and basic human rights. 'It was common knowledge that Fifth Column activities were rife . . . the enemy was at our gates.'[1]

And two of those enemies kept their rendezvous with Pierrepoint on charges, not of espionage, but treason. In the shifting sands of law, backed by the even more mobile changes of morality, treason against the crown was once the most ghastly and pernicious evil of them all. In reality, it was at first a con by an outnumbered government (a single monarch and a tiny Privy Council) desperate to keep itself alive and in power. On 22 August 1940, Parliament passed the Treachery Act, demanding the use of the death penalty for all cases of espionage and serious ones of sabotage. In June 1945, a new Treason Act amended earlier examples, which dropped various requirements. Treason had now reverted to the old pattern as the worst crime in the book.

One victim of this new law was London-born Swiss, Theodore Schmurch, who, at the age of fifteen, joined Oswald Mosley's British Union of Fascists, with its headquarters in Smith Street, London. Joining the Service Corps (drivers) of the Army two years later, he was captured by the Italians in North Africa and acted as a spy for them, reporting prison camp conversations. Posing as Captain Richards, he tried to obtain similar information from Lieutenant Archibald Hart, himself a prisoner-of-war in Rome. Hart told him nothing, but appeared as a witness for the prosecution at Schmurch's trial at the Bailey in September 1945. By this time the war, even against Japan, was over and there was a sense of vengeance in the air once the initial euphoria of victory had passed. Tried by court martial, Theodore Schmurch was the last man ever to be executed for treason.

The day before that, Pierrepoint had despatched a far better known traitor, the Irish American William Joyce, known as Lord Haw-Haw. Born in Brooklyn of Irish immigrant parents, Joyce joined the British Fascists in the year after Hitler took power in Germany. He soon quarrelled with Mosley, however, and formed his own breakaway group, the National Socialist League. Applying for a British passport in July 1939, Joyce sensed which way the political wind was blowing and left for Germany days before war was declared. He quickly began broadcasting over German radio on behalf of Dr Josef Goebbels' Ministry of Enlightenment and Propaganda, and his peculiar pronunciation gave rise to his nickname. Many people in Britain tuned in to him deliberately, and not only believed that he was an actual English aristocrat, but that what he said was true. 'We all know about Banstead,' he told the listeners of Bremen radio, 'even that the clock is an hour slow today.' And he was right! In fact, much of Joyce's propaganda was very general, with all-embracing warnings of air raids and it was clear that he knew very little of what was really happening in wartime Britain. His broadcasts became entertainment and many were genuinely surprised to find him in the dock on a charge of treason. He was caught by the British at the end of May 1945 as Nazis all over Germany slipped off their Swastika armbands and denied all knowledge of anything or claimed merely to have been following orders. At his trial, the legitimate problem of his nationality arose. He was an American citizen by birth, claimed to have taken out German citizenship in 1940 and was, therefore, in no sense a traitor. What hanged him was his British passport. By obtaining one, however briefly, he was deemed to owe allegiance to George VI and even an appeal to the House of Lords failed to save him. In the final court of appeal, only Lord Porter spoke of clemency.

Among those who worked on the prosecution case against Joyce was Reginald Spooner, a gifted Scotland Yard detective. He listened to the last broadcast recorded, but never transmitted, by Joyce in April 1945:

I have always hoped and believed that in the last resort there would be an alliance, a combine, an understanding between England and Germany.

And of the likely future relationship between the democratic West and the Bolshevik East, he said:

Just make sure that the end of this world war is not the beginning of a greater world war than you have ever imagined possible.[2]

Two weeks earlier, John Amery, the son of one of Chamberlain's Cabinet Ministers at the start of the war, was hanged at Pentonville. Bankrupt at twenty-four and guilty of providing Franco's troops with guns at exorbitant prices in the Civil War, he too made radio broadcasts from Germany after 1942, before forming the militarily useless British Free Corps (Legion of St George). Caught in Italy in July 1945, Amery tried the same defence as Joyce – he had become a Spanish citizen, therefore the Treason law did not apply. In the Bailey, however, the accused changed his plea to guilty and the whole case lasted a mere eight minutes before the black cap was placed on the head of Mr Justice Humphreys.

Why did men like Schmurch, Joyce and Amery 'go over' to the enemy? And how many more, far more ordinary people, might be tempted to do so, given the right circumstances? To understand the motivation, we must realize two things. In 1940 at least, few people expected us to be able to survive, much less win the war. And in the dark, depressed days of the thirties, there were many who rather admired Adolf Hitler. Some of this admiration was born out of racism. Hitler was admired because he had contempt for Jews. As the pacifist Marquis of Tavistock wrote:

> We should not forget that even in our boyhood the German Jew was a byword for all that was objectionable . . . Even in our own country there are thousands of quite respectable people . . . who have a most venomous hatred against the Jews and would certainly become Jew-baiters of a kind if they had Hitler's power and opportunity. Indeed, there may be a bit of the Hitler even in ourselves . . . [3]

Others were more direct:

> 'Look at our Army!' roared a member of the BUF [British Union of Fascists] at a rally at the end of August 1939. 'Look at its leader – Hore-Belisha! Whenever I see this man's physog [face] in the paper a horrible, revolting feeling comes over my stomach.'[4]

And some people in high places agreed. In a disgraceful episode of British Jew-baiting, Lord Halifax, the Foreign Secretary, engineered Hore-Belisha's dismissal on the grounds that, as Minister for War, he was unpopular with the generals. Winston Churchill, though pro-Zionist and certainly not a fan of Hitler, was impressed by

Fascism's stand against the Left. He wrote to Benito Mussolini, the Italian dictator, in the 1920s:

> If I had been an Italian, I am sure that I should have been wholeheartedly with you from start to finish in your triumphal struggle against the bestial appetites and passions of Leninism.[5]

It would be a gross overstatement to imply there were secret Nazis among the British aristocracy, but political giants like David Lloyd George were bowled over by Hitler's 'economic miracle' – the Führer was 'a natural leader of men'; Halifax had hunted foxes with Goering, *Gauleiter* of Prussia, *Reichsfeldmarshal* of the Luftwaffe and seen by many as second only to Hitler himself. And several of them hovered around the organizations which, after 1939, looked positively sinister – the Anglo-German Fellowship, the Right Club and the Link.

The Fellowship was founded in October 1935 before any of Hitler's aggrandisement became obvious. Its headquarters were near Sloane Square in London and its first secretary was T P Cornwell-Evans, the actual founder being E W D Tennant. All 700 of its members were professional or industrial leaders; three were directors of the Bank of England; and sixty sat either in the Commons or the Lords.

The Right Club boasted such luminaries as Viscount Rothermere, the newspaper tycoon; his son, Esmond Harmsworth; G Ward Price, director of the *Daily Mail* and the Fellowship's Tennant. It had been founded by Captain Archibald Ramsay, MP for Peebles.

The least impressive was probably the Link, the brainchild of Admiral Sir Barry Domville, founded in 1938. By this time, Hitler's occupation of the Rhineland and his posturing in Austria and the Sudetenland, left little doubt as to the direction of his foreign policy. Britain was already – desperately – arming. The Link produced a journal, the *Anglo-German Review*, the circulation of which probably never exceeded 400.

How many of these *Fascisti*- and Nazi-wannabees dropped their affiliations on the outbreak of the war we will never know. By the sweeping powers that Chamberlain's and later Churchill's government gave themselves, right-wing heads rolled. In May 1940, the month when Chamberlain gave way to Churchill, Regulation 18B swept thirty-four high-profile dissidents into gaol, among them Ramsay and John Beckett, secretary of the British People's Party. The real prize, however, was Oswald Mosley.

The most famous of all the 'fellow-travellers of the Right', aristocratic Mosley was educated at Winchester and Sandhurst, an officer in the 16th Lancers and Conservative MP for Harrow. Originally a Socialist, Mosley was appalled at the ineffectiveness of Ramsay MacDonald's Labour Party and created the New Party, which developed into the British Union of Fascists (BUF) after his visit of enlightenment to Italy. Always claiming to be more impressed by Mussolini than Hitler (the Italian dictator had by this time been in power for fourteen years), Mosley was, nevertheless, perfectly happy to adopt the Nazi tactics of beating up Jews in the streets. Trouble brewed in 1934 when Mosley demanded a modern dictatorship based on the Enabling Law in Germany, which would keep Hitler in power for the rest of his life. A Fascist rally at Earl's Court was attended by over 2,000 and there were serious casualties. Two years later, in the Jewish East End, lorries were overturned, eighty more people were injured and eighty-four arrests made, mounted police delivering frequent baton charges. As if to prove, however, that Britain was far in every way from Germany, in a pitched battle between the BUF and Communists in Liverpool in October 1937, both sides stopped when the National Anthem was played!

The outbreak of war was clearly a pivotal moment for British Fascists. Mosley continued to oppose the war until his arrest in May 1940, but it is likely that many admirers of Hitler abandoned the Right the previous year, deterred not only by the outbreak of war, but the violence of Mosley's followers. 'This is a Jews' War' proclaimed the Right Club's handbills, but only the most fanatical anti-Semites believed them.

The paranoid government used the Emergency Powers (Defence) Act to round up and intern thousands of aliens who found themselves stranded on the wrong side of the Channel. The various sub-clauses of the Defence of the Realm legislation permitted the arbitrary arrest of anyone who had 'sympathies with the system of government of any power with which His Majesty is at war'. Naturally, anyone with a German name fell into this category. Before the war, an estimated 15,000–20,000 Germans lived here and their number swelled as Nazi persecution in Europe grew.[6] In a move horribly redolent of what the Nazis would do to Jews and other 'undesirables' in the years ahead, the government classified aliens into three categories: 'A' class were interned as likely collaborators, spies and Fifth Columnists; 'B' were carefully monitored and restricted in terms of jobs and movements; 'C' (in fact the majority) were released.

But this was in the autumn of 1939, the time of the 'Phoney War' and the lull before the storm. By May 1940, with the Dunkirk experience and the enemy at the gate, some 2,000 aliens living near the coast were imprisoned. Every 'B' class alien was likewise rounded up and taken to holding camps. There were even a few suicides among people who had only recently escaped from altogether more deadly camps in Central Europe and feared the worst. Men of European ancestry were evicted from council houses and refused entry to the Home Guard.

When Italy joined the war, Italian restaurants and ice cream parlours all but disappeared. Anyone who had not been resident for twenty-five years was interned, even those (like the Austrians) who had run from the very Fascism they were now believed to be supporting. By the end of the summer, there were hardly any free Germans or Austrians and many 'A' and 'B' aliens were suffering wretched existences. They were allowed no post, were not permitted to see their families, were not allowed radios, newspapers or books and were surviving on very meagre fare. The 'C' category had now, in effect, become 'B'. They could not travel, nor were they allowed to own a car, a map or even a bicycle.[7] A straw poll conducted in July showed that nearly half the British public wanted all aliens imprisoned without delay. Gradually, as the paranoia lessened and invasion became ever less likely, thousands were released to join the workforce.

But a far more dangerous threat was believed to exist among the native British population, what Churchill called 'this malignancy in our midst'.[8] The new powers given to the police led to some high-handed behaviour that completely backfired. In June 1940, Dr J J Paterson, Medical Officer of Health for Maidenhead and a friend of Bernard Spilsbury, the Home Office Pathologist, had his house ransacked by police on the grounds that before the war he travelled extensively in Germany.[9]

Churchill's 'malignancy' was countered first by propaganda. In June 1940, the *Sunday Despatch* published a full page entitled 'Forty Steps Britain Must Take Now'. Among those that focused on crime and punishment was a demand for the death penalty for all acts of sabotage and Fifth Column activity. Our prisons, said the *Despatch* should be turned over to war production. Aliens and Conscientious Objectors, should also be made to work. Anyone detained under the defence regulations should have their property and assets confiscated.

Posters appeared everywhere, reminding people that 'Careless Talk Costs Lives' and urging them to 'Be Like Dad – Keep Mum'. And it was monitored by ceaseless vigilance. Whereas an outraged *Picture Post* could rail at the absurdities of censorship imposed by the Ministry of Information, it could be blind to its own effective propaganda. In a crawling caption about Churchill, still First Lord of the Admiralty in April 1940, the editor wrote: 'He made no extravagant claims. He refuted some already made. But when he said a German ship had gone, it had.'[10] Ships, perhaps. Aircraft, no. On the morning after the heaviest Blitz of the war, 10 May 1941, Churchill was happy to concur in the lie that the RAF and anti-aircraft guns had shot down twenty-eight enemy aircraft. In fact, the figure was eight and one of those was not shot down, but crash-landed in Scotland. It was flown by Rudolf Hess.[11]

Writer Alan Bennett has lampooned the paranoia of 1940s Britain perfectly in his *Forty Years On* (1968). An MP, his wife and the wife's ancient nanny are sitting out the Blitz in the basement of Claridge's Hotel, commenting on the absurdities of the world on the streets above:

Moggie: A woman at the canteen said that her son, who's in the Ministry of Food says it's common knowledge that Hitler died six months ago. Only it's being hushed up.

Hugh: *The Times* Correspondent says that air raids are having a serious effect on Bridge.

Moggie: Lyndoe in the *People* says they won't invade until Venus is under Capricorn.

Hugh: When's that?

Moggie: 1947. Apparently they've tried one invasion already. They say that –

Hugh/Moggie together: the Channel was white with bodies.

Moggie: They say that some of the Luftwaffe pilots who've been shot down were wearing lipstick and rouge.

Hugh: A German agent has reported that London is now so demoralized that titled ladies are relieving themselves in Hyde Park.

And in case I am accused of making undue fun of the British of the forties, humour was an essential tool of survival at the time. And the incomparable A P Herbert said it all back in May 1940:

Do not believe the tale the milkman tells;
No troops have mutinied at Potters Bar.
Nor are there submarines at Tunbridge Wells.
The BBC will warn us when there are.

Even something as harmless (and, to the social historian, invaluable) as the Mass Observation Unit could be seen in a sinister light with the outbreak of war. Tom Harrisson and Charles Madge set up this socio-anthropological organization in 1937 to study the habits, attitudes and opinions of the British people. Their reports – War Begins at Home (1940); Clothes Rationing (1941) and People in Production (1942) were the result of a little army of snoopers with clipboards and questionnaires operating out of Kensington.

[33]

Despite this, Mass Observation provided some interesting facts which argue against the paranoia of the age. In April 1940, it reported that

> the majority of people hardly realized what [the Fifth Column] meant. We also found that the level of ordinary people's feelings was much less intense than that expressed in some papers.[12]

The role of the media in wartime – *any* wartime – is beyond the scope of this book, although it is axiomatic that bad news and scare stories sell newspapers. Churchill's government would no doubt have reacted to Mass Observation's findings with alarm – it was precisely that sort of know-nothing complacency that had allowed the Third Reich to invade and dominate Europe.

In the summer of 1940, when the risk of invasion was at its highest, the Ministry of Information set up the Silent Column, designed to counter the debilitation of rumour and defeatism. With hindsight, we know today that much of what the public read and saw in the forties was every bit as propagandistic as the eyewash produced in Berlin. The motives may have been pure, but the use of white and black propaganda was exercised on a scale never seen before. Those members of the public who bought this wholesale were deemed to be 'doing their bit'; those who did not were potential and actual criminals. Harold Nicholson, Parliamentary Secretary to the Ministry of Information, wrote:

> he [the chatterbug or rumour-monger] will say that his brother-in-law – chatterbugs always have innumerable brothers-in-law – was on the train from Derby when a nun entered and started to read a religious book. The book dropped from her lap and as she stooped to retrieve it, she disclosed a manly wrist complete with a tattooed inset of Adolf Hitler.[13]

Chatterbugs were particularly dangerous because careless talk could indeed cost lives. It also landed people in prison. 'National

Socialist Britain is coming,' warned a local government official in Chatham in February 1941. 'England awake!' He was parodying Hitler's famous dictum 'Deutschland erewach!' and was sentenced to hard labour. The fact that in 1941 even military advisers to the Prime Minister also believed that a Nazi Britain was more or less inevitable, did not deter the lawmakers from pouncing. But for every case of Nazi sympathy (and there were very few of these) there were many more of plain carelessness, as the warning posters implied. Englishmen were not used to being watched and spied on and centuries-old habits of speaking one's mind died hard. A 24-year-old man chatting to a mate in a Rochester pub happened to discuss a warship he was building at Chatham docks. Unfortunately for him, nearby sat two members of the Intelligence Corps. For the 'criminal folly of chattering', the shipbuilder got two months. It is most unlikely that this man saw himself as Mr Knowall, Miss Leaky Mouth, Mr Pride in Prophecy, Miss Teacup Whisperer or Mr Glumpot, all of them characters dreamed up by Alfred Duff Cooper's Information Ministry, but he was given a criminal record all the same.

The Silent Column slid into obscurity by the end of 1940 but prosecutions continued, especially where it was believed dissension was being sown in the Armed Forces. The concept of mutiny was alien in the Regular Army, but conscription had put all sorts of men (and women) into uniform and their loyalty might have been suspect. Although few knew it at the time, the behaviour of many of these conscripts in the retreat from Dunkirk had been far from exemplary and it is a mark of the gullibility of the public that nearly all of them bought Churchill's lie of the victory snatched from defeat.

Mass Observation reports by the end of May 1940 spoke of men 'talking freely about their experiences, particularly in pubs' and that this was 'not good'.[14] In November 1941 the *Kensington Post* reported the case of an Army major fined for making defeatist remarks in a London pub:

> Churchill is leading this nation to ruin . . . we have not the tanks to compete with the Germans . . . the country is rotten to the core.[15]

In fact, the phrase 'rotten to the core' appears so often in newspaper and court proceedings of would-be Fifth Columnists that we can be forgiven for believing the authorities were involved in a conspiracy of giant proportions, putting the same hackneyed phrase into the mouths of potential anarchists. Merely for suggesting, in June 1944, that British servicemen should receive the same pay as their American counterparts, a local government official in Hampshire was charged with unlawfully endeavouring to breed disaffection among HM Forces.

When Reginald Spooner, the Yard officer attached to the Intelligence Corps interrogated William Joyce's 'team' in conquered Berlin in 1945, he came across Henry Hicks, a former insurance manager who claimed to have worked with Josef Goebbels' Ministry of Propaganda in order to sabotage it. He rather destroyed his defence when letters were found in his possession dating from 1939 explaining why he had left Britain: 'I have come to live in Germany with my family as political refugees from Jew-controlled England.'[16]

Hicks got four years' penal servitude.

The B feature actor, Jack Trevor, living in Berlin when war broke out, used the tired Nazi defence of having to obey orders[17] to oblige Goebbels' propaganda machine or his family would have been killed. His real name was Cedric Steane and he had won the Military Cross serving with the Manchester Regiment in the Great War. One of his films for Goebbels saw him in Grenadier Guard uniform, changing the guard at 'Buckingham Palace' with German extras. He was sentenced to three years.

The only one of the traitors that Spooner liked was Norman Baillie-Stewart, who had broadcast for the Nazis out of the Studio in Radio Paris. It was Baillie-Stewart's bad luck that an unusually inefficient clerk had not filed his request for German citizenship until 1940, even though he had lodged it two years earlier. Technically, then, Baillie-Stewart had changed his nationality to that of the enemy in time of war. That should have hanged him, but the judge, Mr Justice Oliver, took a more lenient view:

A traitor is a man who will accept and enjoy the protection of his country and then sell it to the other side, but you had abandoned the protection of the country.

He served three and a half years of his five-year sentence.

A much more serious case involved Dorothy O'Grady, of Sandown, Isle of Wight. She was sentenced to death in February 1941 under the Treachery Act because she had sabotaged telephone wires in an attempt to impede Army movements. Mrs O'Grady seems to have been at the hub of a BUF nest centred on Southsea, but since she was clearly unbalanced, her sentence was reduced to fourteen years' penal servitude.

Less spectacular was the case of the mother and son arrested in June 1940 on charges of 'communicating to another person matter which might be useful to the enemy'. This referred to the existence of the new British Broadcasting Station in Stoke Newington. The defendant said to police: 'Why should not we tell the people where to hear the truth? There will be more justice when Hitler comes.'[18]

Conscientious objection posed a peculiar problem. If a man tended a sick soldier, he was in fact aiding the war effort by sending him back to the Front. If he so much as bought a postage stamp, he was still aiding the war effort. The only way to prevent this was to send the man to prison. There was a far more relaxed official attitude to 'conchies' than there had been in the Great War, where such a stand was invariably equated with cowardice. When COs put up posters in London in the summer of 1940 demanding an end to the war, the magistrate who heard the case dismissed it, concluding, 'This is a free country. We are fighting to keep it a free country, as I understand it.'[19]

The figures themselves make interesting reading. Some 59,192 people claimed conscientious objection. Of these, 12,204 were turned down as spurious and were liable for call-up; 14,691 took up non-combatant posts with the Armed Forces; 28,720 continued in work related indirectly to the war effort, such as farming; and 3,577 were exempt. Local feeling swung with the fortunes of war. The toleration of the Phoney War gave way to hysteria in the 'invasion summer' of 1940 and 119 local authorities fired all COs working for them. Some received vicious letters, others were studiously ignored by former friends. Some 214 women were jailed for refusing to take up various forms of civilian work; 555 prosecutions took place against COs who refused to do fire watch duties during the Blitz. George Elphick of Lewes in Sussex went to prison five times for this offence. By and large however, the authorities' decision to allow COs to say their piece, even to bodies of troops on religious grounds, was the right one and totally at variance with their paranoia elsewhere.

Particular targets were Jehovah's Witnesses, fortune-tellers, clairvoyants and spiritualists. The Jehovah's Witness movement saw a huge revival, from 6,000 adherents in 1938 to seven times that twenty years later. It is probable that the large numbers of them in jail – over 200 by April 1942 – resulted from their annoying habit of 'doorstepping' in peacetime. There was a revival too, of spiritualism, but nothing on the scale that it mushroomed in the Great War, because of the emotional need to stay in contact, somehow, with the dead. Magistrates took a dim view: 'to pretend to conjure up [the spirits of the dead] when it is false and a hollow lie is nothing less than a public mischief.'

It was the celebrated trial of the medium Helen Duncan at the Old Bailey in 1944 that brought all this into sharp focus. Despite producing several excellent character witnesses, including the journalist Hannen Swaffer, Mrs Duncan already had two convictions against her. It was not the giving of false hope that she was charged with – after all, all of Churchill's government could have been accused of that throughout the war – but that she was making money out of it. In sending her to jail for nine months, the judge said:

There are many people, especially in wartime sorrowing for loved ones. There is a great danger of their susceptibilities being exploited and out of this yearning for comfort and assurance there are those unfortunately who are ready to profit.

While other mediums the length and breadth of the country were freed, Mrs Duncan was made a scapegoat.[20] Charging her with fraud was fraught with difficulties – if she and her client genuinely believed in a reachable afterlife, who was committing a crime? Accordingly, she was charged under the 1735 Witchcraft Act, which was in fact obsolete, though not actually repealed until 1951.

Industrial sabotage was a notoriously difficult crime to categorize. Shortfalls in Britain were likely to be the result of war-weariness, carelessness or pilfering. To prove that it was the work of an active Fifth Column was vastly more difficult. The Trade Union movement had always been viewed with suspicion by Conservative governments and nobody was under any illusion that the coalition team of Churchill and Attlee was Conservative by another name. Churchill himself had in fact been particularly 'anti' the workers in the 1926 General Strike and set the tone for authorities generally on the lookout for Trotskyites as well as secret Fascists deliberately sabotaging the war effort.

In 1942, the government introduced legislation against the work-shy. In the Leicestershire coalfields in 1944, prosecutions occurred at about one a month. Two brothers, unemployed for ten months between them, were sentenced to a six-week term of imprisonment and a £7 10s fine respectively.[21] When the bone idle of Birkenhead hit upon the feeble excuse that they were slacking in order to be called up instead, the magistrate screamed at one of them:

You are an absolute traitor . . . It is an absolute scandal that men like this should be retained in a sheltered occupation, while others are slogging about in Sicily and elsewhere. It makes my blood boil when our own sons are out fighting and young men like this go scot-free.[22]

One girl offered nine jobs turned six of them down between August 1943 and November 1944 and was prosecuted three times. Others, like the sixteen-year-old runaway Joan Wolfe, stuck jobs for days at a time before drifting on to others – and, in her case, to her death.

Some cases of actual sabotage, which were very rare, were motivated by personal spite rather than political machinations. The Stockton and Tees-side *Weekly Herald* reported in January 1942 on a factory worker who had turned up drunk. On being refused entry to the premises, he climbed a fence and switched off all the machinery he could reach before being restrained. He served three months. A similar case in Hackney the previous year, in which a die-casting factory literally ground to a halt for twenty-four hours, was the result of a dispute over bonus pay.

What we have seen in this chapter is a country, in 1940–41 at least, arguably teetering on the brink of collapse. 'Fortress Britain' survived in part because the heavy hand of government suppressed anything it deemed 'un-British'. Gertrude Green of Croydon wrote to the *Daily Sketch* in 1940 highlighting the paradox:

> Surely it is strange in a country which is fighting for freedom that we should notice more and more frequently in the papers such words as 'imprisonment', 'restraint', 'force' . . . Can you wonder that we sometimes feel we are copying the country we are fighting?[23]

Law-abiding citizens found themselves in the dock on the suspicion that they were part of a huge underground conspiracy. And there was nothing new in this. In the 1790s and 1800s, William Pitt's government – locked in a mortal struggle with Revolutionary and Napoleonic France – instituted a similar raft of legislation because they had no effective way of gauging public opinion. With the mass communications available in the 1940s and the existence of the Mass Observation Unit, not to mention an enemy as obnoxious and terrifying as the Nazis, Chamberlain's and Churchill's governments might have exercised the toleration and spirit of understanding they generally accorded Conscientious Objectors.

But there was a war on . . . and you couldn't be too careful.

CHAPTER THREE

The Blackout Killers

However many new crimes the government might invent to torment the civilians fighting the People's War, the old ones remained. Murder was regarded in the 1940s, as it is today, as the yardstick of social depravity. The Nazis could highlight the decadence, as they saw it, of Weimar Germany in the 1920s by reference to the cases of Fritz Haarman and Peter Kurtin, two of the most prolific serial killers in history. But the odd fact about murder in wartime Britain is that it did not increase. At a time when violent death occurred every day, through the two incarnations of the Blitz in particular, the live-for-today mentality described by Molly Lefebure meant that life was considered cheap, and the number of murders ought to have rocketed accordingly. But when we look at the figures this simply is not so.

Taking the statistics from those actually executed for murder an interesting pattern emerges. If we take a six-year sample (the length of the Second World War) and apply it to other decades, the 1933–38 period saw fifty-nine people hanged for murder, three of them women. The total number of victims was sixty-eight. The average age of the murderers was thirty-two, the youngest being twenty and the oldest sixty-two. If we look at motive, far and away the most common is domestic: husbands and boyfriends killing their partners in a screaming row. Next comes theft, then sex crimes. Three victims were killed in fights, only one for gain (that old chestnut of Agatha Christie, then at the height of her success) and four in killings that appear to have no motive at all and can only be classified as random. In terms of weapon used, twenty-two victims died by being battered to death, either with fists or the proverbial blunt instrument. Ten were strangled, some by ligature, some manually. There were nine fatal stabbings and seven shootings. One victim died by gassing, one by poison (the métier par excellence of the Victorian murderer) and one, bizarrely, by being buried alive. Nowhere emerges as a 'murder capital' in the 1930s, Greater London (with a far larger population than anywhere else) accounting for only nine of the fifty-nine cases.

If we look at the six years that followed the war, (1946–51) we have the following distribution. Ninety-seven people were hanged, including two women and this was in a period that saw the experimental abolition of the death penalty under Clement Attlee's Labour government and its Home Secretary, Chuter Ede. The number of victims was 109, but six of these were attributed to the serial tendencies of the 'acid bath murderer', John George Haigh. The average age of the murderers was thirty-three, the youngest (two of them) being nineteen and the oldest fifty-nine. In terms of motive, domestic violence again leads the field, accounting for thirty-seven of the killings, with theft, sex and fights following in descending order. There were seven that had no clear motivation, none for gain and it was a quiescent period in the history of the IRA. Twenty-seven victims were battered to death, twenty-six strangled, twenty shot and twelve stabbed. There were no cases of poisoning or gassing, but one of drowning and two of asphyxiation.

Can we learn anything from a comparison with the murder rate in the Great War? After all, 1933–38 and 1946–51 were periods of peace. Is there any pattern we can deduce from a country plunged into a prolonged conflict? There are problems here, based on the shorter (four-year) period under analysis, as well as the fact that both world wars saw men executed for spying and treason, for which, technically, there is no specific victim. Between 1914 and 1918, sixty-two people were hanged, all of them men. Once again, domestic violence topped the motive list, but hugely so, accounting for nearly 70 per cent of murders. Deaths in fights came next (five) and gain, sex and theft trailed behind that. Twelve men, however, were hanged for espionage and one, Roger Casement, for treason, because of the Irishman's collaboration with the Germans. Stabbings were easily the most common form of murder, accounting for 50 per cent of the killings. Ten people were battered to death, seven were shot and three strangled. Three were drowned, all by the same killer, George Joseph Smith, the 'brides in the bath' murderer. The average age of the hanged was slightly higher than we have seen, at thirty-five, but again, we must take into account those not actually guilty of murder. The youngest killer was only twenty, but the eldest, Charles Frembd, was seventy-one when he cut his wife's throat, unable to stand her constant nagging any more.

What of the People's War? Between 1939 and 1945, 112 men were hanged and no women. The average age was thirty-one, the youngest 19 and the eldest 62, hanged for murder during a robbery. As in other periods, 'domestics' account for most murders, at 28 per cent, with sex crimes at 20 per cent and murder during robbery at 16 per cent. Twenty-two per cent of those hanged were spies. The weapon pattern does not provide any tangible link with the war. Guns were used in 19 per cent of the cases, as opposed to 23 per cent involving battery. Stabbing and strangulation both account for 14 per cent. For reasons of space I have concentrated here on a series of murders I believe were born out of war. Most of them are well known because of their sheer gruesomeness. A shortage of paper in wartime meant that reporting of these cases was limited, but most of them have become *causes célèbres* in one way or another since the 1950s and whole books have been written on them.

One of the most prolific – and until 1953 successful – serial killers was John Christie, and although his killing spree did not come to light until after the war, it began during it, and he was able to lure unsuspecting victims to his house at 10 Rillington Place, Notting Hill, because he could brag about the medical knowledge he claimed to have picked up as a Special Constable with the Reserve. Christie killed eight women, possibly more, but two of them definitely during wartime. Their bodies were found buried in the tiny 20 square feet of garden at the back of the shabby little house at No. 10.

Christie was born in April 1898, in Halifax, to Ernest and May Christie. His father was a stern, authoritarian figure, a designer in a carpet company and a member of the Conservative Primrose League. His mother, known as 'Beauty' Halliday, was a star of local am-dram in the area. All his life, Reg Christie joined organizations that gave him a sense of superiority and a uniform to wear. He sang in the school choir and became a boy scout, later gravitating to scoutmaster. In his early years, the influences that turned him into a killer were already at work. The flashes of temper, all too obvious in his father, revisited themselves in him – in fact his first 'crime against the person' was for hitting a prostitute with a cricket bat. When he was eight, the sight of his grandfather's corpse laid out for burial had him trembling with fascination and pleasure. Bossed around by his bevy of older sisters, he spectacularly failed to perform in teenaged fumblings with a more experienced girl, who promptly told the neighbourhood and christened him 'Reggie-No-Dick'.

By the age of seventeen he had a criminal record, ironically for stealing while working as a clerk with the local police. Kicked out by his father, Christie drifted from job to job, sleeping in the shed on the family allotment, while his doting mother smuggled food out to him.

In 1916, the wayward lad – along with many others – joined the Army. Hit by shrapnel and caught in a gas attack while serving with the Sherwood Foresters, Christie dined out on his disabilities for the rest of his life and even used the ploy to prove his physical incapacity for murder at his trial. His blindness for six months never happened and his three and a half years loss of voice lasted, in fact, for seven weeks. But the truth and Reg Christie had become strangers long ago.

On 20 May 1920 Reg married the stoical Ethel Waddington and it was allegedly two years before the marriage was consummated. Moving to London, Christie took his pilfering ways with him and received nine months in prison for theft as a postman. He was bound over by magistrates two years later, pleading his war record, but served another nine months in 1924 for larceny. Ethel left him and his movements until 1933 are obscure. Certainly he served six months' hard labour for bashing his prostitute lover with her son's cricket bat. As always, Christie the resourceful criminal had a reason: he was demonstrating his cricketing skills at the time and the bat slipped . . .

In 1933 he was again in prison for stealing a car from a Catholic priest, who had felt sorry for the balding little man with the hoarse whisper, especially since Christie had been knocked down by a car on his arrival in London and had undergone genuine surgery. The same year, Christie asked Ethel to return and she did, effectively sealing her own death warrant. A hypochondriac (he visited his doctor 173 times over the next twenty years), liar and frequenter of prostitutes, like many killers over time, Christie showed to society his pompous, respectable side. He was fussy, fastidious and an appalling snob. He also had this totally false view of himself as a charming ladies' man – 'More like Charles Boyer, me,' he once said, comparing himself to the suave film star, who was a heart-throb in those years.

In 1938, as Adolf Hitler took first Austria, then the Sudetenland, in the run up to the war that forms the backdrop of this book, the Christies moved into 10 Rillington Place, renting the ground-floor flat of the three-storey house. When visiting Ethel's family, Reg spoke of their grand house in London with its servants' quarters, and because he illegally sub-let to tenants like the luckless Evans family, who arrived in March 1948, many people believed that he actually owned the premises. In fact he was working as a junior clerk and never earned more than £8 a week.

On the outbreak of war, Reg Christie joined the Police Reserve of Specials. The fact that he had quite an extensive criminal record proves how desperate the authorities were for manpower, and for four years, it gave Christie the chance to patrol at night and mix with shady characters in Notting Hill's pubs and cafés. One of these was twenty-one-year-old Ruth Fuerst. After his trial, ten years later, with another seven victims to his credit, Christie reminisced:

It was thrilling because I had embarked on the career I had chosen for myself, the career of murder. But it was only the

beginning . . . The Sixth Commandment – 'Thou Shalt Not Kill'
– fascinated me . . . I always knew that some day I should defy
it.[1]

As Ludovic Kennedy says, in what is still the definitive study of the
case:

War is a time when people are expected to go into uniform . . .
Police uniform was almost as good as military uniform and a
good deal safer . . . His duties not only allowed him to go on
leading the shadow life he loved, but specifically encouraged
him to.[2]

Ruth Fuerst was a student nurse, born in Voeslau, near Vienna,
in March 1922. She arrived in England in June 1939 and although
no accounts that I have read explain it, it is possible that she was
one of the last Jews to leave Nazi-occupied Europe before the
ghettos and camps began in earnest. This would explain why Fuerst
did not contemplate leaving England when war broke out. Instead,
she gave up nursing and took a job in a munitions factory, the
Grosvenor Works, in Davies Street. Poorly paid and friendless
(bearing in mind the general attitude of the public to 'Germans') she
seems to have taken to part-time prostitution and had a baby by
an American GI. It was the summer of 1943 and the American
contingent was already making their presence felt. She met Christie
either in a café in Ladbroke Grove or while he was walking his beat
and they met several times after that, the girl possibly visiting
Rillington Place when Mrs Christie was out at work.
     Christie's account of her murder, which he gave freely once he
had been convicted of the murder of Beryl Evans in 1953, insisted
that Ruth made the first move. This was possible, since Fuerst was
an experienced street girl and may have believed that the Special
could do her a few favours, even if that meant just looking the other
way while she was on the 'night shift':

'She undressed,' Christie said, 'and wanted me to have intercourse with her. I got on the bed [this was in the back bedroom

which overlooked what would later become her grave] and had intercourse with her. While I was having intercourse with her, I strangled her with a piece of rope. I remember urine and excreta coming away from her. She was completely naked. I tried to put some of her clothes back on her. She had a leopard-skin coat and I wrapped this round her.'[3]

In the middle of all this, like a scene from a bad melodrama, a telegram arrived to say that Ethel Christie was returning from a family visit to Sheffield later the same day. In a frenzy of panic, Christie ripped up the floorboards in his living room and stuffed Ruth Fuerst and her clothing underneath. The same spot would become Ethel's grave years later. The next day, when his wife was at work, Christie dug up the body and prepared a grave in the garden, 'on the right-hand side towards the rockery'. Obviously he needed darkness to put a body in it, so he stashed Fuerst in the wash-house, which would serve as a temporary resting-place for later victims, and at ten at night – telling Ethel he was going to the toilet – hastily buried the girl and levelled the ground the next day. Although in his later confessions Christie claimed that his first two murders, in particular, were meticulously and coolly planned, the most difficult aspect for any murderer is the disposal of the body and here, Christie was inept. Having buried Fuerst, he then decided to pull up as much of her clothing as he could and burn it in the garden incinerator. Months later, while gardening, he found the dead girl's skull and hid it in a dustbin.

It is inconceivable that in a house and garden as small as 10 Rillington Place, no one, especially Ethel Christie, should not have become suspicious. Perhaps that is why she ended under the floorboards.

'Women who give you the come-on wouldn't look so saucy if they were helpless and dead,' Christie told a *Sunday Pictorial* reporter. Most commentators believe that Christie's intercourse with Fuerst, as with all of his later victims except his wife, took place after death, not before it, making Christie that most revolting of killers, a necrophiliac.

We know a great deal more about the patterns of killing than in Christie's day because of research carried out, mostly in America, over the last thirty years. There are widely acknowledged to be seven phases in which the lust to kill grows, becomes inevitable and dies away after the event, only to repeat itself later. For Christie, it happened again the following year. Resigning from the Police Reserve at the end of 1944, he took up a job at the Ultra Radio Works in Acton and here he met his second victim, Muriel Eady.

Christie's tactic here was very different. Eady was thirty-one, totally respectable, living with an aunt in Putney and had a 'gentleman friend'. The couple were invited on several occasions to Rillington Place to have tea with the Christies. When Ethel yet again visited her family in the north, Christie was able to put his murderous plan into operation. Muriel Eady was a martyr to catarrh and the pompous know-it-all ex-policeman convinced her that he had an inhalation device at home that would cure it. Completely trusting, Eady accepted Christie's cup of tea before sitting in a deckchair to inhale the Friar's Balsam through a tube. Behind her back however, a second tube in the contraption was attached to the room's gas supply and on releasing a bulldog clip, Christie was able to gas the woman as she sat there. When she was unconscious, the killer switched off the gas, took Eady into the bedroom and 'had intercourse with her at the time I strangled her ... Once again, I experienced that quiet, peaceful thrill. I had no regrets.'

In fact, this emotion is atypical of serial killers, who often feel a sense of anticlimax and serious depression once the deed is done.

With more time on his hands, Christie prepared Eady's grave next to Fuerst's and further from the house. As she was fully clothed, except for knickers, disposal of the garments was not a problem.

Why was so little fuss made about the sudden disappearances of two young women in the same area? The simple answer was the war. Street girls like Ruth Fuerst were always on the move, following the bright lights or the Army camps. The year 1944 saw the terrifying arrival of the Doodlebugs with their lethal whine: people went missing every day and an overstretched police force could not be everywhere.

It was the totem phase of Christie's killing spree that left un-answered questions. The head of Ruth Fuerst was not kept as a totemic trophy. Buried temporarily in the dustbin, Christie threw it later into a bomb-damaged house in St Mark's Road nearby. Its 110 pieces were painstakingly reassembled by pathologists at his later trial. Among the grisly totems found in the kitchen at Rillington Place was a tobacco tin containing four different lots of pubic hair. One of these may have been Ethel Christie's, but the others did not come from the semi-mummified bodies of later victims stashed behind wallpaper in a cupboard. Two of them may have belonged to Fuerst and Eady, but at least one remains unidentified. When asked at his trial whether he had killed anyone between 1943 and 1949, Christie replied, 'I might have done. I don't know whether I did or not.'[4]

Another serial killer whose crimes only came to light after the war was John George Haigh. Executed for the murder of Henrietta Olivia Durand-Deacon on 10 August 1949, he confessed to three more murders during wartime. Like Christie, Haigh came from a household dominated by a stern father. John and Emily Haigh were strict Plymouth Brethren, which gave the boy a sense of superiority that would, in the end, prove fatal.

Haigh was born in Stamford, Lincolnshire in July 1909. Lazy at school, he quickly realized that he could lie and get away without retribution from man or the terrifying God his father warned him about. He became an adequate forger and a reasonably successful con-man. He left school without qualifications in the year of the General Strike and took to car theft, and obtaining money on hire-purchase agreements by using aliases and fictitious addresses. He was sentenced to fifteen months and on his release worked briefly for a cleaning company before being sacked for dishonesty. Setting up as a solicitor (he would trawl lists of genuine firms to find an actual name to use for authenticity's sake) he defrauded clients of over £30,000 before the scam was rumbled and served four years' penal servitude in Dartmoor.

He was released in the 'Spitfire summer' of 1940 and should have been called up, but with the sheer brass neck for which he was already well known, claimed to be in a reserved occupation and began a career of burglary from evacuated houses. The following year saw him in prison again, with twenty-one months' hard labour. He used his time inside profitably, studying (albeit superficially) the law and allegedly dissolving mice with sulphuric acid. In September 1943 he went to work for a company based in Crawley, Sussex, which is referred to in various accounts of the man's life as either an engineering firm or a small goods factory. Making contacts with his undeniable oiliness and outward charm, Haigh rented a basement in Kensington from Donald McSwann, where he repaired pinball machines from amusement arcades. Like Haigh himself, McSwann was a 'call-up dodger' and Haigh saw huge financial possibilities in this. Always a sharp dresser, the ex-choirboy with the glib tongue rather enjoyed the good life of the West End clubs, seemingly untouched by the rationing and privations that affected most people – but all this cost money.

On Saturday, 9 September 1944, Haigh 'bumped into' McSwann in The Goat pub in Kensington High Street. Discussing draft-dodging and Haigh's ability to help because of the people he knew, the two men ended up in Haigh's basement in Gloucester Road. Fascinated by the 40-gallon drum of acid standing in one corner, McSwann was obligingly bending over it with his back to Haigh when the deadly employee smashed in the back of his skull with a hammer. With gloves, an apron and a variety of saws, Haigh dismembered his landlord's body and lowered the portions into the acid. No one seems to have noticed the oddly attired man in rubber gauntlets and gas mask coming up for fresh air during that frantically busy night, nor the corrosive stench of acid coming from the basement. By the next morning, all that was left of Donald McSwann was dumped as sludge from buckets into London's sewerage system.

Haigh now used his forgery skills to produce letters, ostensibly from the dead man, to his parents, persuading them that he had gone north for the duration to avoid call-up and that he had given Haigh legal rights to run the amusement arcade company for him. The fact that he could convince Amy and William McSwann that all this was above board speaks volumes for his ability, their gullibility, or both. He even – at a time when frivolous journeys were still frowned on because of petrol rationing – drove north to Scotland to provide bona fide postmarks from the dead Donald.

This was only a temporary expedient, however, because Haigh wanted the McSwanns' money as well. He lured them both to the Gloucester Road basement on 10 July and they followed their son into oblivion via the drum of sulphuric acid. Again, Haigh's forgery persuaded the authorities that the McSwanns had signed their properties over to him. He sold their shares and their furniture, made £4,000 and moved on.

If Christie and Haigh were two high-profile murderers whose crimes began, but did not end in wartime, Gordon Cummins was one whose murderous career was, mercifully, short. Elderly people in February 1942, reading the *News of the World*'s banner headline – 'Another Jack The Ripper At Large' – must have been transported back to another world. In the autumn of 1888, five prostitutes had been murdered by the same hand in the neighbouring parishes of Spitalfields and Whitechapel. Today, Gordon Cummins' crime spree would have filled newspapers for weeks. Superintendent Robert Higgins, writing his memoirs years later wrote:

> Had Cummins committed his crimes in peacetime he would undoubtedly have become one of the world's most celebrated and infamous murderers . . . But we were at the height of the war then and the papers were too full of other 'life-and-death' matters.[5]

With a shortage of paper, and grimmer headlines like the advance of Rommel's Afrika Korps and the fall of Singapore – plus the fact that Cummins was extraordinarily inept – relatively little attention was paid. For example, the *Daily Telegraph* and *Morning Post* of 13 February only allotted 2 inches of column space to the murders of his first two victims.

Like Christie and Haigh, Cummins was a fantasist with delusions of grandeur, which are the stock-in-trade of the con-man. He was born in New Earswick near York in 1914 and educated privately at Llandoveris in Wales and Northampton Technical School after a family move. An undistinguished scholar, he trained as an industrial chemist with a London firm after leaving school, but was sacked because his work was unsatisfactory. He drifted, like Christie, from job to job, slapdash work and a lack of commitment characterizing his performance. In 1935 he joined the Royal Air Force as a rigger, checking aircraft before the pilots took over. When war broke out, his ambition was to fly Spitfires or Hurricanes and he relished his association with the men of the Battle of Britain, whom Churchill was famously to call 'The Few'. His messmates were quickly irritated by his snobbery. He claimed to be the illegitimate son of a peer (his father actually ran a school for delinquent boys), spoke with a cut-glass accent and carried a photo in his wallet of his 'father', an equerry, escorting the King to some function or other.

The year after Cummins joined the RAF, he married Marjorie Stevens, the secretary of a West End theatrical producer, a woman who would remain loyal to him throughout his trial. We know so little about Cummins' psychology that explaining his sudden impulse to kill is very difficult. There seem to have been no scrapes with the law or any sign of violence towards women before 8 February 1942, when he met Evelyn Hamilton. She was forty-two, originally from Newcastle, and a qualified pharmacist. She had recently resigned as manageress of a chemist's shop in Hornchurch, Essex, and was carrying £80 on her on the night she died, intending next day to move north again, where it was safer.

Superintendent Frederick Cherrill, the doyen of fingerprint analysis, took up the tale in his autobiography[6]:

> When I arrived at Montagu Place it looked to me as though the body had been hurriedly pushed through the narrow door of the [air raid] shelter after strangulation. It lay upon the floor against the seat, face upward. Round the mouth the murderer had wound tightly the woman's own silk scarf as a gag.[7]

Her hat, a matchbox, powder compact and torch all lay nearby. In the dim light of his own torch, Cherrill recognized the tell-tale bruising around the throat that he knew was caused by a left hand.

He had only just got back to his office at Scotland Yard the next morning, 10 February, when he received a phone call to go to Wardour Street, where another corpse had been discovered:

> Lying across a bed . . . with not even a sheet as covering, was the almost nude body of a woman. She was a ghastly sight. She had been the victim of a sadistic attack of the most horrible and revolting nature.[8]

Lying nearby were the bloodstained weapons that the killer had used after strangulation – a tin-opener and a piece of broken mirror. The papers at the time – and Cherrill in his account – glossed over the wounds for reasons of susceptibility, but the Wardour Street victim's injuries to her vagina were precisely what gave Cummins the grim epithet of 'Ripper'. Nita Ward was the street alias of Evelyn Oatley, thirty-six, a former actress and Windmill girl, who had left her husband and turned to prostitution in Soho.

The police interviewed a neighbour who had heard Oatley return the previous night at about eleven fifteen with a man. Their voices and the wireless could be heard through the wall. The dead woman's husband was traced to Blackpool, but he had not seen his wife for months and was eliminated from the enquiry.

Two murders so close together, even with the backdrop of appalling stories of the war, led to something akin to panic in London. *This* Ripper was striking in the West End, not the East, and although the occupation of Evelyn Oatley was given in the vaguest terms, her address alone spoke volumes. The 'sexual maniac' referred to by the Home Office pathologist, Bernard Spilsbury, was targeting *any* female, regardless of class. The *Evening Standard* of 13 February announced a third killing in a flat in Gosfield Street behind Tottenham Court Road. Even in the privations of wartime, Cherrill was struck by the spartan appearance of the murder scene – a single bed, a table, a small carpet, a rug and two chairs. A 'much-darned' silk stocking was wound around the corpse's neck and her naked body had been viciously mutilated *à la* Evelyn Oatley. Once again, Cherrill's nose for useful dabs came into play and he found left-handed fingerprints on a brass candlestick and a half-drunk bottle of stout on the premises:

> It now seemed pretty certain that a killer was abroad who murdered not only for gain – in each case the handbags of the

women had been rifled – but in order to indulge in a wicked and insensate lust to perpetrate the most diabolical injuries on the women he killed.[9]

The victim was Margaret Lowe, 'a handsome and finely built woman who was known locally as "Pearl"'[10] Cherrill recalled. She was forty-three, a widowed prostitute who had once kept a boarding house in Southend. Cherrill had literally just returned from Gosfield Street when his Yard telephone rang to announce a fourth murder, this time at Sussex Gardens, Paddington. Once again, the same MO – strangulation with a scarf as ligature, and the semi-naked body ripped open. In life, she had been Doris Jouannet, the wife of a French hotel manager, Henri Jouannet, who had taken British citizenship in the thirties. The couple had been married eight years and had a flat in Sussex Gardens. Henri's statement to the police, of a last supper with his wife and of his returning the next day to find the milk not collected and the bedroom door locked, gave no hint that the dead woman was a part-time prostitute. It is likely, if astonishing, that the hotel manager had no idea of this.

If Cherrill was the fingerprint boffin on the case, Chief Inspector Edward Greeno was now put in charge and was officially leading what the newspaper hoardings called 'West End Search for Mad Killer'. Greeno estimated that it took Margaret Lowe fifteen seconds to die:

> Fifteen seconds to die and God knows how long it took to do what happened next; or maybe the savagery started before the silk stocking round her throat was twisted to strangling pressure.[11]

When Greeno looked at the mutilated remains of Jouannet with Bernard Spilsbury, the pathologist assured him that he had 'a madman on parade here' and 'when you catch him, I'd like to know if he is left-handed'. The murderer had held up the dead woman's breast and almost sliced off her nipple with a razor blade.

On 12 February, before Doris Jouannet's body had been found, Greeno and two women were to get extraordinarily lucky. On that evening, Greta Haywood – Cherrill merely calls her Mrs H – was picked up by a tall, handsome young airman in the Trocadero in Piccadilly Circus. She agreed to meet him later in a pub and after saying their goodnights, she was aware of him following her along St Albans Street. He asked her for a kiss, put his gas mask down to take her in his arms, then choked her into unconsciousness. He was rifling her handbag when a delivery boy on his way to the nearby Captain's Cabin, happened by and the assailant dashed off into the blackout darkness.

'The lust for blood must still have been upon him,' mused Cherrill, and the airman went off in search of more prey.

Cherrill's 'Mrs M' was Mrs Mulcahy, who worked in the Piccadilly area under the pseudonym Kathleen King. The airman, now without his gas mask, which the police had already picked up, talked her into a taxi and they went back to her flat in Southwick Street, Paddington. While she tried to sort out a broken light, he attacked her with his hands around her neck. She fought and screamed, which all his earlier victims seemed to have failed to do, kicking his shins and making such a row that he fled the scene, this time leaving the blue webbing belt of his RAF greatcoat and thrusting £5 into her hand, presumably in a weak attempt to keep her quiet.

What followed was hardly dazzling police work, but Greeno and Cherrill were experienced professionals and they did not put a foot wrong. The gas mask left in St Albans Street bore the unique number: 525987. It belonged to an officer cadet named Gordon Frederick Cummins. Greeno picked him up at his billet in St John's Wood and put him in an identity parade. Mrs Mulcahy, clearly still traumatized from the attack, could only be sure about Cummins' cold green eyes. Greta Haywood had no doubts at all – Cummins was the man from the Trocadero. In taking his fingerprints, Cherrill noticed that the airman signed the necessary authorization with his left hand. He was charged with the murders of Oatley, Lowe and Jouannet and the attempted murders of Hayward and Mulcahy. The case against him for the first killing, of Evelyn Hamilton, was left in abeyance for the moment.

While Cummins was on remand in Brixton gaol, Greeno did the

round of narks and snitches, which were the lifeblood of city policemen the world over. His uniformed team, working out of Tottenham Court Road police station, interviewed hundreds of prostitutes and one of them, Phyllis O'Dwyer, told Greeno that on the night of 12 February before the attack on Haywood, a young airman with the distinctive white flash of an officer-cadet on his field cap, had picked her up and tried to strangle her with her necklace in her flat:

> It was a large necklace . . . he said to me 'Do you always wear a necklace in bed?' – he was sort of turning the centre stone around in his fingers – and I said 'Well, sometimes.' Well, he still had hold of this stone and suddenly he started to twist it. Then he sort of grabbed a whole handful of the necklace and twisted it like mad. It was choking. And I could see his eyes – in fact, that was all I could see of him, his eyes. They were very wide apart, a sort of light green and they were blazing. Just like a madman's. I was in agony.[12]

She had fought him off and ordered him out. He had given her £10 for the trouble he'd caused, saying he was very sorry, and that he had 'got a bit carried away'.

In the meantime, Cummins denied everything and had an alibi for the nights in question by virtue of the signing in and out times at the St John's Wood barracks. Greeno was aware that the attacks and murders had happened on every night except Wednesday. When it became obvious that the cadets were in the habit of falsifying times to cover their comrade's illicit 'nights on the town', Cummins' alibis crumbled. The one night he could not escape was his fire-duty night, Wednesday. As a typical serial killer, but of the disorganized type, Cummins had taken souvenirs from his victims and Greeno found them: Doris Jouannet's wristwatch, fountain pen and comb; Evelyn Hamilton's pencil (and brick-dust from the Montagu Place air raid shelter found in his uniform trouser turn-ups); and cigarette cases belonging to both Evelyn Oatley and Margaret Lowe.

Even so, the prosecution at Cummins' subsequent trial almost blew it. Mr Justice Asquith presided over the Old Bailey proceedings on 27–28 April, G B McClure appearing for the prosecution. Mrs Cummins sat in the courtroom, smiling encouragement at her husband as the police built their case against him for the murder of Evelyn Oatley: only one victim, which was the usual practice in the case of multiple killings. As Cherrill was giving his evidence, he realized to his horror that the jury were being shown photographs of the wrong set of fingerprints and he had to tell the judge accordingly: 'It was the first time in the history of the Old Bailey,' he wrote later, 'that a trial had ever been stopped for such a reason.'[13]

A new jury was hastily empanelled and the case was relaunched days later. Cummins was found guilty, despite defence counsel John Flowers' best attempts to shake the jury over the fingerprint evidence, and his appeal failed. Albert Pierrepoint took society's revenge at Wandsworth on Thursday, 25 June.

Killers like Cummins were not fully understood at the time – the Yard seems to have regarded theft as his primary motive – and the pressures of war meant there was insufficient time to study the man or his crimes in detail. 'You may wonder,' Cherrill wrote, 'what manner of man was this who, night after night, set out to murder and mutilate women with such wanton savagery . . .'[14]

What is marked about the judicial process in the war and post-war years is the speed with which justice was done. Cummins was on remand for sixty days, which is one of the longest terms in the period. The jury only deliberated for half an hour before finding him guilty: 'I shed no tears for Cummins,' wrote Greeno, who formally identified the man's body dangling at the rope's end in Wandsworth, 'I thought he was the lowest form of man.'[15] And Robert Higgins pulls no punches either:

[Cummins] was by far the most vicious killer I encountered, or in fact, heard about during the whole of my police career . . . [He] had not a trace of pity or conscience in his entire make-up.[16]

The statistics that began this chapter are based on convictions – they do not take into account unsolved murders. In October 1941, nineteen-year-old prostitute Maple Church was found strangled in a bombed-out building in Hampstead Road. She worked the Soho streets and was strangled by a killer whose left hand was stronger than his right. Was she the seventh victim of Cummins, the Blackout Killer?

If Cummins grabbed the headlines in his brief murder spree, and Christie and Haigh were to do so in far more detail later, other killings did not go unreported. One of the most bizarre murders was the political assassination of Sir Michael O'Dwyer, former Lieutenant-Governor of the Punjab. On the afternoon of Wednesday 13 March 1940, the Tudor Room at Caxton Hall echoed to the crash of gunfire as the Sikh extremist, Udham Singh, emptied his revolver into the guests on the podium. Lord Zettal was hit twice in the chest, Sir Louis Dane took a bullet in the arm and a shot shattered Lord Lamington's wrist. It was O'Dwyer who came off worst, bullets hitting both his kidney and heart. At his trial, Singh claimed the whole thing had been an accident, that he had intended to fire over the heads of speakers just to frighten them. The jury did not believe a word of it and Singh hanged at Pentonville on 31 July. It may be that the wrong man died and that Singh thought he was firing at General Reginald Dyer, who had given the fatal order for the Amritsar Massacre in the rioting of 1919. If so, it had taken over twenty years for vengeance to come calling.

On Saturday, 2 November 1941, in a war-torn Liverpool that would not be adding more pyrotechnics for Guy Fawkes Night to those already provided by the Luftwaffe, fifteen-year-old Mary Hagan went out in the evening to fetch a paper for her father. When she had not returned by a quarter past seven, a search was instigated and the girl's raped and strangled body was found in a concrete blockhouse near the Brook Vale Bridge. It was not a difficult case for the local police. William Hindley had seen a soldier near the bridge and Thomas Todd went one better by identifying him as Samuel Morgan, from a local family, and serving with the Irish Guards. He was arrested in London eleven days later and returned to Liverpool for questioning. The bandage left in the blockhouse matched that missing from his medical field kit and forensics were able to find tell-tale soil samples in the folds of his battledress. A shaky alibi of drinking in a hotel in Seaforth fell apart quickly and Morgan tried a defence of manslaughter. Thomas Pierrepoint did the duty in Walton Gaol on 9 April: Mary Hagan would have been sixteen nine days later.

Gunner Harold Hill put forward a plea of schizophrenia when charged with the double murder of eight-year-old Doreen Hearne and her friend Kathleen Trundell, six. The grey, grainy, press photographs of the time show him in the back of a Railton police car, eyes closed in shame as he is taken away for questioning. The girls' bodies were found a few yards apart in Rough Wood, a copse 4 miles from their homes in Penn, Buckinghamshire, on Saturday, 22 November 1941. George Hatherill of the Yard was called in that night. They had both been strangled and stabbed in their chests and throats, although there was no obvious sign of sexual interference.[17]

The obsessions of wartime meant that a whole army of snoopers and nosey-parkers were on constant alert. Children had seen the girls climbing into a lorry and one of them, Norman Page, was able to recall the vehicle's registration number. It was a lorry that leaked oil and Hatherill was able to trace it to the Army camp at Yaxford, Suffolk. An identification parade led to Harold Hill's arrest. His lorry odometer showed an extra 20 miles for which he could not account, and there were specks of human blood on his battledress. Most damning of all was the handkerchief Hill had dropped at the murder scene, with the laundry mark RA [Royal Artillery] 1019, the same as on all other items of Hill's clothes. His fingerprints were found on Doreen Hearne's gas mask, the one no doubt her distraught mother would have insisted she carry at all times.

'Not,' as Hatherill admitted later, 'a very difficult case to solve,' but one in which the work of the detectives was of the highest methodical order.

The name of the hangman is not listed for the execution in Oxford Gaol on 1 May, but it was one of the Pierrepoint double acts.[18]

Winifred Evans was twenty-seven and went to a dance on Wednesday, 8 November 1944, in the village hall at Beccles. She was a wireless operator in the WAAF, according to friends 'quiet and reserved'[19] and she got back for duty at 12.05 a.m. Her friend, Corporal Margaret Johns, making her way to bed at the camp, bumped into an aircraftsman, loitering around the darkened corridors, drunk and apparently lost. He asked Johns if this was 'Number One Site' and looked to her like a sober man putting on an act. Less than an hour later, Evans' body was found face down in a ditch: she had been battered, raped and asphyxiated. Whoever had killed her had attacked from behind, bursting her liver and bruising her lungs as he landed on her and ramming her face into the mud.

The Yard was called in and Chief Inspector Greeno arrived with Keith Simpson. It was snowing that hard autumn and the dead woman's body was still under a tarpaulin, laced in white. An identity parade of the entire camp that day confirmed the 'drunken' airman was 37-year-old Arthur Heys. Older than his comrades, with a wife and two children, Heys had been at the dance the previous night but had broken away from the group to report a stolen bicycle to the police. Heys' uniform was torn, as though by barbed wire from a perimeter fence. A 'jigger' button found near the body was missing from his overcoat. There were rabbit hairs on his trousers, as there were on Evans' clothing and long, mousey human hair which, Simpson was convinced, came from the dead woman.

The most bizarre feature of this case was the anonymous letter sent to the camp Adjutant on 8 January 1945. It was signed with the initials 'RCAE' and was written in block capitals with a blue crayon and some odd spelling mistakes, purporting to come from the real killer rather than 'the airman so wrongly accused':

She had her cycle-lamp [the letter ran]. No one will ever find this. We stopped at the road leading to the SSQ [Signals Office]. She told me she could not stay long being nearly half past twelve. She should have been on duty. She accepted money from me which I got back, finding she was unclean. This is the type of girl she was, a gold-digger. I have known her go with three Yanks in one night. I must have gone mad. I don't remember exactly what happened. I know we struggled and I tore her tunic and slacks and believe other things and I was most indecent.

Although Heys refused to reprint any of this while in custody and his lawyers prevented Greeno from forcing the issue, it became evident that the aircraftsman was the author. His knowledge that Winifred Evans was 'unclean' (i.e. having a period) was correct and her bicycle-lamp, which she used as a torch was, indeed, never found. What was totally wrong was the good-time girl reputation that the killer had given her: Simpson was able to prove that the dead woman was a virgin.

After the jury found him guilty of a murder the judge described as 'more savage and horrible than any it has been my experience to try', Heys wrote another letter, this time in his own handwriting, and to Greeno, accusing him of breaking his wife's heart. Heys died at Norwich on 13 March 1945.

The war threw up three totally bizarre cases that have no parallel in the history of British murder, two of which might be connected. In the summer of 1940, Florence Ransom blasted three women to death in the garden of their Kent home. The subsequent case reads like a 'who's who' of criminology. Fred Cherrill, the Yard's finger-print man, dusted the weapon and the crime scene for prints. The legendary Bernard Spilsbury carried out the post-mortems, writing on his card-index system, 'shock due to gunshot injuries' as the cause of the deaths, 'Murder.' Robert Churchill, the gun expert, had no difficulty identifying the weapon. It was a single-barrelled, single-loader shotgun, heavy and with a stiff pull. Loaded shotguns were liable to go off accidentally if a shooter stumbled while carrying one. Not so with this weapon. The killer would have had to have reloaded five times to inflict the fatal injuries. And the trial made legal history. During the day, the Observation Corps kept watch on the roof of the Bailey for enemy air raids, listening for the snarl of the sirens and the deadly drone of the bombers. The court-room had a glass roof. Instead of the custom of keeping the jury in a hotel room overnight so that they could not be influenced by outsiders, they were allowed home for reasons of safety – most air raids happened at night.

In the classic style so beloved of 'B' features in the cinema of the following two decades, the local Kent police, under Detective Inspector Frank Sneed, called in the Yard. The officer given the case was Detective Chief Inspector Peter Beveridge, who only that day had been transferred from the Flying Squad to the 'Murder Squad'. The Yard team then quickly uncovered a bizarre 'ménage à quatre' involving Mr and Mrs Fisher and their respective lovers. Mrs Fisher was actually a widow, Florence Iris Ouida Ransom, a somewhat Bohemian woman currently with a Danish lover: a fact happily tolerated by Mr Fisher, who had a mistress of his own. It was Mr Fisher's ex-wife and daughter, as well as their housekeeper who had been blasted by a shotgun. Beveridge's task was to trace the drinker of a fourth teacup he found in the kitchen of Crittenden Cottage, the murder scene. And to find the owner of a lady's glove on the path that led to the killing field.

Despite the fact that all this activity coincided with the beginning of the Battle of Britain, with Heinkels and Messerschmitts screaming through the skies over Kent, a cohort of more than twenty Fleet Street journalists descended on the otherwise sleepy village of Matfield. Percy Hoskins, doyen of crime reporters, led the field; Edwin Tetlow was there from the *Mail* and Norman Rae from the *News of the World*. O'Dowd Gallagher of the *Daily Express* came with laurels of his reporting of the Spanish Civil War, the Italian attack on Abyssinia and the Japanese invasion of China. The *Daily Mirror*'s Ewart Brookes had been among those who took his own motor-launch across to Dunkirk, no doubt to get a colourful first-hand story as much as to save lives.

The situation at Matfield and nearby Piddington Farm, which 'Mrs Fisher' ran was impossibly convoluted, especially as most of the participants in the saga used nicknames. Florence Ransom, as well as calling herself 'Mrs Fisher', was known as 'Julie'; her husband Walter was 'Peter'; one of the dead women, the real (ex) Mrs Fisher, actually Dorothy, was known as 'Lizzie'. Three people who worked at Piddington were actually Florence Ransom's family, but they all denied it for reasons best known to themselves.

The net closed on Florence on Friday 12 July. After increasingly irrational behaviour she was tracked down to High Holborn tube station and a nosy press photographer (were they tipped off?) took what is probably a unique photograph in the history of British crime. Peter Beveridge is shown tipping his bowler-hat to the murderess prior to arresting her on suspicion. She is standing, very stylishly dressed, with holdall and the padded shoulders that were all the rage. 'Oh, yes,' she said, in a matter-of-fact sort of way, 'but I must first see my husband. He's in an office round the corner.'[20] Mrs Ransom began behaving even more oddly in Tonbridge Police Court on Tuesday, 16 July. Local reporters observed that she was distressed and half-dazed, sitting in a huddle, resting her head on the shoulder of a policewoman.

At the Bailey, defence counsel Stuart Horner, who had only been given a week to prepare for the case, argued instability and lapses of memory. The judge, Mr Justice Hallett, was having none of it: 'I do not understand lapses of memory. A person is either sane or insane. I am not aware of any third stage.'[21] British justice relied on the McNaghten rules, laid down a century earlier, as a yardstick for measuring legal sanity. It was hopelessly inadequate in terms of actual psychiatric assessment, and the Mental Deficiency Act of 1913 was no better, but under them both, Mrs Ransom was held fit to stand her trial. Four days later, the jury found her guilty. When her appeal failed, she sat rocking in the dock, whispering, 'I want to go home.'

And go home she did in the January of 1967. Her death sentence was commuted in December 1940 by the Home Secretary – the 'man who rations mercy' – Herbert Morrison. Mrs Ransom spent the next twenty-seven years of her life in Broadmoor.

The linked cases take us back to a time, potentially, long before the Second World War. 'Anybody can become a witch,' wrote Detective Superintendent Robert Fabian, and explained the centuries-old ritual. 'You do not believe such nonsense and neither do I,'[22] he concluded. But the still unsolved murder of farm-labourer Charles Walton gave everybody, on St Valentine's Day 1945, pause for thought. Perhaps there was more time to reflect now that the Allies were closing in on the Third Reich, and not only was the potential invasion of Britain a memory, but the deadly Doodlebugs had stopped too. The day before Charles Walton died, the German city of Dresden was flattened in a terrible firestorm, which left a trail of slaughter. Estimates of the dead ranged from 30,000 to 200,000. Few people worried about a single old man when figures like that hit the headlines of British newspapers. Few that is except Superintendent Alec Spooner of Warwickshire CID, based at Leamington, the dead man's neighbour, Harry Beasley, and his employer, Alfred Potter. When Walton, rheumaticky, cantankerous and seventy-four, failed to return from hedging, the two civilians had set off in search of him. They found his body by torchlight in a field on the slopes of Meon Hill, above the village of Lower Quinton, where they all lived.

Walton's pitchfork had been thrust though his throat, pinning him to the frozen earth beneath. His billhook had been used to carve a crude cross into his chest and it was left in a deep gash across his throat. Spooner's initial enquiries in the village drew a blank, so he called in the Yard. Fabian's assistant was Sergeant Albert Webb, who would work on the Haigh case in the years ahead, and the two of them were slightly thrown to find that Spooner, whom Fabian described as a 'highly scientific' policeman, was already steeped in the folklore of the area. Nearby were the Rollright Stones, an ancient circle near Long Compton, long associated with Druidic sacrifice and witchcraft. And Walton had died on St Valentine's Day, the Druid festival of Imbolc, in which humans had once been sacrificed so that their blood seeped into the earth and replenished it for spring.

Nor was Walton's murder the first in the area. In 1875, farm-labourer, John Haywood, skewered old Ann Turner with a pitchfork, threatening to kill all sixteen of the witches who lived in Long Compton. This link gained credence when the redoubtable Margaret Murray entered the arena seventy-five years later. An archaeologist, Egyptologist and one-time Suffragette, Dr Murray was in her eighties when she investigated the Meon Hill murder and wrote a detailed report for the *Birmingham Post*. Although long discredited, the ideas of the woman who wrote *The God of the Witches* were then state-of-the-art. Murray did not arrive until 1950, posing as a dotty old Miss Marple on a sketching holiday. She was sharp as a needle, however, and found exactly the same kind of sinister silence that Spooner, Fabian and Webb had encountered five years earlier. 'Cottage doors were shut in our faces,' Fabian remembered, 'and even the most innocent witnesses seemed unable to meet our eyes.' When the police arrived to question locals at the College Arms, conversation stopped and people left. Weird incidents began to happen. A police car ran over a dog; a black hound was seen by several investigators, but no one knew whose it was; a calf was found dead in a ditch.

Fabian's investigation, nevertheless, stayed in the here and now. His team interviewed all 493 villagers and questioned boot repairers in Salisbury. Nearby was Long Marston prisoner-of-war camp, only 2 miles from the murder scene and home to some 1,043 Italians, Germans, Slavs and Ukrainians. Although no prisoner ever escaped from Britain, their presence caused problems. There was a serious breakout attempt in Comine, Perthshire, shortly before Christmas, which left one man dead and four seriously injured. Security was slack in many camps, with prisoners working in the area, drinking in pubs and chatting up local girls.[23] Fabian called in the extraordinary DS David Sanders of Special Branch, who spoke fluently all the languages in the camp! Blood found on the coat of an Italian prisoner proved to be that of a rabbit: the man was a poacher, not a murderer.

An Avro Anson spotter plane flew low over the fields, photographing the area. A detachment of the Royal Engineers combed the place with mine-detectors, looking for the victim's missing watch. Blood-spattered twigs, flattened grass, Walton's saturated clothes were all studied relentlessly in the West Midland Forensic Science laboratory and . . . nothing.

'So we had to leave it,' Fabian wrote. His chief suspect was Alfred Potter, a taciturn farmer who had fallen on hard times. It was said that he owed Walton money and that when the old man came for repayment, something snapped:

Maybe [mused Fabian ten years later], somebody in that tranquil village off the main road knows who killed Charles Walton, who lies buried among the neat, grey tombstones of

[65]

Lower Quinton churchyard? Maybe one day somebody will talk? Not to me . . .

The pathologist who examined Charles Walton's body, J M Webster of the West Midlands laboratory at Birmingham, had also been engaged in April 1943 on the case of a corpse found stuffed into the hollow trunk of a wych elm in Hagley Wood, not a long crow's flight from Meon Hill. Four boys were out birds' nesting or rabbit catching on Sunday, 19 April. It was Bob Hart who climbed up through the spindly branches of the wych elm and saw in its hollow, half rotten trunk, a skull he took to be a fox's. Prodding it out into the open with a stick, the boys realized to their horror that it was human.

Contact with Sergeant Richard Skeratt of the local police led to Worcestershire CID cordoning off the entire area and treating it as a crime scene. Scattered bones were found in the leaf mould for yards around and the right hand, virtually intact, led detectives into a bizarre sideways look at the supernatural.

Webster pieced together what he could of the corpse and arrived at a useful physical appearance. The dead woman was about thirty-five when she died, 5 foot tall and wearing a dark skirt, a cheap mock-gold wedding ring and unusual blue, crepe-soled shoes. Her hair was brown, but most noticeable were her irregular teeth in the lower jaw. Such evidence traced to dental records has been known to hang men, but, in this case, police drew a blank. In fact, all leads proved fruitless.

Two men heard screams coming from Hagley Wood one night in July, but a search of the area at the time had found nothing unusual. There had been a gypsy camp nearby at the same time, but there was nothing tangible to link the corpse with them. One major problem was the murder scene. Why would anyone go to the lengths of stuffing a body, even that of a small, relatively light woman, in the trunk of a tree over 5 feet above the ground? Could the feat have been carried out by one person or must there have been two involved? Then came the graffiti. On a number of walls in the area, chalk marks appeared: 'Who put Bella down the Wych Elm – Hagley Wood?' In some variants the name Luebella was used. It is entirely possible that this line had no direct connection with the killer, but was merely the work of a hoaxer. In the event, it led nowhere.

Letters began appearing in the Press too, not purporting to come from the killer, but suggesting all sorts of possible motives. Looming largest among them was witchcraft and when Dr Murray began to investigate the case seven years later, she was able to point up the fact that 'Bella' and 'Luebella' were names commonly associated with the Black Arts. The severed hand, originally hacked from a corpse, especially a hanged felon on the gallows, was thought to possess magical powers. It could open locks, paralyze victims and, as the 'hand of glory' (*main de gloire* in the French) was linked to the lethal plant mandragora. The journalist 'Quaestor' writing in the Wolverhampton *Express and Star* ran articles in 1945 that linked the Hagley Wood murder with that of Charles Walton on Meon Hill. In fact, of course, the links were tenuous in the extreme. 'Bella' was young and female and the cause of death could not be identified (any more than she could). Someone went to considerable lengths to hide the body and the scattered bones and severed hand was likely to be the work of foxes. Whoever killed Charles Walton made sure he was found and that his overtly ritualistic wounds were obvious.

Into the ring, in the 1950s, stepped the ex-spy Donald McCormick, who concluded that 'Bella' was probably an agent with the code name of 'Clara' and that she may have been related to the Dutch spy Johannes Dronkers, caught and executed in 1942.[24] McCormick – who had a colourful take on life – postulated that 'Clara' was obsessed with horoscopes and astrology, and was in fact escaping the Aktion Hess, the rounding up of various fakirs who were said to have influenced the Deputy Führer's unfathomable flight to Scotland in May 1941.

More prosaically, locals were convinced that gypsies were responsible, and that perhaps 'Bella' was one of them, guilty of some crime against her people, and they had executed her in a ritual of their own. Like the murder of Charles Walton, the case remains unsolved.

The novelist and critic Graham Greene became an Intelligence Officer on the outbreak of war and wrote in 1941 *The Ministry of*

Fear. 'Nobody troubles,' he wrote, 'about daily deaths . . . in the middle of a daily massacre.' But this was simply not true. Society, for all the pressures put upon it, had not fallen apart. Life was cheap, but it was not free. The police worked ridiculous hours to control crime. The public were astonishingly vigilant. And people up and down the country were avid to scan their newspapers for details of grisly crimes like those dealt with in this chapter.

CHAPTER FOUR

The Black Market

Throughout history there have been certain crimes that most members of society do not regard as crimes at all. Today we would include parking on double yellow lines and speeding, where no motorist is happy to accept the injunction that 'twenty is plenty'. Such is the contempt for driving and parking law that thousands of us break it every day. A better parallel with wartime restrictions is, perhaps, the smuggling of the eighteenth century. Occurring all around the coast, men and women smuggled because the government had imposed swingeing duties on various goods. To avoid paying the hated revenue, people went to extraordinary and ingenious lengths to smuggle contraband, knowing there was a ready market, even among the otherwise honest, great and good.

In September 1939, identity cards were introduced to a free people who had never known such strictures. The carrying of papers was a European notion, not British, but anyone who felt resentment at having to produce their identity card was doubly outraged in December, when they were issued with ration books containing coupons with which to buy produce. The reason for this was obvious. During a war as total as the 1939–45 conflict, trade was seriously disrupted. Goods that were wholly imported – like bananas – disappeared from the shops. Meanwhile, home-produced goods, like silk, had more important uses than ladies' lingerie – it was the best material for parachutes.

The Board of Trade, via posters to be displayed in shop windows, reminded everybody of the new uses of what once had been household goods:

In Wartime, production must be for war and not peace. Here are examples of the changeover from peacetime products to wartime necessities:

Corsets become Parachutes and Chinstraps
Lace Curtains become Sand fly Netting
Carpets become Webbing Equipment
Toilet Preparations become Anti-Gas Ointments
Golf Balls become Gas Masks
Mattresses become Life Jackets
Saucepans become Steel Helmets
Combs become Eyeshields

Butter and bacon were rationed that December. The weekly allowance was 4 ounces of butter, 12 of sugar, 4 of bacon and ham. From March 1940, meat was rationed; tea, jam, cooking fat and cheese from July. Officially, the British public could eat one egg a fortnight.

Policing all this, from its Whitehall offices, was the Ministry of Food, which became positively Orwellian in its arbitrary behaviour as the war progressed. Under its organizer, Lord Woolton, it tried to impose a healthy – but above all, cheap – dietary regime on a nation that had not yet recovered from the economic privations of the thirties.

'War and Peace' pudding from Canada was a rare treat. With little dried fruit available, housewives put diced carrot into Christmas puddings. Carrot croquettes and carrot fudge were recipes found in magazines and Marguerite Patten became the acceptable face of constrained cooking long before the advent of the celebrity chefs. Lest the public start to believe that the Ministry was obsessed with carrots, they also promoted 'All-Clear sandwiches' and 'Woolton pies', thus proving their fixation with parsnips. Even bread, the staple diet of Englishmen for centuries, was rationed soon after the war, and the fact that there was no open revolt against this proves how cowed the public had become by constant control from above. But even before bread rationing, the 'British loaf' was coarse, grey and not very tasty. In major cities, 'British Restaurants' sprang up as a cheaper rival to Joe Lyons' Corner Houses, backed by an enthusiastic Winston Churchill. Prominent on the menu were . . . parsnips and carrots.

The Ministry of Agriculture tried to persuade people to 'do their bit' by planting carrots and parsnips rather than begonias and a fortune was spent on the propaganda war to encourage people to 'Dig For Victory'. Bones were saved and boiled down to make glue that held aircraft parts together. Pots, pans and railings were handed in at special centres to be recycled for tanks, planes and battleships. The fact that little of this was actually used made no difference to the call.

Clothing coupons were introduced in June 1941. Gone were the wide billowing 'Oxford bags', fashionable with young men in the 1930s – their turn-ups disappeared too. Skirts lost their pleats and hemlines got shorter, much to the delight of young men, but quite shocking to the older generation. Deprived of silk for stockings, the trendier girls coloured their legs with gravy browning and got a friend to draw a seam up the back with an eyebrow pencil.

In July 1943, the *Sunday Pictorial*'s John Ridley went undercover to show how easy it was to obtain clothing coupons illegally: 'It was a seedy little man in a shiny blue suit who started it all for me. "Want some clothes coupons?" he asked.' The article was addressed to Hugh Dalton at the Board of Trade, asking for readers to let Ridley know of their own similar experiences: 'It is up to everyone to help trap these rats.'[1]

Eventually, even cosmetics were hit. Soap was rationed in March 1942 and men could only buy five razor blades at a time. The budget of 1943 increased the price of all cosmetics by 50 per cent. An ordinary lipstick was now twelve shillings and sixpence (in today's terms about £25) and face powder £1 5s (£50). The Toilet Preparations Order limited the amount that could be produced. Real wages were rising in 1941–42,[2] so that even the working class, traditionally the poorest end of society, could actually afford more in the way of life's luxuries than at any time in the past. The coupon system, however, prevented this from happening. Angus Calder highlights the problem by looking at the clothing industry. In the spring of 1942 the official allowance meant that a man was entitled to buy: a topcoat once every seven years; a pullover and waistcoat every five; a jacket every two; a shirt every twenty months; a pair of shoes every eight months; and a pair of socks every two. As Edward Smithies points out, this 'represented an intolerable lowering of standards'[3] for the better off.

How did the public respond to all this? As is usual, everybody moaned, but as we have seen, moaning itself was a dangerous pastime in the war years. It could be interpreted as defeatism and that could mean a prison stretch. Some people organized defiant groups – for example, the Langdale Street Housewives' Circle in Stepney in the summer of 1941 – outraged at the 'food racket'. Shops that broke the law were boycotted.

But this was not the norm. Many people – from professional criminals who realized there was money to be made in an adaptation of their usual work, to upright citizens – were quite prepared to bend the rules, in order to maintain what they saw as their usual lifestyle, thus stepping outside the law.

The traded goods came from three principal areas: theft from the workplace, illegal sale of farm produce and illegal manufacturing. Pilfering became endemic very quickly, partly because – for all the camaraderie that people remembered with the glow of nostalgia in the years after the war, and for all the 'gung-ho' solidarity Churchill's government presented to the world – there was something of a 'them and us' attitude between the front-line troops and the civilians expected to supply them. Nor was this the first war in which this gap was noted. The Minister of Munitions in the First World War said in his first speech: 'We must keep on striking, striking, striking,' and the poet, D S MacColl, summed up the situation brilliantly in 'The Miners' Response':

We do: the present desperate stage
Of fighting brings us luck;
And in the higher war we wage
(For higher wage) *We Struck*.[4]

Strikes in both world wars were regarded by fighting men as little better than treason, but in fact, working men who were told their workplace now manufactured tanks rather than cars, felt mightily aggrieved. After Dunkirk there was a certain pulling together for the war effort, but by 1941, with the threat of invasion receding, there was something of a return to the pre-war shop floor versus management animosity that characterized the thirties. Some 1,354,000 working days were lost through strikes in 1939 and 1,077,000 in 1941. But for every man prepared to face the flak of more patriotic neighbours by standing on a picket line, there were half a dozen content to strive to meet the government's almost impossible demands – as long as there was something in it for them.

The docks were inevitably a focus for pilferers. In Liverpool in May 1944, five dockers were arrested with ties and handkerchiefs hidden in their clothing. One had 60 yards of silk wrapped around his body!

There were two types of dockyard pilfering. The first – and more serious – was the link with organized crime. In one case, a docker's home was raided in Birkenhead and the police found 250 'hot' items, ranging from cooking stoves to dog collars. When questioned, the docker explained that he had obtained these items from men in pubs, and this typifies the problem for the police throughout the war – no receipts, no surnames, no friend-of-a-friend and the Black Market trail went cold. Professional pilferers sold their stolen goods on to a 'fence', who would then distribute elsewhere. Sometimes, whole factories or companies were involved in disseminating goods in this way.

The second type of dockyard theft was casual, carried out by amateurs, sometimes spontaneously, because security – despite all the wartime precautions – was so lax. Regular police were appointed eventually because the scale of pilfering was getting out of hand. Most of this theft was for the dockers' own personal use, to supplement food or clothing allowances, and in the Liverpool area in particular, running battles with the police sometimes occurred when an individual was caught. Where fines were imposed, a docker's mates would chip in, since many of them knew it might be their turn next. Mass pilfering at the docks occurred occasionally, as endemic briefly became epidemic.

The railways were, inevitably, other centres of theft, and at Shoreditch in 1942, the entire staff at the LMS depot were found guilty of stealing oranges, ladies' stockings and milk-powder to the value of £60. In the following year, at Daventry, cigarettes, men's shirts and whisky were stolen from LNER freight wagons and here, most of the guilty were given prison sentences for three to six months. Prosecutions like these, however, were only the tip of a huge iceberg. A magistrate wrote in the *Hackney Gazette*:

> Just now no good citizen can be anything but profoundly disturbed by the number of cases of larceny from the employer.[5]

Firms of all shapes and sizes were hit by this crime. Ford's, Plessey's, Berger Paints, Kearley and Tonge, Ever Ready, Odeon Theatres and the Co-op were just some of the high-profile companies – all household names – which were suffering huge losses. Even more alarmingly, among the victims were various ARP centres and even some canteens of the Metropolitan Police!

Police Forces routinely raided firms and searched employees on their way out of the gates. By 1942, vast quantities of alcohol and tobacco were being stolen, both acting as an unofficial currency in the Black Market. One tobacco company in Hackney lost an estimated 2 million cigarettes (in today's terms worth £320,000) in less than a year.

The scale of pilfering was such that arrests were unusual – token at best. Magistrates, too, took as lenient a line as possible, in the largely mistaken belief that the British, in the face of adversity, did not behave that way.

It was in the Black Market that the honest citizen came face to face with the professional criminal. If goods were pilfered – and that, in itself, was a euphemism for stolen – then there had to be a market for such goods. The racketeer who made all this possible was that legendary character, the Spiv. The term comes from the inter-war racecourse gangs who used polite society's 'spiffing' to mean splendid. The image was one of 'Jack-the-Lad' – a genial sharp dresser who lived by his wits and flitted in and out of the shadows of the underworld. Spivs were actually a wide cross-section – crooked businessmen (many of the cases of pilfering were inside jobs involving management), old lags, deserters and draft dodgers.

Black Marketeering and racketeering themselves also came in various shapes and sizes. There was a brisk market in the illegal printing of identity cards and ration books. These items were also a target for theft, to the extent that, by 1942, the whole rationing system in London was under threat of collapse.

Chief Inspector Ted Greeno's experience is telling. In September 1943 his informants told him that a staggering 5 million coupons were available on the Black Market, having been obtained from an Army depot at Earlsfield in South West London. They were held here because they were specifically for discharged servicemen or Blitz victims whose clothes had been destroyed in air raids. With his instinct for gambling, Greeno was looking for someone who knew his way around the depot, could gain access without attracting attention, and had the necessary contacts to pass the coupons on. He found just such an individual: 'a young man with a major's crown, a taste for dog racing and a perpetual desire to change into civvies.'[6] In fact, the target – trailed by Greeno's Yard officers and an 'underworld scout' – was a second lieutenant with a room in a hotel in Seven Sisters Road, Holloway. The chambermaid told Greeno's men that he kept a locked trunk there, full of secret papers and a revolver. Confronted by Detective Sergeant Hodge at the American Bar of the Charing Cross Hotel, the 'major' turned out not to be carrying his identity card, refused to open a briefcase he was carrying, and dropped a few senior police names to attempt to bully Hodge into letting him go. It didn't work and the 'major' found himself facing Greeno at the Yard. He soon cracked, explaining that he hired two men to steal the coupons through windows he knew would be left open, selling the coupons in batches to various contacts all over London.

Early in 1944, 14,000 ration books were stolen in Hertfordshire and a lorry was needed to shift them. In Preston, a middleman distributing clothing coupons told the court prosecuting him that he had a waiting market for 20 million. In both these cases, those caught were unwilling or unable to name their numerous contacts, relying on the old lag's favourite tag line – 'somebody I met in a pub'.

A London postman took advantage of the system of posting books by helping himself. Police found 50,000 coupons in his flat. Inevitably, the easiest place to acquire coupons illegally by fraud, rather than outright theft, was at the printers and the pulpers – the beginning and end of a ration book's life. Forgery had declined in terms of convictions in the inter-war years but coupons were badly printed and much easier to copy than currency. Where forgers were caught, they risked jail sentences of up to four years. Because of the rationing system, coupons acquired a currency status of their own and it was possible to sell them for ready cash. Poor families did this on a regular basis; each book was worth between 10s and 12s 6d. At the other end of a transaction, retailers collected the coupons they alone, by regulation, were allowed to tear out of books and hand them in to the Post Office in exchange for a voucher. Unscrupulous shopkeepers, knowing that GPO officials did not have the time to check, falsified the number of coupons contained in their envelopes. In the rare instances of this scam being discovered, the shopkeeper pleaded an honest mistake in counting and sometimes got away with it.

Many illegal goods changed hands at illegal prices in street markets around the country. Petticoat Lane (Middlesex Street) in London was one notorious centre, but the best chronicled was Romford in Essex. Tic-tac men, well used to spotting policemen at a distance from the days of the racecourse gangs, were used to warn dodgy stallholders of the Law mingling with the crowds. Much of this involved the rag trade, the clothing industry which, as we have seen, was badly hit by wartime regulations. Some people complained – with a deep irony bearing in mind what was happening all over Nazi-occupied Europe – that large numbers of Jews were involved in this. There were certainly large numbers involved in the legal clothing trade, but the numbers of prosecutions of Jews for racketeering of all kinds was remarkably small.

The most sophisticated and complicated end of this trade involved the notorious 'L Triangle' of London, Leeds and Liverpool. The northern port was particularly useful in obtaining illicit goods from the United States (before their troops arrived and afterwards) and from the Irish Free State. Such was the extent of this operation that Scotland Yard assigned three senior officers in 1942 to combat it. Leeds had been a centre of the wool trade for centuries (part of the city's coat of arms is a sheep) and much of the economy of London's East End had belonged, as we have seen, to Jewish clothes sellers.[7] Messrs Barker, Yandell and Sands, all of superintendent rank, were assigned to the Board of Trade, which technically issued arrest warrants for Black Market crimes such as these. Yandell found that in Leeds millworkers by the dozen were walking out of their workplaces with rolls of cloth under their arms in broad daylight. Using 'narks' and 'stoolies', many of whom had already tried blackmail, he was able to close down at least some of this racketeering. He knew only too well that the operation would continue until rationing ceased, and that meant long after the war ended. In a single case, Yandell brought forty-eight culprits to court at Harrogate, some charged with theft of cloth worth £1,600 and others as receivers of stolen goods. The prosecution summed up the problem when it said of these people (including housewives, civil servants and a dentist):

> they may be small fry involved in small transactions, but it is owing to the stupidity and anti-social tendencies of these small fry that this racket goes on at all.[8]

If the clothing Black Market was a problem, that in food was probably worse. Receivers of dodgy clothes ran the risk of being spotted wearing something suspicious every time they left their homes; illicit food was gone in a mealtime. And, unlike clothing, the sale of Black Market foodstuffs implied a potentially serious health threat. Today's environmentalists would blanch at the dietary routines of wartime. Sell-by dates had not been invented. The majority of people did not own refrigerators, an American gadget that did not become *de rigueur* until long after the war. Butchers, even honest ones trading before the advent of the coupon, often sold tuberculous meat, relying on the fact that the overstretched Sanitary Inspectors and Meat and Foods Inspectors could not be everywhere at once. Wartime privations made all this worse. Sometimes steak was grey with infection; sometimes, it was horse. The coupon price of an egg was threepence three farthings; one dealer in North London was charging 15 shillings a dozen. Fish, of poor quality even at Billingsgate, the country's largest fresh-fish market, could be obtained if you knew the right people. Deep-sea trawling was largely a thing of the past with wolf packs of U-Boats prowling the Atlantic and the Channel. 'Everyone must pay,' one Black Marketeer told the court, 'or go without.' Faced with that stark choice, many people were prepared to pay. In the whole arbitrary creation of the nearest thing people had seen to a police state since the rule of the Major Generals,[9] the Ministry of Food seems to have been the most obnoxious.

In January 1941, the Ministry made inflation an offence by criminalizing price increases in a vast range of consumables, from coffee to nuts. The other side of the coin was food wastage. In 1940 the *Western Mail*'s headline ran: 'Food Wasters May Get Two Years Imprisonment'. And the Ministry again enlisted the aid of police to get results against lawbreakers. In February 1945, Police Commissioner, Sir Norman Kendall, working with Charles Tegart of the Ministry of Food, identified fifty leaders of the Black Market, many of whom were already behind bars. In fact, as fast as one gang was broken, another emerged, as slippery and streetwise as the last.

William Barker carried out an operation on a premises in Eastcheap in March 1942 and his team trailed a lorry that picked up cases of tinned sardines and sacks of cornstarch, which it proceeded to unload in the West End. When the Yard men pounced, the lorry was found to be stuffed with rationed goods bound for Mayfair restaurants. When the Black Marketeer, Seymour Sidney – aka 'Skylinski' – was arrested, he had £644 in his wallet and the Lord Chief Justice told him, 'You have committed, in effect, acts of sabotage against this nation.'[10]

The Ministry used highly underhand methods to trap the unwary, sending 'daffy' young women into butchers' and grocers' shops, persuading the proprietors to part with produce without the necessary coupons and then returning with a policeman to have them arrested. Lord Woolton believed this sort of thing was absolutely necessary, but few of the public agreed.

In Essex, unscrupulous poulterers were selling birds kept supposedly for breeding, to London restaurants. A journalist visiting the Braintree livestock market noted that many of the hens were blind or lame and totally unsuitable for breeding. Presumably, however, even a blind chicken tastes nice at a dinner table. The prices charged represented 100 per cent mark-up and butchers and poulterers throughout the land received gaol sentences for this sort of offence. Such was the contempt for the authorities and their petty regulations that egg dealers regularly signed themselves 'Neville Chamberlain' or 'Winston Churchill', depending on what year it was, and nobody seemed to notice!

Where retailers were caught charging excessive prices, they invariably blamed a huge mark-up from the wholesaler. Lord Woolton himself was said to be keenly interested in this, knowing full well that the occasional prosecution was regarded by most entrepreneurs as a legitimate business risk like any other vagary in the market. The attitude of the courts to crimes like this was, to say the least, schizophrenic. On the one hand, crimson-faced magistrates ranted about treachery and self-interest in the face of national desperation. On the other, they doled out fines that completely failed to act as any sort of deterrent. At Chelmsford market in the last December of the war, undercover inspectors discovered a stall selling hairgrips at a profit of 450 per cent: the stallholder was fined £5. When an enforcement officer was locked in an office by an unscrupulous greengrocer in Wallasey, having sold goods at inflated prices, he was fined only £6 for what might have been regarded as a kidnapping offence.

The scarcity of goods led to something like 'auction fever' in a deprived, but relatively wealthy, population. Razor blades, nail files, combs, jewellery, stationery and toys went for ludicrous prices from the suitcases of street-traders and from market-stalls rented by fences. Christmases were particularly 'silly seasons' as a depressed populace desperately tried to cheer themselves up. Like all contraband, the Black Market relied on dishonest people persuading the gullible that, since everyone was involved, where was the harm? Everyone knew 'someone who knew someone' and deals were struck at all levels. And it succeeded because the authorities were swamped and inconsistent. In the North East, in 1944, 860 complaints were received by the Price Regulation Committee, mostly from members of the public furious at being 'ripped off'. Some 239 incidents were deemed criminal, but of these only twenty-seven came to court. The rest were dealt with simply by a caution (which, it is a safe bet, was ignored).

From this arose the widespread belief that corruption reached the highest level. Home Office pathologist Keith Simpson could dine very comfortably in the élite London restaurants. Clubland continued to flourish, flouting almost every regulation in Churchill's book. It really was a case of Rudyard Kipling's 'brandy for the parson, baccy for the clerk' and if not everybody was prepared to watch the wall, as the poet suggested we should to avoid incrimination, most people did. And senior policemen had other fish to fry. Chief Superintendent Arthur Thorp, dealing with a murder enquiry in Wales, found a leg of ham hidden under his hotel bed: 'I went through the motions,' he wrote later, 'of inquiring how [the culprit] had come to be in possession of the meat, but soon discovered I was getting nowhere. And anyway – I was busy.'[11]

There was a noticeable increase in Black Marketeering as the war went on. After D-Day – and particularly as the V1 and V2 rocket bases were captured by British and American troops – the fortress mentality of the early years vanished and large numbers of people began to look forward, not just to peace, but to an end of privations. But the fact that rationing continued after VE and VJ Day – on certain goods until 1952 – meant that the *raison d'être* for the Black Market continued too. Goods were now streaming back into Britain from a grateful, liberated France, often via American airbases in Lincolnshire and East Anglia. War production was now seen as less relevant. Even Rupert Bear annuals were produced as 'War Economy Issue' with soft covers rather than the pre-war hardbacks and manufacturers continued to produce non-essential goods like toys, even from their own garden sheds and front rooms. In one case in Hemel Hempstead, a worker at an aircraft factory was stealing Perspex (not available on the open market) and making toy planes with it. In the first six months of 1944, prosecutions in Willesden uncovered the illegal manufacture of 7,666 chairs, 4,040 clothes-horses, 2,952 bread boards and 26,146 items of costume jewellery.

The total value was £20,965 and, as in the Hemel case, production was carried out by companies working on government contracts.[12]

The other development that concerned the authorities greatly was the merging of the Black Market with organized crime. What had been a largely amateur business in 1940 was, by 1945, linked to the Underworld, especially in London, providing cash for the betting and gaming frenzy that specialist police units were being set up to deal with. The London *Evening Standard* quoted a detective in January 1945:

> Night after night, in so-called social clubs, you can see as much money on the gambling tables as you would normally see in peacetime Cannes, Le Touquet and Monte Carlo.[13]

Three years earlier, Defence Regulation 42CA had fixed penalties of three months' imprisonment and a fine of £500 against those involved in gambling. Any 'party' involving more than ten people intending to play for gain was liable. For some reason (presumably because of the different legal system) Scotland was exempt.

Ask anyone what image the Second World War conjures up and most people would say the Blitz and the Black Market. In the research for this book, I asked a small cross-section of people who were children during the war what their criminal memories were: 85 per cent had some recollection of mothers and fathers obtaining goods from the Black Market, as though this was the norm.

There was a general perception at the time – and since – that in terms of food privations, country-dwellers had a far better time of it than 'townies'. Imports of food literally halved during the war and the need to use every available piece of land became a necessity.

ITMA's Tommy Handley, of course, had his own take on egg production at a time when the humble egg became something of a symbol of the country's ability to muddle through: 'Hello, yolks – have you ever tried *ITMA* eggs? They're all singing, all humming and all bumen.'[14]

The 'Basal Diet' – 12 oz of bread, 1 lb of potatoes, 2 oz of oatmeal, 1 oz of fat, 6 oz of vegetables and 6/10 of a pint of milk a day –

never really took off, largely because the Black Market found ways around it.

By the middle of the war, consumption of vegetables was up by 30 per cent, potatoes 40 per cent, and milk 30 per cent over pre-war levels. Meat, however, had dropped by more than 20 per cent, sugar 30 per cent, citrus fruits by 50 per cent. Whereas worried wireless doctors warned of health dangers, the death rate among civilians, excluding Blitz casualties, was falling in the forties, especially in terms of a sharp downturn in tuberculosis.

Foodstuffs were notoriously tampered with in a way that had not happened since the introduction of the Food and Drugs Act, under Disraeli in 1876. Flour, salt and baking powder were packaged as 'milk substitute' for 5 shillings a pound. Onion substitutes were often little more than water accompanied by a smell.

There was a sense, in the case of rationing and prosecutions of the Black Market, that what was being waged was not a war against crime, but a perpetuation of the class system's unfairness. Hovering like a spectre out of the depressed thirties was Communism – or at least Socialism – now made more acceptable because Fascism was seen as the enemy and Soviet Russia, after the summer of 1941, was our ally. Many of the Left welcomed Chamberlain's and Churchill's restrictions because they gave a balance to a system that, pre-war, did not exist. In theory, the lord of the manor could now obtain only the same number of bacon rashers as the lowliest denizen of an inner city. In practice, of course, this was not so, and it gave an almost political edge to dodging regulations and buying and selling illegal goods.

With only one person in seven unhappy even with the idea of rationing, the Black Market appeared to have its work cut out to make any headway at all, and at least according to one survey in 1942, most support for rationing came from middle-class, Southern English housewives. The Black Market of course was run almost entirely by men at its large-scale, organized end and flourished in areas where poverty and hardship had been the norm pre-war. Steelworkers, miners and dockers proved to be less well-nourished than agricultural workers, merely adding to the notion that the countryside was better off and providing a ready urban market for illicit goods.

Despite Woolton's 900 inspectors regularly snooping for the Ministry of Food, trying to implement the 415 regulations that the government had brought in by the end of 1944, the Black Market continued to be a problem, especially when the 'grey market' of shopkeepers putting a little aside for favourite customers, is taken into account. Angus Calder sums it up:

How big the [Black Market] was, no one will ever know; it was in the nature of a successful black market transaction that it was left out of official statistics and evaded courts of law.[15]

A total of 114,000 people were prosecuted, 30,000 in the 'worst' year of 1943, but this figure almost certainly represents the tip of a vast iceberg.

War profiteering was the most distasteful end of the Black Market, often categorized as a separate crime. Brothels and good-time girls overcharged American servicemen and the Free French. Hotels did the same. One Price Regulation Committee in the Midlands came across examples of boarding houses upping their tariffs by 700 per cent when the Yanks arrived. Four servicemen told them they had all squeezed into one room and that had cost them 30 shillings, at a time when the normal price was 3s 6d.

All kinds of 'fiddles' were carried out by demolition workers on a bomb-site to high-powered companies providing vital government contracts. Meanwhile, fraud was notoriously difficult to prove, especially where building costs were involved, because competition almost ceased to exist and the construction industry became almost exclusively a seller's market. In West Ham, after an air raid, it was noted that:

out of two gangs of ten men each, four men in one case and three in the other, were actually working; in a gang of twelve men, five were working and in a gang of twenty men, ten were working. In nearly all cases, those who were working were doing so in a very desultory way, chucking one brick on to a lorry and then resting before repeating the process.[16]

This was 'shirking' or 'malingering' and although it constituted negativity and let the side down, was hardly a crime in the accepted sense and virtually impossible to prosecute.

Such self-interest was very noticeable in the housing market. With so much destruction of property in major cities, prices soared. *The People* in 1943 complained that a house costing £700 in peacetime now fetched £1,500 or £1,600. Terraced houses doubled their value in three years. It was all characteristic of a dog-eat-dog society, which would continue into the post-war years, when the daily uncertainties of wartime life had gone, and perhaps nothing remained but cynicism and self-interest.

The Black Market remains an enigma. The number of prosecutions brought probably barely scratched the surface of its breadth and depth. Whereas other types of crime show an increase – murder, armed robbery, rape for example – selling and receiving on the Black Market was endemic. It was notoriously difficult for the authorities to obtain evidence against culprits – hence the alleged need to 'snoop' by undercover agents. Anyone would be happy to co-operate in the catching of a killer, but a Black Marketeer was the bloke on the corner who, while he might charge inflated prices, was doing society a favour. It was that most difficult problem – the victimless crime. The other problem was that little distinction was made between the casual amateur who had the bad luck to be caught and the professional, big-time racketeer, who used the war as a cloak for large-scale moneymaking.

Like every other type of crime we have encountered in this book, the Black Market would flourish long after they sounded the last All-Clear.

CHAPTER FIVE

'Overpaid, Oversexed and Over Here'

There is probably more mythology concerning the Americans than any other topic from wartime Britain. In fact, one woman from Suffolk went so far as to say: 'I still remember the Yanks almost more than I remember the war itself.'[1]

The first myth was that the first GI[2] to come ashore was Private First Class Milburn H Henke from Hutchinson, Minnesota, who landed on the quay at Belfast with the 34th US Infantry Division. As such, he became something of a celebrity, although *The Times* could not resist the irony that his father was a naturalized German. In fact, Henke was technically the 501st – the actual advance guard were already on their way to a makeshift camp before the photographers and the media arrived.

It seems lunacy in hindsight that Germany should declare war on the United States four days after the Japanese attack on Pearl Harbor, the day that President Roosevelt said 'would live in infamy'. At the time and since, most people merely attributed it to Hitler's insanity. In fact, it made far more sense in 1941. America had been resolutely isolationist in the twenties and thirties, Roosevelt not making threatening noises until after *Kristallnacht*, the pogrom against German Jews in November 1938. And there was a strong anti-Semitic lobby in the States too, which, Hitler believed, would never allow Congress to go to war for the Jews. If they would not fight for Europe and they would not fight for the Jews, why should they fight at all? Hitler was gambling on appeasement until he had won the European war; and in 1941 the American Armed Forces were not the juggernaut they have since become. The Army was only the twentieth in the world in terms of size – smaller than the Dutch. At most, they could raise 245,000 trained men – five divisions to the 141 that the *Wehrmacht* already had in place in the West.

But America had not, in fact, been sitting idly by before December 1941, any more than Britain had before September 1939. In June 1940 conscription was brought in for the first time in American peacetime history, 900,000 men between the ages of twenty-one and thirty-five being 'drafted' in the first year. By the end of the war, the Army had reached a vast 8.3 million, with an age range of eighteen to sixty-five.

A fast and tough training programme, where regular drill sergeants screamed at their recruits for days on end in an attempt to make soldiers of them, led to the harbours of Boston and New York. There the 'doughboys' – still wearing the uniform of 1918, complete with canvas puttees and British-style tin hats – crowded onto troop steamers and ocean liners to risk the torpedo run of the U-Boat-infested Atlantic. The food was terrible and the lavatories awash as the ocean rolled. At least the new-style helmets – issued to the second wave of recruits – made excellent sick bags.

Punch magazine in 1942 showed an American tank convoy, spearheaded by the Statue of Liberty, thundering through an English countryside where cheery locals, young and old, waved a friendly greeting from the Rose and Crown pub. Except that it wasn't quite like that . . .

Dear old England's not the same,
The dread invasion, well, it came.
But no, it's not the beastly Hun,
The god-damn Yankee army's come.

The 'invaders' had been issued with *A Short Guide to Britain*, in an attempt to explain the differences between two nations who had once been one. Written by novelist Eric Knight, it contained some home truths:

> You will find that all Britain is a war zone . . . the British have been bombed, night after night . . . thousands of them have lost their houses, their possessions and their families . . . there are housewives in aprons and youngsters in knee-pants who have lived through more high explosives in air raids than many [US] soldiers saw in first-class barrages in the last war.[3]

And it put things in perspective. Britain was about the same size, in square miles, as the single state of Minnesota (Texas, of course, was three times the size). Sixty thousand British civilians had been killed in air raids, rationing had taken its toll on food supplies and luxuries. Cars were a rarity, petrol impossible to find and girls painted their legs with beetroot juice to resemble 'nylons'. 'The British,' Knight reminded the American troops, 'are tough, strong people and good allies. Don't be misled by the British tendency to be soft-spoken and polite . . . The English language didn't spread across the oceans and over the mountains and jungles and swamps of the world because these men were panty-waists.'[4]

But despite the attempts by both governments to paper over the cracks of national differences, it was destined not to go as smoothly as all that. The sheer scale of the operation was mind-boggling.

In June 1942, when the Americans established their ETO (European Theater of Operations), there were less than 60,000 troops here and most of these were based around Belfast. By the build up to D-Day, on 6 June 1944, there were 1,526,965 Americans here, massing by that time all over the south of England, ready for embarkation to Normandy to challenge Hitler in his own front yard. Convoys of trucks and jeeps rattled along country roads designed, essentially, for farm carts and horses. Giant B17 bombers, the Flying Fortresses, growled over the tarmac in USAAF bases in Lincolnshire and East Anglia. Their larger cousins, the B24 Liberators, rattled windows as they rumbled overhead. More than 1,100 cities, towns and villages were home to this friendly invasion force, occupying 100,000 buildings from evacuated schools and country houses to aircraft hangars, Nissen and Quonset huts and canvas bell tents.

But the locals began to notice niggling little annoyances. The Americans had none of the staid conventions of their British counterparts. Privates danced with squire's daughters and colonels danced with tarts. In fact, the American uniforms were so superior, in cut, colour and style, with the chocolate tunics and aurora[5] trousers of the airmen, that many Britons had serious difficulty telling officers from other ranks. What rankled with some was the fact that NCOs wore their chevrons 'upside down' to the British way[6] and John Keegan, today a leading military historian, remembered as a boy evacuated to the West Country: 'How different they looked from our own jumble-sale-quality champions . . . armed with glistening, modern, self-loading rifles.'[7] Keegan was particularly impressed by their vehicles:

> Towering GMC six-by-sixes, compact and powerful Dodge four-by-fours and . . . tinny and entrancing jeeps, caparisoned with whiplash aerials and sketchy canvas hoods which drummed with the rhythm of a cowboy's saddlebags rising and falling to the canter of his horse across the prairie.[8]

Molly Lefebure was fascinated by jeeps too, until she rode in one driven by Military Police in London and was so jolted around, she was glad to get out, never to repeat the experience.

But the biggest difference between the American and British Armed Forces, and between Americans and British civilians, was the extraordinary wealth of the GIs. The troops themselves might counter that they were 'underfed, underpaid, undersexed and under Eisenhower', but it rang a little hollow when the reality was that American troops earned five times that of their British counterparts. A British private earned 14 shillings a week in 1942, a sergeant 2 guineas. The GI drew the dollar equivalent of £3 8s 9d and the sergeant £5 7s 2d. Added to that, in a country barely affected at all by rationing, the visitors had access to limitless amounts of PX (Post Exchange) goods, candy, nylons, tinned meat and tinned fruit.

This imbalance was a motive for crime that cut in two directions. 'Townies' or civilian lads on limited income were naturally incensed

The British Union of Fascists was a prime target of the government even before the war began. Their leader Oswald Mosley spent two years in prison under the Defence of the Realm Act.

The acceptable face of the Fifth Column. Under the fierce wartime regulations, Dorothy O'Grady was sentenced to death for espionage. In the event, she served fourteen years in prison.

EVACUATION

THE GOVERNMENT HAVE DECIDED THAT IF THERE ARE AIR RAIDS YOU WILL HAVE ANOTHER CHANCE OF SENDING YOUR CHILDREN AWAY.

THIS TIME THE CHILDREN WILL NOT GO UNTIL AIR RAIDS MAKE IT NECESSARY.

THE NEW SCHEME WILL BE FOR SCHOOL CHILDREN WHO WERE AT SCHOOL LAST JULY, OR WHO HAVE REACHED THE AGE OF FIVE SINCE. IT APPLIES TO NO OTHERS.

NOW IS YOUR OPPORTUNITY TO REGISTER YOUR CHILDREN FOR EVACUATION. FILL UP THIS PAPER AND RETURN IT AT ONCE.

You are free to make up your mind, but you must MAKE UP YOUR MIND NOW. It is your duty to do so for the sake of your children. The authorities cannot make their plans at all if they do not know how many they have got to provide for.

If you want any help or there is anything you do not understand go to the nearest school, where you will either be able to get help or you will be told where you can.

The scheme that was not working. This leaflet gave parents a second chance to ge their children to safety.

Did they know there was a w on? According to behavioural psychologists, these children, from Tile Hill in Coventry, we among the most disturbed an lawless ever recorded.

WAR DAMAGE ACT, 1941 (PART I)

CONTRIBUTION PAYABLE IN RESPECT OF LAND, BUILDINGS AND OTHER IMMOVABLE PROPERTY

Explanatory Notes

These Notes explain the provisions of the Act regarding the contribution which are likely to be of general interest. *Please keep them for future reference.*

1. Risk period.

The Act provides for a contribution to be made towards the expense of payments for war damage to land, buildings and other immovable property (including rateable plant and machinery) occurring during the period beginning with 3rd September, 1939, and ending on 31st August, 1941. (There will be further legislation for any subsequent risk period.)

2. Properties on which the contribution is chargeable (contributory properties).

The contribution will normally be charged in respect of each property for which a separate valuation for Income Tax under Schedule A or for rating had effect in the risk period.*

3. Amount on which the contribution will be calculated (contributory value).

This will usually be the net Schedule A assessment† (before allowance of personal or special reliefs) in force at 3rd September, 1939. Where, however, during the risk period* new Schedule A assessments have come into force by reason of lands being split up into new units, or new and higher Schedule A assessments have come into force by reason of structural alterations, the new assessments are to be taken.

If there was no Schedule A assessment, the contribution will be calculated on the net annual value for rating (usually the value as at 3rd September, 1939).

4. Payment by instalments.

The contribution for the risk period ending 31st August, 1941, will be payable by five annual instalments, becoming due on 1st July in each of the years 1941, 1942, 1943, 1944 and 1945.‡

5. Amount of the instalment.

In general each of the five instalments will be charged at the rate of 2s. in the £. The rate of each instalment will, however, be 6d. in the £ for—

(a) agricultural properties (*see* Note 6);
(b) properties used for open air games, etc. (*see* Note 7);
(c) waste land and property valuable solely or mainly for shooting or fishing (*see* Note 8).‡

6. Agricultural properties.

The agricultural properties chargeable at the 6d. rate comprise—

(a) properties entitled to be de-rated as agricultural land or as agricultural buildings;

(b) farmhouses occupied in connection with agricultural land; and

(c) agricultural cottages which are occupied in connection with agricultural land and are on or contiguous to that land. ("Agricultural cottage" means a dwelling-house of a person who is employed in agricultural work on the land by the occupier of the land and is entitled, as tenant or otherwise, to the use of the house only while so employed.) Where cottages are included in the Schedule A assessment on a farm, the 6d. rate will be applied to the whole of the property included in the assessment.

Allowance of the 6d. rate is subject to the condition that the property was within the above descriptions throughout the risk period*, but any temporary diversion from normal use or occupation by reason of circumstances arising from the war will be disregarded.

7. Properties used for open air games, etc.

A property which was throughout the risk period* used solely or mainly for open air games, open air racing or open air recreation is chargeable at the 6d. rate. (Temporary diversion from such use by reason of circumstances arising from the war will be disregarded.) If the property comprised at the beginning of the period buildings which cost £5,000 or more, the buildings are chargeable separately at the 2s. rate.§

8. Waste land and property valuable solely or mainly for shooting or fishing.

A property which throughout the risk period* was waste land or was valuable solely or mainly for shooting or fishing is chargeable at the 6d. rate. Any dwelling-house comprised in the property is, however, chargeable at the 2s. rate.§

---

* For the purpose of assessing *the first instalment*, due on 1st July, 1941, no account will be taken (a) of Schedule A assessments or rating valuations which did not have effect until after 1st January, 1941, or (b) of the purposes for which a property was used, or the kind of land or buildings of which it consisted, after that date.

† The interest portion of any redemption annuity payable under Section 4 of the Tithe Act, 1918, may, however, be deducted.

‡ Provision is made in the Act whereby the number of instalments, or the amount of future instalments, or both, may be increased at any time with the approval of the House of Commons in the light of the expected receipts from the contributions and the expected payments under the Act in respect of war damage. The Act also provides that Parliament shall determine the disposal of any expected excess of contributions over such payments.

§ Any necessary apportionments of values are to be made by the Commissioners of Inland Revenue and will be subject to appeal to the Special Commissioners of Income Tax.

ven in the midst of destruction, there were people keen to falsify information to get cash.

Saucepans
or steel helmets

EVERYBODY knows that our normal peacetime standards of living must be cut during a war. Everybody knows that ships must carry war needs; that material and labour must all work for the war effort. But does everybody realise that while a shortage of supplies means inconvenience to the buyer, it must mean hardship to the seller?
All honour then to the great mass of traders who accept the new conditions with good grace.

ISSUED BY THE BOARD OF TRADE

This government propaganda tried to encourage traders not to profiteer from the war. Large numbers of them did.

In the paranoia of war, every adult was expected to carry a card like this. Failure to do so led to fines, imprisonment or both.

At the war's end, thousands of service came home to a country still in the gri authority, the black market … and cr

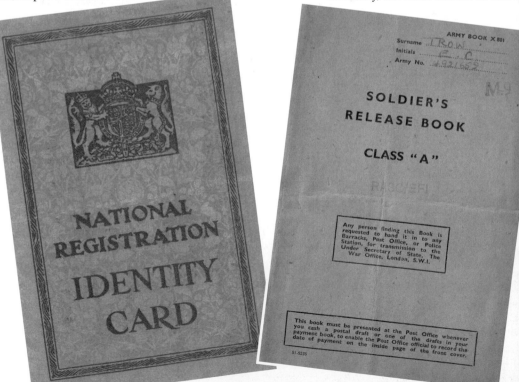

NATIONAL REGISTRATION IDENTITY CARD

ARMY BOOK X 801
Surname .....TROW.....
Initials .....E. C.....
Army No. ...4921855...

M.9

SOLDIER'S
RELEASE BOOK

CLASS "A"

Any person finding this Book is requested to hand it in to any Barracks, Post Office, or Police Station, for transmission to the Under Secretary of State, The War Office, London, S.W.1.

This book must be presented at the Post Office whenever you cash a postal draft or one of the drafts in your payment book, to enable the Post Office official to record the date of payment on the inside page of the front cover.
51-5235

DON'T . . .

THIS is intended for YOU. Read it, remember it, pass it on to your friends. First, and most important of all things is

Don't Listen to Rumours

You will get all the news that matters—bad or good—in your newspapers. Disbelieve anything else you hear — particularly alarmist news. Next thing to remember is

Don't Broadcast Information

You may know that there is an anti-aircraft gun cunningly concealed in the field next to your garden. But that's no reason for passing on the information. It may reach someone who should not know it.

Don't Lose Your Head

IN OTHER WORDS—KEEP SMILING. THERE'S NOTHING TO BE GAINED BY GOING ABOUT WITH THE CORNERS OF YOUR MOUTH TURNED DOWN, AND IT HAS A BAD EFFECT ON PEOPLE WHOSE NERVES ARE NOT SO GOOD AS YOURS.

SO EVEN IF A BOMB FALLS IN YOUR STREET— WHICH IS UNLIKELY — KEEP SMILING.

Don't Listen to Scaremongers

You will always find scaremongers about. Just treat them as you would a smallpox case— move on quickly. The enemy loves to spread rumours. Part of his campaign was to panic Britain—and he will still try it, hopeless although it is.

Don't Cause Crowds to Assemble

THE POLICE HAVE ENOUGH TO DO. IF YOU SEE PEOPLE GATHERING AND THERE IS NO REASON FOR YOU TO JOIN THEM— WALK ON. IN OTHER WORDS—MIND YOUR OWN BUSINESS.

AND ABOVE ALL DON'T FORGET THE OLD ARMY ADAGE.

Be silent, be discreet, enemy ears are listening to you.

NOW GET AHEAD, DO YOUR JOB AND DON'T WORRY.

The Government takes command on the first full day of the war. Alongside this grim warning, the *Mirror* readership was no doubt encouraged by an advertisement that read 'Sausages go better with HP sauce'. It was not long before sausages just went.

This is as good as it got. Meat and three veg cost 6d. Pudding was 2d extra – a 'legal' meal bought with coupons could only be supplemented via the Black Market.

Harvest in Britain 1941. Prisoner of war camps were always potential scenes of breakouts and crim

During the war, 'CKS' wa
the new boy in Home Offi
Pathology, elbowing out t
increasingly fallible Sir
Bernard Spilsbury in
presiding over the forensi
of the war's most celebrat
murder cases. He is holdi
the skull of a 16-year-old
Joan Wolfe and the army
issue knife used in the fat
attack on her.

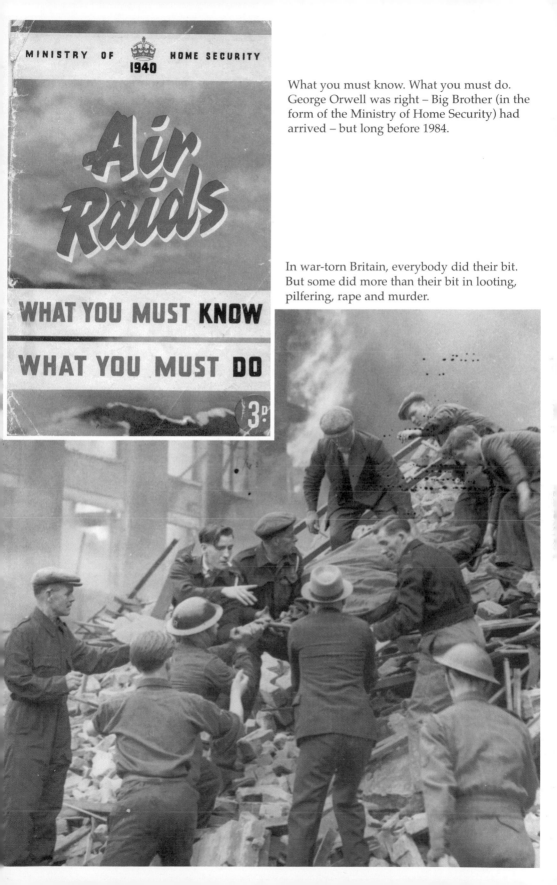

MINISTRY OF HOME SECURITY
1940

Air Raids

WHAT YOU MUST **KNOW**

WHAT YOU MUST **DO**

3ᴅ

What you must know. What you must do. George Orwell was right – Big Brother (in the form of the Ministry of Home Security) had arrived – but long before 1984.

In war-torn Britain, everybody did their bit. But some did more than their bit in looting, pilfering, rape and murder.

Fire guards carried out an important job, but a surprisingly large number of them looted the buildings they were supposed to be guarding.

In London, the Underground stations served as free air raid shelters but conditions in them were appalling, encouraging crime.

when local girls swarmed around the Americans like bees around a honey pot and that led to fisticuffs. On the other hand, locals saw the Americans coming. For every streetwise 'Dead-End Kid' from the Bronx who could look after himself, there were dozens of hick farm boys from Iowa who had never seen a big city before. Taxi-drivers cranked up their prices – so did the ladies of the night the GIs called 'hookers'.

The New World had sent troops before the Americans arrived. Just before Christmas 1939, with the war only four months old, 7,500 troops of the 1st Canadian Division arrived. As part of the Empire, it was naturally assumed that the Dominion would provide support for Britain. They were based in transit camps all over the country as numbers grew, training in woodland and heath for what was the disastrous Dieppe raid in August 1941. On that day, of the 4,384 casualties, 3,379 were Canadian. The Germans were impressed; after D-Day, *Wehrmacht* general von Vietinghoff wrote in his diary: ' . . . only Canadians attack like that.'

Like all armies, the Canadians had their own Military Police, which maintained discipline, but an important distinction was made that in wartime, crimes committed on British soil were to be investigated by the British police, and trials and punishment should conform to British laws, run exclusively by the civil authorities. By comparison with the Americans, the Canadians were well behaved. In September 1942 a report revealed 923 who had been convicted of all crimes since the war began. Considering there were nearly 205,000 of them here by then, the ratio is four or five criminals for every 10,000 Canadians. Only six men stood trial for murder in a six-year period, but one of them provided 'the last of the classic cases' and was a window display for the combined talents of Superintendent Edward Greeno of Scotland Yard and Dr Keith Simpson, the Home Office Pathologist.

In October 1942, a party of Marines training in Houndown Wood near the village of Thursley in Surrey, came across the badly decomposed body of a girl. Local police cordoned off the area, moving the Army beyond the perimeter, and sent for the Yard in time-honoured tradition. With Greeno came Keith Simpson and Molly Lefebure, his secretary, crouching on the hilltop as the maggots crawled and writhed in the body cavity at their feet.

Once the body could be moved to Guy's Hospital, Simpson was able to calculate, from the degree of maggot infestation, approximately when the murder was committed. The body was that of a teenaged girl and the killing had been carried out elsewhere with the corpse dragged and hastily buried on high ground. When the fragmented skull was reassembled, Simpson could reconstruct what had happened. The girl had been attacked from the front with a knife that had left curious bevelled circular holes in the forehead. Terrified, bleeding and dazed, she had run away from her attacker until he had felled her with a silver birch branch found lying near the body. Blood and hair were matted into the bark. She had hit the ground so hard that her left cheek was shattered and her front teeth were knocked out. Greeno's enquiries, in conjunction with the Godalming police, soon matched the green and white frock fragments to a sixteen-year-old runaway, Joan Pearl Wolfe, who had been living, against the express wishes of the authorities, with a French-Canadian Cree Indian, August Sangret. The pair had been living as man and wife as often as Sangret could slope out of Witley Camp, first in a cricket pavilion in Thursley village and then in a series of 'wigwams' he built in the woods, which gave the case its famous name – the Wigwam Murder.

The problem for Greeno was that there were 100,000 Canadians in the Witley–Thursley area and 'camp followers' like Joan Wolfe knew any number of them. Three other names emerged at Sangret's subsequent trial, any one of whom could have been the father of the child that Joan claimed she was carrying. In the end, what hanged Sangret was his Army-issue knife. He had used it to hack the branches to make Joan's love nest in the wood and the tip of the blade had broken to form what was described in court as a parrot's beak. It was this that had made the peculiar, circular holes in the dead girl's skull. That skull was produced in the Old Bailey, the first time that such an exhibit had been placed before a jury, who were horrified.

Sangret died at Wandsworth on 29 April 1943. Molly Lefebure saw his body as Keith Simpson duly certified that he had died by judicial hanging:

He lay there . . . muscular, well built, his handsome bronzed skin marked only by the imprint of the hangman's noose around his neck.[9]

The American legal situation was different. Parliament, anxious to keep the GIs and their government sweet, passed the United States of America (Visiting Forces) Act in 1942, which stipulated that all infringements be tried by US military courts. This in itself led to tension and a sense that the Americans were 'protecting their own'. This was not actually true. A twenty-year-old naval rating who shot two British marines in June 1944 was found to be borderline mentally deficient. Because of this, his death sentence was commuted to forty years' hard labour. If anything, the American Military Police – called 'Snowdrops' because of their white helmets – were a little overzealous in the use of their nightsticks (British policemen still carried the 14-inch-long truncheon), screaming through city streets in their jeeps and breaking up fights in clubs, pubs and dance halls.

Ted Greeno found himself working with 'a dapper little Texan', Colonel Moroney:

One day, he shot out of a side turning and followed my squad car in Coventry Street. He was in a huge de Soto and as we weaved through the traffic he cut in with the 'wailer' that every cinema goer knows. The crowds scattered. We tore down Haymarket . . . and before I could get out Moroney shot in front of me. All four doors of the de Soto burst open and his 'snowdrops', whose seats swivelled for the manoeuvre, leapt out like a landing party. They whipped out pistols and marched ahead of me.[10]

Every American tried and found guilty by US Court Martial was hanged at Shepton Mallet. The only British involvement was that hanging was carried out along more or less British lines, sometimes by the American military hangman, Master-Sergeant John C Woods, or by Albert Pierrepoint.

Two days before Christmas 1942, when the inmates of

Desborough Camp in Northamptonshire had entertained local children with tinsel, Hershey bars and tinned fruit, an incident took place in the 827th Engineer Battalion. Perhaps Private David Cobb was lacking in the Christmas spirit when he told passing Second Lieutenant Robert J Cobner that he had been on guard duty for long enough. Cobner was officer of the day and in any case had a right to expect civility from an enlisted man. He upbraided Cobb for not standing to attention and called for the sergeant of the guard, Mason, to arrest the man. In the scuffle that followed, Lieutenant Cobner was shot at virtual point-blank range by Cobb. The soldier was the first American to die on the gallows in England.

Eleven days after Lieutenant Cobner was killed, the same fate befell Private Harry Jenkins. New Year's Day 1943 saw Private Harold Smith go AWOL – 'over the hill' as the Americans called desertion – from Chisledon Camp, Swindon, and gravitate as did thousands of others to the magnet that was London. He met an old buddie, Harry English, and the two of them drank and impressed the girls until the cash ran out and then Smith decided to go back to camp, face the wrath of his CO, and no doubt spend some time in the 'cooler'.

When he got there, he found that most of his unit had moved on, leaving only a skeleton 'depot' troop behind. On 9 January he helped himself to an automatic pistol in the squad room, and was making his way to the Mess Hall, when he was challenged by Private Jenkins. The two men staged a bizarre shoot-out, which any Saturday matinee kid would have recognized, and Jenkins fell dead. Smith fled the camp again, catching a bus to nearby Marlborough and a train to London. Two days later, Constable James Watson asked the 'Yank' for his identity card and arrested him. Tried at Bristol, Smith was hanged on 25 June.

If Cobb and Smith had used violence on one of their own, in the confines of American Army camps, the case of John Waters was different. One of the major problems in Anglo-American relations – and the cause of a great deal of tension – was the GIs' propensity for picking up girls. Lonely, far from home, and with very few female service personnel, the GIs inevitably took up with local girls. For some, it was drinking the night away, gyrating across the dance floor to the frantic rhythm of the jitterbug. To others, it was promises of a new life in the West and invitations home to tea with a suspicious and not altogether enamoured Mum and Dad. For yet others, it was a roll in the hay. And for others still, it meant murder.

In February 1943, Doris Staples was thirty-five – slightly long in the tooth, perhaps, for the average 'GI Bride'. She worked in a draper's shop in Greys Road, Henley on Thames, and began 'walking out' with Waters, who was based nearby. He seemed keener on the relationship than she did and her coolness led him to believe that she was seeing other men. Matters came to a head on 14 July, ten days after the Americans had staged as spectacular an Independence Day party as they could, given the circumstances of wartime. Shots were heard from the draper's shop and both the local police and the Snowdrops laid siege, eventually lobbing tear gas into the building.

When they entered, the bullet-riddled body of Doris Staples was found in the smoke. Waters, hiding in a toilet, shot himself in the head but the wound was not fatal. He faced trial in Watford in November and was executed at Shepton Mallet the following February, four months before his unit moved south to mass for the invasion of Fortress Europe, code-named OVERLORD. The fact that there was an appeal for clemency from Waters' own unit is perhaps not surprising. The 'draft', like its counterpart in Britain, was no respecter of persons; neither was there time for proper medical assessment of recruits. Given the vast numbers involved, it would be extraordinary if there were not unstable psychopaths and sociopaths with various units, whose aggression was not necessarily directed towards the enemy. However, the fact that the Henley townsfolk also organized a petition for mercy is telling. Violence and crime was often the result of disharmony between the GIs and the locals, but it would be totally wrong to imagine that this was the norm. Most people from both races realized that the American presence was essential if we were to do more than survive. There was understanding, give and take, and warm and lasting relationships that were, in many ways, the start of the 'special relationship' that exists to this day.

What is apparent so far in American wartime crime is the ready availability of guns. Not only did the visiting forces carry such weapons, but they came from a culture in which the ownership of guns was commonplace, enshrined in their constitution, as it was once enshrined in ours. That would have a serious echo in the years ahead. The case of J C Leatherberry did not follow this pattern.

An abandoned taxi was found in Haynes Green Lane, Marney, near Colchester, on the morning of 8 December 1943. Investigating officers found a bloodstained jacket inside and in the pocket a driving licence with the name of Henry Claude Hailstone. What raised suspicion among the Colchester CID was the fact that the cab had been parked on the 'wrong' side of the road. There were large numbers of Americans in the area and later that day, a bloodstained coat was discovered not far from the abandoned taxi. The sheer bureaucracy of wartime undoubtedly helped the police with their enquiries. Everybody carried identity cards and other papers and any military personnel had their belongings and equipment stamped with tell-tale numbers.

The bloody coat belonged to a Captain J J Walker, who told police he had had the coat stolen, along with a Rolex watch and a bottle of bourbon on 5 December. The thief had left behind a gas mask with the name of J Hill. He was a coloured American soldier. On the following day, the body of Henry Hailstone was found in the gardens of Birch Rectory. He had been strangled with a ligature and badly beaten, mostly around the head. Hailstone weighed over 11 stone and the body had clearly been carried some distance, implying that more than one man was involved.

Hill, the gas mask owner, was traced via meticulous police work and he explained that he lent the mask to a comrade-in-arms, George Fowler. His quarters revealed a pawn ticket for a Rolex watch in the name of Charlie Huntley. And Huntley had been given the watch by Private J C Leatherberry. Fowler cracked under police interrogation and turned the equivalent of king's evidence by implicating Leatherberry as the killer. He had strangled Hailstone from behind, although the motive remained unclear.

Both men were tried at Ipswich in January 1944 and found guilty. Under the British law of joint culpability, they would both have hanged. American law was different: Leatherberry kept his rendezvous at Shepton Mallet but Fowler was given a life sentence.

'A coloured American soldier'. It had been a mere twenty years since lynchings and beatings of Blacks were a commonplace in the states that had once been the Confederacy. It was only two generations since the abolition of slavery in the US and attitudes and prejudice died hard. 'They fought separately and died equally,' wrote the black GI musician, Ralph Ellison, stationed in Wales during the war. But there were many white Americans who only paid lip-service to the notion of 'separate but equal'. For them, the Jim Crow laws still existed; the Ku Klux Klan had recently reached the 5-million-membership mark, and Roosevelt's much vaunted New Deal had had little impact on poverty in black communities.

There were 12,000 coloured soldiers in Britain by the summer of 1942. Many of them had joined the Army pre-war to escape poverty and, almost exclusively, they were given menial jobs such as loading and unloading, labouring, kitchen and domestic work. They were not allowed to join the élite units of the Marine Corps or the Air Corps. The joke ran at the time: 'What do you call a Negro with three Purple Hearts? A fiction.'[11]

Racial attitudes like this needed careful adjustment on both sides. On the one hand, American troops were told to 'cool it', that there was no colour bar in Britain. On the other, in keeping with our general feeling of gratitude, the British were supposed to accept prejudice, at least in part. Some did it with relish. Mrs May, the wife of the vicar of Worle, near Weston Super Mare, called a meeting of local women in which she laid down six rules of how to deal with black soldiers. To summarize, they should be discouraged from using shops, move away from them in cinemas, cross the road if meeting one on a pavement, have no social dealings with them and never invite them into your home.[12] General Eisenhower's plan was to send coloured units to the major cities where there was a small black population already – Bristol, Cardiff and Liverpool. Elsewhere, 'furlough passes'[13] were distributed so that it was unlikely black and white soldiers went out on the town together. Locals found themselves having to set up 'black' and 'white' dances in village halls. In Launceston, Cornwall, there were even 'black' and 'white' fish and chip shops. In the event of trouble, it was noted that the Snowdrops tended to use their batons with great alacrity on the black soldiers.

The official British line was published in September 1942 with a Home Office circular to all chief constables:

> It is not the policy of His Majesty's government that any discrimination as regards the treatment of coloured troops should be made by the British authorities. The Secretary of State, therefore, would be glad if you would be good enough to take steps to ensure that the police do not make any approach to the proprietors of public houses, restaurants, cinemas or other places of entertainment with a view to discriminating against coloured troops.[14]

Most British people had only ever seen blacks (especially American ones) in supporting comedy roles on the big screen. Steppin Fetchit re-enacted the amiable, harmless 'Sambo' role that had once saved the slaves from beatings, brandings or worse if the whites believed them to be 'uppitty niggers'. Some of the younger generation were enthralled by coloured musicians – Satchmo, Hutch, the Ink Spots – but this was hardly the same as having armed coloured men on street corners and dancing with white girls. Without exception, black soldiers were more polite and courteous than whites when dating British girls, knowing they ran a risk of a beating from white 'comrades' if discovered. Attitudes drove many Britons into an opposite frame of mind. One wrote: 'I don't mind the Yanks, but I can't say that I care much for the white chaps they've brought with them.'[15]

In Birmingham, white troops kicked blacks off the 'sidewalk', calling them 'black trash'. A white soldier of the 11th Armoured Division told a Chippenham woman in a very matter-of-fact way, 'Ma'am, we shoot niggers where I come from.'[16]

Violence between black and white units of the American Army was frequent and usually centred on cinemas and especially dance halls. Before one particular balloon went up, a white serviceman said to a girl, 'Go take a ride. Where I come from [Kentucky] black men don't go out with white women.' The resulting brawl led to broken heads and a lot of damage to a London pub. The magistrate rather feebly fixed a one-shilling fine on the troublemakers and £5 costs. His task, however, was to maintain cordial relations, and the only reason this case came to court at all was that the Kentuckians had enlisted in the Canadian Army before Pearl Harbor. Generally speaking, white troops could not understand the leniency and equality with which the British treated blacks. In Manchester, there were so many racial incidents that the entire American Army was banned from the city centre for two weeks.

On 5 October 1944 ten black soldiers, drinking in the Crown at Kingslake, near Basingstoke, were found to be without passes and sent back to camp by the Snowdrops. The men collected rifles back at their base, returned to the pub and opened fire in an ambush on the Military Police, killing one and wounding another. This was a reflection of a similar attack in Launceston, Cornwall, thirteen months earlier, when a black versus white gunfight erupted in the town square.

There were, of course, some locals who fully supported the racist attitudes. A woman in sedate Leamington Spa reported that it 'was horrible to see white girls running around with the blacks – but they do say once a black, never a white, don't they?'[17] There is little doubt that many of the racial slurs that caused so much tension revolved around sex, and a large proportion of the crime involving black and white Americans related to sexual assault or prostitution.

German propaganda attempted to capitalize on the situation. Leaflets were dropped onto known black units from raiding aircraft, asking why coloured soldiers fought for a race that so consistently degraded them? Similar literature fluttered down on British troops serving in the Western Desert (the Eighth Army), reminding them that while they risked life and limb, Americans based in Britain were enjoying their womenfolk.

Three[18] men were hanged for rape during the Second World War: all three of them were Americans. Private Edward Hefferman had gone to a dance at Bishop's Cleeve in Gloucestershire with his

sixteen-year-old girlfriend Dorothy Holmes. It was Sunday, 4
March 1944 and on their way to the girl's home, Hefferman was
attacked by two men, one of whom hit him in the face with a bottle.
While he staggered around, bleeding and trying to get help, his
attackers, black soldiers Elija Brinson and Willie Smith, dragged
Dorothy into a field and raped her. Footprints left in the recently
fallen snow sealed the soldiers' fates and they were hanged at
Shepton Mallet on 11 August, by which time most of their buddies
were crossing the Loire, liberating France.

Madison Thomas was not executed until October. On the night
of 26 July, he had 'got fresh' with Beatrice Reynolds at Gunnislake
in Cornwall, as she walked home late at night from a meeting in the
local British Legion Hall. Not content with chatting her up, he made
a play for a friend, Jean Blight, whom they met on the way. Once
Thomas had shaken Jean off, he tired of small talk with Beatrice,
knocked her to the ground, raped her and ran off with her watch.
At an identity parade next day at Whitchurch Down camp,
Tavistock, Jean picked out Thomas, whose fatigues were found to
have bloodstains that matched Beatrice's.

'The only thing that was cheap in Britain,' many Americans used to
joke, 'were the women.'[19] Indeed the oldest profession welcomed the
Americans – and everyone else – with open arms and I have included
prostitution in this chapter not because it was by any means purely
an American vice, but because the Americans were more ripped off
by it than anyone else. Robert Fabian wrote:

> The prostitutes can spot the Mug coming. They can pick him
> out by his way of walking, by the manner in which he carries
> his head and moves his eyes. They do not see him as the
> romantic character he imagines himself to be and even though
> he is a six-footer in Service uniform, with a chest full of medals,
> he is just another Mug to them . . . They are as hard as nails.[20]

If the Mug was American, prices rocketed. In 1943, the going rate
in London (always *the* magnet for visiting forces) was £3 or £4 for
an all-night session; by the end of the war, GIs were being charged

£5 for a 'quickie'. Everyone knew the disparity of pay between British and American forces, so this seemed only reasonable.

Prostitution had always drawn to its ranks a wide variety of women, from all social classes. The rigid class structure of Victorian and Edwardian England, which still had its dying echoes in the 1940s, called for 'courtesans', who once rode in Rotten Row and lived in fashionable apartments in Duke Street, to the denizens of the bordellos of Soho and the Haymarket, to the tragic apparitions that plied their trade standing up in the dark labyrinths of Spitalfields, Whitechapel and any Army or Navy town the length and breadth of the country. Wartime produced far more casual prostitution. The professional 'good-time' girls – known to the Americans as 'Piccadilly Commandos' – had always been there, working their shifts and their patches, usually watched over by sinister pimps, who were also busy avoiding call-up. It was the others that caused more concern to the churches and welfare officials: 'At 7 o'clock,' a Shropshire man remembered, 'on a summer's night and local girls all dolled up and scrambling aboard jeeps after first asking their escorts not to forget to give some gum or candy to their kids left behind in the street . . .' [21]

Gum and candy, *the* currency of Anglo-American relations, could hardly be classed as payment for sex, but among the girls who merely wanted to dance the night away to a Glenn Miller number and sip a port and lemon (assuming that either of these was available in rationed England) some were married, separated from their fighting husbands and in need of cash. Evelyn Oatley, one of the victims of Gordon Cummins, was an actress who turned to prostitution to make ends meet. Doris Jouannet, another of the Blackout Killer's targets, had a husband whose income as a hotel manager ought to have been sufficient to keep her off the streets, but was not.

By December 1942, cases of sexually transmitted diseases (still known universally as VD – venereal disease – in the forties) had escalated by 70 per cent since the Americans' arrival. There were nearly 2,000 cases of gonorrhoea and 166 of the infinitely more dangerous syphilis. A conference called in March 1943 concluded that the reasons for this increase were the fact that so many rich, physically fit Americans were here without the stabilizing effect of home; the relaxation of parental control among young girls because of the war; and the 'handiness' of the blackout.[22]

The hub of the prostitution trade was Piccadilly – one reason why the US Military Police Headquarters was established there:

> The girls were everywhere [remembered Robert Arbib of the 820th Engineers]. They walked along Shaftesbury Avenue and past Rainbow Corner, pausing only when there was no policeman watching. Down at Lyons Corner House on Coventry Street they came up to soldiers waiting in doorways and whispered the age-old question . . . Around the dark estuaries of the Circus, the more elegantly clad of them would stand quietly and wait – expensive and aloof. No privates or corporals for these haughty demoiselles. They had furs and silks to pay for.[23]

Cockney newsmen selling London newspapers also sold condoms – French letters as they were usually known. The Snowdrops, who patrolled regularly, were endlessly moving copulating couples on, out of doorways, alleyways, air raid shelters. Girls were sometimes robbed or beaten up, especially if arguments erupted over payment. 'Marble Arch style' meant sex standing up, fully clothed, and a surprising number of prostitutes believed that pregnancy was unlikely in this position.

Before the war, the more exotic end of prostitution was the white slavery market. Rather like hit-men and nymphomaniacs, white slavery was the stuff of novels and film, but there was a kernel of truth in all of it. In 1936 the body of Max 'the Red' Kassel was found in a ditch near St Albans. Under the cover of selling diamonds in the West End, he was, in fact, an upmarket pimp for French girls working out of Soho for a Parisian gang. One of these, Jeanette Cotton, was found dead in the same year in her flat in Lexington Street. Two others, Josephine 'French Fifi' Martin and Leah 'Stilts' Hines, had both died by strangulation within fifteen months of each other in 1937–38. It is likely that these girls had refused to hand over the agreed chunk of their earnings to Paris and died as a result.

Kassel may have gone the same way from his failure to keep the girls in check. The crimes remain unsolved.

The police handbook called *Moriarty's Law* made it clear to policemen everywhere that prostitution *per se* was not a crime – soliciting was. So was pimping or 'living off immoral earnings' and 'keeping a bawdy house'. The Blitz may have driven women off city streets in 1940–41, but they had returned by 1942 and the Doodlebug attacks took place in daylight anyway, so had little effect on crime of this sort. In the mid-1930s the Flying Squad, not regularly involved in vice, estimated that London prostitutes worked about four hours a night, servicing fifteen to twenty clients. Their earnings averaged between 10 shillings and £1 a client (a weekly take of £80–100 fifty years before the arrival of the minimum wage). This was forty or fifty times what a shop girl at the time could earn. In wartime business rocketed, especially after the Americans arrived. They now worked fourteen or fifteen hours a day, with a commensurate increase in clientele and, as we have seen, charges.

The image we have of prostitutes at any time has largely been imposed on us by moralists who find the 'trade' offensive. Research carried out on prostitution in the 1950s likened them to a trade union, looking out for each other and leading contented lives. The more successful (and generally older) girls had flats and apartments, sometimes with maids, and left the streets as soon as they could. Inspector Sharpe of the Flying Squad once counted seventy-six girls strung out along Piccadilly: the number probably trebled by 1944 and the creation of the GI centre at Rainbow Corner.[24]

The hardest group of prostitutes to uncover were the high-class call-girls who had private apartments and made their arrangements by phone. They often provided 'special services' like flagellation and it is difficult to know what effect the outbreak of war had on them. Next came a group who had 'rooms' provided for them in guest houses, Bed and Breakfasts or even shops. Those nearest to railway stations did the best trade. These rooms qualified as brothels and their owners could be sentenced to weeks of hard labour. Of those who operated in the open air, most were single girls working on their own and consequently the most vulnerable. While most were happy to use doorways or dark corners, some actively sought out the parks – the 'Hyde Park Rangers' as the Americans called them. The fact that arrests for prostitution dropped in the Metropolitan District between 1938 and 1940[25] is likely to be more to do with the fact that blind eyes were being turned and that female favours were more available for free.

The war years were a golden age for prostitutes. Migration from the capital (and other major cities) meant that apartments and sometimes whole houses were available for rock-bottom rent. By 1942 such rents were rocketing, but the girls simply upped their prices accordingly. As the build-up to D-Day grew in the south, the number of brothels increased. One of them, in Brighton, 'entertained' 154 American servicemen (between fourteen girls) in a single twenty-four-hour period. One of the girls was fourteen years old. The St Marylebone Record reported a case on 17 June 1944, in which the madam's response to the police officers who arrested her was: 'The boys belong to a bomber crew. They might be killed tomorrow. Surely you don't mind them having a good time with the girls?' It was a fair question, all things considered.[26]

The most spectacular prostitute of the war was probably Marthe Watts,[27] originally from Paris, who appeared before Bow Street magistrates over 400 times between 1940 and 1945. She operated under the aegis of the Messina brothers – the most notorious of the underworld figures before the advent of the Krays. On VE night, when total strangers hugged each other and kissed and cried, Marthe was busy until six the next morning servicing forty-nine clients.

Some cases were tragic. The Paddington News of December 1944 painted a less than rosy picture of a serviceman returning home on leave. A sergeant in the Royal Engineers opened the front door of his house in Camden Town to find two women in bed with two black soldiers and his wife in bed with a third. His children were locked in the Morrison shelter in another room. The London County Council took the children into care and his wife was given two months' hard labour.

In December 1941 conscription was introduced for single women between twenty and thirty. Most prostitutes avoided this by writing their occupation on their call-up papers and the authorities usually left them alone; they were not the sort of girls needed for the war effort – they were 'doing their bit' already.

Police action against prostitutes varied. Since officers patrolled regular beats, they could hardly miss the girls on their patch. Robert Fabian quotes one pimp introducing him to a new girl: 'Ursula, this is Mr Fabian, Chief of the Manor – you don't give him any nonsense and he'll treat you fair.'[28] Constables often arrested girls on a rota basis and most of the prostitutes pleaded guilty at the magistrates' courts, paid their fines, and earned the money back over the next few nights.

In London at least, there seems to have been a crackdown on brothels as the war wore on. In 1940, 142 people were convicted in connection with brothel-keeping; in 1943, the figure was 843. The year 1944 saw a peak at 944. The figures for Birmingham, Britain's second largest city, are tiny by comparison: 1940, only five, and in 1945 no figures are available. The peak year of 1944 only registered a total of forty convictions.[29] Punishments varied from fines of less than £10 to imprisonment, the latter almost always the case if children lived on the premises.

'Georgina Grayson' was precisely one of those good-time girls that caused moralists and the authorities most trouble. Her real name was Elizabeth Jones and she was eighteen years and seven months old when she was sentenced to death for her part in the Cleft Chin Murder. The case itself was, in the words of one of the counsel involved, 'sordid and drab', but it caught the public imagination for a number of reasons. The war was nearly over and although men were dying daily, they were doing it in France and the ghastly days of bombing terror were at last over. The murder involved a relatively glamorous young blonde girl. And above all, it was the only case in the entire war when an American serviceman was handed over to the British courts for trial. George Orwell, in *Decline of the English Murder*, wrote: 'Jones and Hulten committed their murder to the tune of V-1 and were convicted to the tune of V-2.'

On the day that the American First Army broke through the Siegfried Line north of Aachen, Second Lieutenant Ricky Allen of the 501st Airborne was introduced by a civilian friend, Leonard Bexley, to a girl called Georgina Grayson, in a café in Hammersmith Broadway. Bexley was a coach trimmer who lived locally and his daughter worked as a waitress in the café. Apart from that, neither Allen nor Grayson was what they seemed.

Georgina Grayson was originally Elizabeth Maud Baker and had been born in Neath, North Wales, in July 1926. She moved to Canada with her family for five years. On their return, relations between 'Betty' and her mother deteriorated, largely because Mrs Baker's time was taken up with an older, semi-invalid sister. Her father was undoubtedly the apple of his daughter's eye and when he was called up in September 1939, Betty was heartbroken and ran away from home three times, once reaching Usk, where her father was posted. Nothing of the difficult, wayward liar emerged in court, but Betty claimed she had been sexually assaulted by a man when she was thirteen and she had learned to dance at an approved school. She had married Lance Bombardier Stanley Jones in 1942, but, beaten up on her wedding night, she had run away again, this time drifting to the bright lights of wartime London to find work as a waitress, barmaid and striptease dancer.

The dramatist, linguist and all-round nosey parker George Bernard Shaw became involved in the case. He wrote to *The Times* on 5 March:

> She [Jones] has earned her living as a striptease girl, which I, never having seen a striptease act, take to be as near to indecent exposure as the police will allow. Clearly we have either to put such a character to death or re-educate her.[30]

Betty worked in shady, down-at-heel clubs like the Blue Lagoon in Carnaby Street and the Panama in Knightsbridge. At the time of the Cleft Chin murder she was living at 311 King Street, Hammersmith, a rather dingy Victorian thoroughfare with terraced houses and a semi-cobbled surface.

Lieutenant Allen was actually Private Karl Gustav Hulten, a native of Stockhom, Sweden, who was born on 3 March 1923. As a toddler he was taken to America by his parents, where his mother worked as a lady's maid in Boston. He attended a farm and trade school in the city and worked as a mechanic with the Firestone Tyre Company before being 'inducted' into the Army in May 1943. The uniform he wore on the day he met 'Georgie' was not his own, although he told the truth about his unit. He arranged to meet the girl that night at 11.30 outside the Broadway Cinema and turned up driving a ten-wheeled truck and drove towards Reading. The conversation almost at once took on an aura of *folie à deux*. He bragged that he ran with 'a mob' (and it may have been The Mob[31] in Chicago) and routinely carried a gun. She told him she longed to do 'something dangerous' (which at the trial turned out to be a bombing raid over Germany). And 'Ricky' had a gun in his belt.

The next day, the couple drove again towards Reading and Ricky, on a whim, stopped, having seen a girl on a bicycle. As she passed, he pushed her off the bike and stole her handbag, hanging on the handlebars. 'Georgie' kept the cash in it and 'Ricky' sold the coupons to an anonymous Black Marketeer the next day.

On Thursday, 5 October, the pair attempted to rob a taxi-driver. Hulten followed the chosen vehicle from Marble Arch to Cricklewood and blocked it with the truck. He held his gun on the driver and demanded his cash, but there was a passenger in the back seat and Hulten clearly didn't like the odds. Baulked of one prey, they looked for another and picked up a girl somewhere along the Edgware Road, who gave them the unlikely name of Tablo. Near Windsor, Hulten pulled the truck over, feigning tyre trouble, and when both girls got out, proceeded to batter Tablo over the head with an iron bar. Together, the pair carried her to a ditch and threw the potential murder weapon into a stream before driving back to Hammersmith with the girl's suitcase and handbag. Tablo was in fact nineteen-year-old Violet Hodge, found by the police. She survived the attack and was not called to the trial because the other assaults and robberies carried out by Hulten and Jones would have been prejudicial to the case.

'The case' developed in the early hours of Saturday 7 October. Hulten had returned to stay with a previous girlfriend, Joyce Cook. When Jones and Hulten said they slept together, they meant it literally. Jones denied vehemently that she was a prostitute, but a rash on her stomach deterred Hulten – 'That put me cavy,'[32] he said at his trial, 'because the Army is always telling us to watch out for things like that.'[33] On Friday night, the pair went out and at nearly midnight tried to hail a cab. The first one to stop was a grey Ford V8 saloon, registration number RD 8955, and its driver was the man with the cleft chin who gave the case its name. He was George Heath, aged thirty-four, from Ewell in Surrey. Although his wife attended the Old Bailey trial in January, Heath carried a photograph of his mistress in his wallet on the night he died. Technically, he was breaking the law by picking up Jones and Hulten because he was operating a private hire car for Messrs Godfrey Davis, for whom he drove. It would prove a costly error of judgement.

As the car left the roundabout onto the Great West Road, Chiswick, Hulten ordered Heath to stop. As the driver turned to open the door to let Jones out, Hulten blasted him with a single bullet to the back. Still alive, but clearly in shock and dying, Heath slumped to one side and Hulten got behind the wheel, his gun trained on the driver, with the command of 'Move over, or I'll give you another dose of the same.' Heath obliged, mumbling something incoherent. Then Hulten drove off while Jones rifled the dying man's pockets and removed his wristwatch, cigarette lighter, fountain pen and propelling pencil. Near Staines, Hulten dumped the body in a ditch and drove back to London.

On the Sunday, the murderous pair sold the dead man's lighter and watch and Jones even won some money on the dogs that night at the White City. They ate out and went to the pictures, the big feature being *Christmas Holiday* with Deanna Durbin and Gene Kelly.

But this was a careless crime, casually executed, and it did not take a Sherlock Holmes to solve it. To begin with, William Hollis, the nightwatchman at the Hudson Motors Depot in the Great West Road, had heard a single shot at about 2.30 a.m. Less than six hours later, John Jones, an electrical apprentice on his way to work found the scattered contents of a wallet along Gains Lane nearby. They included the identity card and driving licence of George Edward Heath. And an hour after that, auxiliary fireman Robert

Balding found the driver's body in a ditch on Knowle Green, Staines.

Dr Donald Teare, who carried out the post-mortem, found that a single bullet had entered Heath's back level with the sixth rib and a little to the right of the midline. The exit wound was clearly visible, level with the third rib, ripping the spinal cord and rupturing a lung on its way. The cause of death was internal bleeding. Heath, said Teare at the Old Bailey, would have been paralyzed within half a minute of being hit and could not have lived for more than a quarter of an hour.

That Sunday, the full horror of what she had done hit Betty Jones hard. She picked up an anonymous airman in a Hammersmith pub (Hulten was back with Joyce Cook) and, depressed and under the influence, told him about the murder and asked what she should do. He told her she must do as her conscience dictated. Her reply spoke volumes about the real Betty Maud Jones, from Neath: 'What if I have no conscience?'

The next day, Monday 9 October, Constable William Waters of F Division was walking his beat when he came upon Heath's V8 parked in Lurgen Street. Since there was an urgent look-out for this vehicle, Waters contacted headquarters and a number of officers under Inspector Percy Read, kept watch until about 9 p.m., when an American officer emerged from a nearby house (Joyce Cook's) and got into the car. They grabbed him before he could start the engine and found a Remington automatic pistol in his pocket, the hammer cocked and the safety catch off. At any moment, Karl Hulten could have killed himself just by sitting down too sharply.

It was on the Wednesday that a War Reserve constable, Henry Kimberley, met Betty Jones in Paul's Café, Hammersmith, where she worked. He had last seen her when she first arrived in London and was shocked at how ill she looked. 'Since I saw you,' she told him, 'I have turned a bad girl and have been drinking heavily.' The bad girl was spoken to by police as a result of this chance meeting. 'If you had seen someone do what I had seen done, you wouldn't be able to sleep at night.'[34] Kimberley passed the conversation to Inspectors Albert Tansill and Wilfred Tarr of T Division, who interrogated the pair separately. They had already interviewed Jones but now Hulten implicated her further and the inevitable recrimi-nations started. He claimed that she had egged him on, both to rob and to kill. She claimed he threatened her at every stage.

Hulten gave two long and contradictory statements to Lieutenant Robert De Mott of the 8th Military Police Criminal Investigation Section. In civilian life, De Mott was an attorney in Colorado and although Hulten tried to suggest that he put words into his mouth at the trial, De Mott proved to be a solid witness. Whereas the Judge's Rules made it very clear what the regulations of questioning suspects were in the British legal system, the Americans were under no such obligations. Hulten's defence counsel tried to imply that De Mott had exceeded his jurisdiction by interrogating Hulten for too long without a break, but this did not get very far when Hulten told the court that he had been treated well by both British and American police: 'It is your privilege to remain silent,' were the American words of caution prior to charging. 'You need make no statement whatsoever. Any statement that you do choose to make may be used either for or against you in the event that this investigation results in any trial. Do you thoroughly understand your rights?'[35]

While the case was pending, the American presidential elections took place and a few days later, the new government decided to waive its rights under the Visiting Forces Act and Hulten became, uniquely in wartime, the responsibility of the British justice system. Such were the sentiments and prejudices of the time that Bechhofer-Roberts could not help commenting on the fact that Jones's solicitors

> added a minor sensation to the already abundant crop by briefing for her defence Mrs Lloyd Lane, this being the first time, I imagine, in English legal history that a woman barrister appeared in a case of such gravity.[36]

He also commented on Hulten's appearance in court:

> he looked an ordinary, stocky, dark-haired youth *with only a somewhat receding forehead to suggest criminal tendencies* [my italics].[37]

'The very decent chap' as Hulten was described by almost everyone who knew him, took the death sentence like a man, but Betty Jones screamed and cried as they took her down. The *News of the World* had got an exclusive from the girl's parents they had brought from Wales to attend the trial, and they waited to find out whether the Home Secretary, Herbert Morrison, would grant a reprieve. The British public, fickle as ever, went in every conceivable direction in reaction to the sentences. The jury had recommended mercy in the case of Jones – she was young, she was pretty, she was female, she was blonde and, at the end of the day, did not actually pull the trigger. Most women, however, wanted her dead. Female workers at a Scottish factory threatened a strike if she walked from the gallows.

'Psychologists,' wrote Bechhofer-Roberts, 'who can explain everything, can perhaps explain this.' Some people feared that America would be outraged if Hulten alone hanged. Others believed the pair were young and foolish and should be released with a warning. Bizarrely, some thought Jones should hang and Hulten should go free. The oddest angle came however, as we have seen, from George Bernard Shaw. Not only was he horrified by striptease dancing (although he had never seen it) the great socialist had a very unusual take on the punishment that Jones should receive. On 5 March he wrote to *The Times*:

> We have before us the case of a girl whose mental condition unfits her to live in a civilized community. She has been guilty of theft and murder and apparently her highest ambition is to be what she calls a gun moll, meaning a woman who thinks that robbery and murder are romantically delightful professions . . .

Finding the decision to kill her admirable, he went on to decry hanging as hopelessly outmoded:

> [It] must be replaced by state-contrived euthanasia for all idiots and intolerable nuisances . . . If the striptease girl had been told simply that her case was under consideration and she were

presently to be found dead in her bed some morning in a quite comfortable lethal chamber not known to her to be such, the relief to the public conscience would be enormous.[38]

As always with Shaw, we cannot be sure how firmly his tongue is embedded in his cheek. His angle had always been to shock, but bearing in mind the reality of 'state-contrived euthanasia' in the T-4[39] programme in Nazi Germany, the joke (if joke it was) fell a little flat.

The next day, Jones was reprieved and Morrison was harangued for his leniency even by his boss, Winston Churchill. Even in the girl's home town of Neath, graffiti artists daubed walls with figures hanging from gallows. And George Orwell was closer to the mark than he knew when he wrote: 'it is difficult not to feel that this clamour to hang an 18-year-old girl was due partly to the brutalising effects of the war.'[40]

As for Hulten, he was executed at Pentonville by the now inevitable Albert Pierrepoint on 8 March 1945, five days after his twenty-third birthday. A 200-strong crowd outside the prison were a reminder of earlier, darker days when whole families had taken a picnic to watch someone being 'turned off'. Among them was the extraordinary Violet Van Der Elst, one of the best-known eccentrics of the century. Turned away from the prison gates, she shouted at the police cordon, 'You let the girl off, but you hang the man. It's a damn shame.'[41] Then she and a slaughterman named Smith started up a lorry parked nearby and attempted to ram the prison gates. In the process, they collided with Sergeant Horace Jarvis, resulting in Smith losing his licence on a rather feeble charge of driving without due consideration. Mrs Van Der Elst put a £20 donation into the Poor Box as she left court.

Almost as suddenly as they came, the Yanks were gone, taking nearly 70,000 British women with them, or shortly after them, as 'GI Brides'. They left behind used 'rubbers', pregnancies, broken hearts and a subculture of violence that has never gone away. In 1944 A P Herbert wrote:

Goodbye, GI,
Don't leave us quite alone.
Somewhere in England we must write in stone
How Britain was invaded by the Yanks,
And under that, a big and hearty 'Thanks'.

Today, most people take these lines of gratitude at face value. I wonder . . .

CHAPTER SIX

The Violent Playground

Some of the most haunting photographs of the Home Front during the Second World War are of children. They are lined up, bewildered and apprehensive, carrying cards with their names and addresses and clutching their gas masks along with their toys. This, child psychologists would declare years later, was the most delinquent and disturbed generation in modern history. In 1939–40, they were being evacuated in vast numbers from the cities that would become killing zones. By late 1940, hordes of them were already coming back.

Government evacuation notices spelt out the problem all too clearly: 'If you do not wish your children to be evacuated you must not send them to school until further notice.' Thus, at a stroke, stabilizing influences were vanishing from the lives of thousands of children. The call-up meant that fathers went to the Armed Forces. Evacuation meant that mothers disappeared too, in the chaos and grime of the railway stations. For those who stayed with mother, school was suspended, either because teachers were part of the call-up or the building itself was utilized for a more immediate purpose or became, courtesy of the Blitz, a hole in the ground. The *Sunday Pictorial* in September 1942 devoted a whole page to this problem. John Watson, Chairman of a London Juvenile Court, gave anxious mothers (in particular) some advice as to how to cope, ending with:

Above all, keep firmly fixed in your mind that the magistrates are not your enemies; they know as well as you do that Tom is not really bad at heart; they are for your child, not against him.[1]

Two of the most famous children of the war, the princesses Elizabeth and Margaret, broadcast to the nation on *Children's Hour* in October 1940:

My sister and I feel so much for you, as we know from experience what it means to be away from those we love most of all.

They had stayed in Balmoral, far from the bombs, while their parents returned to Buckingham Palace, if only so they could 'look the East End in the face'.[2]

Those public schools that stood in the danger zones were evacuated *en masse*, the buildings themselves often becoming the secret headquarters of Something-Or-Other. Cheltenham doubled up with Shrewsbury, and Dulwich with Tonbridge. Malvern College moved into Blenheim Palace, its staff and pupils blissfully unaware that the Churchills' home was the headquarters of state-of-the-art radar research.

Life magazine's 'most human picture of the war' shows a scruffy crowd of children sheltering in a trench and staring skyward. They were hop-pickers in the Kent fields – 'Hellfire Corner' – which had provided extra cash and a breath of fresh air for East Enders for half a century. The picture was enlarged and displayed in the British Embassy in Washington, adding no doubt to the growing support for Britain in the States.

In the public consciousness, as well as in the reality of actual cases, children were usually victims. Among the working class of 'the England of the Dole' in the depressed 1930s, children were often left to fend for themselves, playing in the streets of the 'Victorian slums' while their parents tried to find what work they could. A scattering of black-and-white photographs catches the children in happy mode – the literal freeze-frame of a generation. On a sunny day in 1931, a crowd of street urchins scamper curiously behind a police 'ambulance' carrying a drunk to Wapping Police Station. A lad who can be no more than eight is wheeling himself along a road inside a car tyre, his shirt ripped, his hands and arms filthy. A toddler is brought safely home by a policeman after the adventure of a lifetime along a street in Spitalfields. The more inventive stage a puppet theatre show for their mates on the pavement. Girls with short cropped hair and pretty print frocks buy toffee from an Indian street vendor.

The photograph most frequently shown from the thirties is of the unemployed labourer standing on a street corner, his head hung low, his hands in his pockets, kicking the stones in silent frustration. Beside him, looking up into his face, two children, not fully understanding the extent of the problem. But they are no more than five or six years old – perhaps this is how it had been for them all their lives.

The pressures of war led to a soaring increase in child abuse. In England and Wales in 1938, there were 932 reported cases of cruelty and neglect. In the years of evacuation, 1939–40, the figures dropped to a slightly more stable 751 and then 671 respectively. There was a jump in 1941 (the year that saw Hitler at his most powerful, the year in which Churchill's military advisers told him we could not win) to 968. But the rest of the war is alarming. In 1942, 1,413 cases were reported. The next year it was 1,612; the year after that 1,721. In 1945, at 1,643, there was a slight reduction, but nothing like a return to pre-war levels. 'The war is to blame for this,' said a soldier whose wife locked her three children in their flat at Coggeshall in Essex while she went out on the town, drinking and dancing. 'My wife has been left on her own.'[3]

In cases of neglect, the incidences seem to increase because of a new awareness of problems among well-to-do pseudo-parents. Evacuation meant that children from city slums were appearing in genteel villages where wretched physical conditions were noticed and not taken for granted. In Birkenhead, in 1941, a mother was convicted for neglect:

David . . . was wearing only a jersey and trousers, which were filthy. He had no underclothing or shoes. The boy's head was covered with septic sores, in which were traces of lice.

In August 1945, as the euphoria of VJ day loomed, another mother was sent to gaol, as reported in the *Hackney Gazette*, for neglecting her toddler. The little girl was 'plastered in excreta from the waist downwards. She was clothed only in a filthy vest and the bedding was covered in excreta'.[4] In the previous year another mother was sent down for two years after bringing her dead child to hospital:

> The body was wasted [the paper wrote] and emaciated and large areas of the skin were raw and wet and undergoing putrefying changes. There were also maggots in the body.[5]

The Americans, of course, came in for their fair share of blame for all this. In Bath, the sedate Georgian spa, which was a surprising hotbed of crime in the forties, three women were fined for neglect of their children:

> the police have received far too many complaints of women leaving their children to the tender mercies of the world and going out in the evenings leaving the house locked up.[6]

When one such child told an NSPCC inspector that he had both an American daddy and a sailor daddy, the local press had a field day.

Poor families, coping with the terrors of the Blitz, the deprivations of rationing and no doubt the lure of rich Americans with their candy, their nylons and their gum, did the best they could under *very* difficult circumstances. And some succeeded. Some, however, failed and their failure went unreported or even unnoticed. For every case of neglect that appeared before the courts, how many did not? As the war went on, and the number of cases rose, there is the tendency to see the authorities leaning ever more harshly on delinquent parents, determined to keep standards of morality high, to prevent the anarchy that hovered near the surface for most of the six long years of the war.

Some children of course were more spectacularly victims of the war; not those who were killed under the rubble of the Blitz and the Doodlebugs, but those who happened to be in the wrong place at the wrong time. As we have seen, fifteen-year-old Mary Hagan was raped and strangled by Samuel Morgan in a concrete blockhouse in Waterloo, Liverpool, on 2 November 1940, the day the Italians call the Day of the Dead. Eighteen-month-old Eileen Crocker was poisoned with cyanide and her little body buried with that of her mother on 20 May 1941. Their killer was Lionel Watson. Their 'crime'? They represented a second family who were becoming burdensome. We know that Doreen Hearne, eight, and Kathleen Trundell, six, were the victims of sex killer Harold Hill in Rough Wood, in November 1941. And that Sheila Wilson would be molested and strangled by Patrick Kingston in July 1942. The only American convicted of child murder was William Harrison, who took seven-year-old Patricia Wylie for a walk to the shops in Killycolpy, County Tyrone, then sexually assaulted and strangled her in a field.

One of the oddest cases of child murder in the war was that of three-week-old Dawn Digby, and again featured a bigamous second marriage. Ernest Digby married Olga Hill in March 1943, but already had a wife of twelve years, Violet Thurley. Olga had already presented Digby with a daughter, Doreen, the previous May, only to have the baby vanish two weeks later, put out for adoption by her father who said they could not afford to keep her. When a second baby, Dawn, was born in October 1943, Digby suggested the same solution. While trudging to a station with heavy luggage on 15 November, Digby lagged behind Olga and when he caught up, little Dawn had gone. Astonishingly, Olga did not get round to asking where she was until several hours later and the couple's new landlady was told that Digby had given the child to Olga's mother. None of this made sense to either landlady or police and first Olga, then Digby, was arrested on suspicion of murder. After two highly spurious statements, Digby finally confessed to battering the baby with a suitcase and burying her body in local woods. He died at the rope's end in Bristol, in March 1944.

More bizarre still was a death reported in June 1940 when thirteen-year-old Francis Fortnum was found hanged with a dog collar from a beam in his father's garden shed. Dr Eric Gardner, the Surrey pathologist, found a home-made armoured car and an imitation Bren gun in the shed along with loops of iron tape. Rather generously he said: 'I don't suggest anything improper was done, but I believe that torture was in the minds of these boys.' [i.e. Fortnum's gang.]

The verdict of the coroner's court was misadventure, perhaps because no one liked to think that children so young could be responsible for murder.[7]

Moriarty's Police Law has a great deal to say about children. Abortion was still a crime in the forties and would be for many years to come. Under a statute of 1861, three types of people were involved: the woman herself, who would be breaking the law if she used any 'poison or other noxious thing' or instrument; a second person who may be the abortionist; and a third party who might supply the means. The Infanticide Act of 1938 involved the wilful killing of a child under twelve months and took into account post-natal depression – 'the balance of her mind was disturbed by reason of her not having fully recovered from the effect of giving birth . . . or to the effect of lactation' – in which case manslaughter, rather than murder, was the charge.

Concealment of birth – so beloved of the darkest Victorian melo-dramas – was also an offence, but it had to involve actual 'secret disposition' of a baby, alive or dead, not mere denial that the birth had ever taken place. Five Acts related to the care of children and 'young persons' (it would be another twenty years before the term 'teenager' became widely accepted) and the term 'child' meant anyone under fourteen. A 'young person' was fourteen to seventeen. The law being the ass it is, even humdrum terms had to be explained so there could be no ambiguity. So 'place of safety', 'street', 'public place' and 'guardian' all required definition.

Cruelty to children, which kept police, the NSPCC and other authorities busy during the war years came in a number of guises. The neglect angle, itself a factor of the grinding poverty of the thirties and the dislocating experience of the war itself, we have already discussed. 'Seduction or Prostitution' concerning girls under sixteen was classed as a misdemeanour and, as we have seen, magistrates were more likely to be severe on brothel keepers with children on the premises (the relevant ages were deemed to be between four and sixteen). Begging with children or teaching children to beg was also an offence, exposing the young to 'moral danger'. Quite what the authorities made of thousands of young-sters asking Americans for gum is anybody's guess! No child under five could be given intoxicating liquor and children under fourteen could not be in the bar of any licensed premises. 'Smoking by Juveniles' came into a special category. It was illegal to sell tobacco to anyone under sixteen. Constables and park-keepers had the right to confiscate cigarettes, tobacco and cigarette papers from juveniles and owners of automatic machines were expected – somehow – to take precautions that the young were not using them or they were to remove the machine. Nobody under fourteen could be served in a pawnbrokers'. No one under sixteen could sell to a 'dealer in old metals'. There were laws about vagrancy, which included children being kept away from school. No child under twelve could be employed, except where certain bye-laws permitted a little light agri-cultural or horticultural work.[8] Choristers and BBC employees were exempt from the usual regulations. There were rules about the number of hours a 'young person' could work and people under fourteen could not lift heavy objects or work for more than two hours on a Sunday or any schoolday. The laws concerning employ-ment abroad clearly fell into abeyance the day that Hitler invaded Poland.

But if people were concerned that the conditions of wartime exposed children to danger, they were equally concerned that they turned them into criminals. The term 'juvenile delinquency' dates from 1817 and it is interesting that that was a period of adjustment after twenty-two years of war against Revolutionary and Napoleonic France. It was also a time of rising crime and the two are not unconnected. Those who find no harm in 'the youth of today' habitually trot out quotations from the great and good of (even ancient) history to 'prove' that every generation is disappointed and even appalled by its successors. The point was, however, that the 'People's War' was one without parallel in modern history. On the one hand, there were more regulations than ever, more people in authority (by dint of wearing uniforms) and more control of the population than had ever been known. On the other, the 'live for today' mentality produced a generation for whom the natural prohibitions of society had effectively broken down or were in danger of doing so.

Part of this feeling – that the new generation was bordering on the out-of-control – can be explained by the breakdown of a class structure that was happening anyway, war or not. Vita Sackville-West summed it up: 'I hate democracy. I hate *la populace*. I wish education had never been introduced . . .'[9] Education was doing what it could. Schools had always been a controlling influence, the best teachers (and the most vicious) being remembered by children well into their adult life. By a coincidence, 1 September 1939 was the day when the school-leaving age was to have been raised to fifteen. This would now have to wait until after 'the duration' and in practice that meant 1947. The evacuation process meant that city schools – London in particular – found themselves entrained, staff and pupils, to somewhere in the country, with all the chaos that inevitably caused. In some cases, whole classes found themselves wandering leafy lanes in search of suitable accommodation, with opportunistic teachers delivering improvized 'nature study' lessons, which would have had Aristotle gasping in admiration. Most schools were open by the middle of September in reception areas, but in neutral areas, the picture was less rosy. An estimated half a million city children were left largely to their own devices. Some of them broke all sorts of regulations by taking on part-time jobs. Others turned to rampant vandalism. At a time when the new Anderson shelters were believed to be vital in saving lives, children targeted them to such an extent that ARP wardens had to lock them.

In these early months of the war, free school milk was stopped; free meals were no longer available; scabies, headlice, ringworm and impetigo became rampant. Teachers were called up and classes instantly doubled in size. School buildings were lost too, long before the Blitz started flattening them. About 2,000 schools were wholly or partly requisitioned for defence and other purposes between 1939 and 1941. The major cities were worst hit – 66 per cent of London schools went; 60 per cent of Manchester's. Teachers tried to mount a peripatetic service, using anything from youth club premises to private homes, but inevitably this had a limited effect.

By January 1940, with the drift back of evacuees, about a quarter of children in the cities received as near to normal service as was possible. A further quarter had some sort of part-time provision. The rest, however, had inadequate home tuition and an estimated 430,000 children received no education at all.

The Blitz made matters worse. Emergency residential nurseries were set up for orphans under five. And the loss of a mother when a father was elsewhere was the equivalent of being an orphan. Nationally, one in five schools was damaged by bombing raids, although, of course, by definition these were concentrated in the cities, making any localized situation far worse than the mere statistic implies. There is no doubt that the Blitz had an appalling traumatizing effect on children, as it did on the adult population. A teacher's report from Bristol claimed that those who remained in the city were eight times more likely to become seriously psychologically disturbed than those who left. Morrison shelters, Anderson shelters, gas masks in cardboard boxes, the dreadful wail of the sirens – these were the outward trappings of a young generation who lived with the prospect that any night could be their last.

One casualty of the war who would not die until seven years after it was Derek Bentley. He was six when war broke out and although the blow to the head that may have triggered his epilepsy happened before the war, when he was seven the air raid shelter in which his family were hiding took a direct hit. He had to be dug out. Weeks later his sister, grandmother and aunt were all killed in a bombing raid. Derek became increasingly withdrawn and in September 1944 a Doodlebug hit the Bentleys' flat, raining concrete and tiles on the eleven-year-old as he slept. His education was similarly disrupted. Friar Elementary School in Webber Street was closed in 1940 because of bomb damage. For two years, all was relatively well for Derek at Camrose Avenue School, in the slightly safer Edgware, but this too was destroyed by a Doodlebug and the family moved to Walworth. When Derek's functional illiteracy became obvious, a doctor wrote 'wartime conditions' on the lad's medical records. It was happening everywhere. On 29 January 1953 they hanged Derek Bentley for murder.

Between 1939 and 1941, the crime rate among young persons under seventeen rocketed by more than a third. Malicious damage rose by 70 per cent; petty theft by 200 per cent. Some children took to looting, aping their elders. Four boys in London, two aged eleven, the others ten, were sentenced to birching for stealing from a bombed house. Writer Leslie Paul found this harsh:

> I can excuse a ten-year-old who wondered whether, in this orgy of destruction, he might not salvage something precious for himself. Indeed, it would seem a kind of sanity.[10]

As Angus Calder points out:

> Whether these figures meant that more children were breaking the law in circumstances of chaos which encouraged them to do so or merely that more adults made it their business to catch and punish them for doing it, this was an important by-product of war.[11]

One ARP warden, however, said of these children:

> If we had as little trouble with adults as we do with children, it would be all right. Hitler'd pack up if he could see some of these London kids.[12]

We shall see how the penal system reacted to this in another chapter, but the trend was to come down hard on offenders, in order to – in Voltaire's cynical phrase – 'encourage the others'.[13]

Accidents involving children increased. Because of petrol rationing, there were fewer cars on the road in wartime, yet child mortality on those roads increased. Long before cot deaths became a recognized, if controversial, area for debate, infant mortality climbed more sharply than in peacetime. The health authorities galvanized themselves to create vaccines to prevent epidemics – almost 7 million children were inoculated against diphtheria during the war – but the emotional and psychological damage to the young was incalculable. As R M Titmuss wrote five years after it all ended:

Not until over three years had passed was it possible to say that the enemy had killed more soldiers than women and children.[14]

Those who ascribed the rise of delinquency to the war did not take into account the pre-war figures. If we take two of the country's largest cities, Manchester and Liverpool, there was a serious increase in juvenile crime (162 per cent and 103 per cent respectively) in the years 1933 to 1936. It was also worrying that *adult* criminals of the 1940s had begun their careers as children in the 'England of the Dole' and this pattern was likely to recur. It is one of the anomalies of the time that what appears to us as a relatively law-abiding period (the inter-war years) should have the seeds of its own destruction visible just below the surface. Rather in the trend of today, increasingly officials took complex legal action rather than the traditional 'clip round the ear'. If this is the case, then there is no 'crime wave' among the young, merely a different way of dealing with the problem.

In the thirties, those who were impressed with the 'economic miracle' of Hitler's new Germany, pointed to the low crime rate there as having been effected by the positive influences of the various Hitler Youth movements. Those who looked into the causes of crime could not decide what the issues were. Were families now less cohesive? Fathers less strict? Was it a simple lack of income and job opportunities in the depressed areas? The Commissioner of the Metropolitan Police, Philip Game, went a stage further by blaming shops for displays from which thefts could occur easily, providing an impossibly strong lure for the weak-willed exponents of spontaneous stealing. As always, churches, youth clubs and above all, schools, were expected to stop the rot endemic in a society widely believed to be going to the dogs. Ever harsher punishments were also advocated and the well-to-do worried about a generation that had too much time on its hands. Fifty birchings were ordered on boys under fourteen (girls were exempt) in 1939. The following year the figure was 283 and in 1951, more than 500.

Juvenile crime statistics for the war years mask, as ever, a complex situation. Evacuees were typical of the problem. In some areas, because of the privations such children had already suffered, shopkeepers turned blind eyes to the odd bit of pilfering that went on under their noses. In others, horrified by the feral nature of their intake, the book was thrown at them. In one week in October 1939, twenty-two children, described as 'defiant' and 'intractable' were taken to court in Northamptonshire, mostly on theft charges. Over half the young people convicted in Cambridge in 1940 were London overspill, changing the character of twee 'middle England' in no uncertain measure.

Most concern was expressed over those children who stayed or returned to the Blitz cities. Boys played dangerous games in bomb craters, smashing windows and stealing what they could. Girls, it was feared, would be encouraged in underage sexual experiments in the rubble that could lead to pregnancies and prostitution. Several of the brothels discovered in London and the south coast during the build-up to D-Day contained girls of fourteen: they had to have learned their trade somewhere.

The need for additional workers now that the call-up was in full swing meant that 'young persons' were earning more money than ever and *still* juvenile crime increased. Those, especially the Socialists, who had blamed the hungry thirties were now at a loss to find a cause and most fell back on the old collapse of the family theme, even more acute and accurate now than in the pre-war years. This was borne out by the fact that the greatest increase in crime seemed to be happening among the under fourteen age bracket, who were not employed in the same way as their elders, if at all.

And most of the crime was, after all, minor. Petty theft, especially of sweets, cigarettes and bicycles covered most of it. The most delinquent age was thirteen, as surging hormones conspired to produce, in some, ever more ludicrous acts of bravado among a generation that had no immediate male role model.

But some juvenile crime was serious. There were gangs in every major city and many small towns and the danger here was not merely the loyalty of the gang members, who would refuse to 'grass' on mates, but the sheer numbers meant they were more likely to egg each other on than a criminal acting alone. The Chief Constable of Liverpool reported that there may not be an overall leader, but there was a great deal of co-operation between gangs involved in a variety of crimes from perjury to manslaughter. A gang operating out of Maidstone, Kent, in 1940 became so adept at stealing bicycles that they were able to strip down machines, swap parts and repaint the frames in a matter of minutes. It is rather difficult to understand the government's decision to release all Borstal boys who had served more than six months. Of the 2,817 released in 1939, 1,419 were back inside by 1946. The rate among girls in terms of percentage (56 per cent) was even higher.

As a child who was to make his name in the annals of hard crime later in the century, the wartime experience of Ron Kray is telling. Although autobiographies of felons should be treated with the same caution as autobiographies of policemen and judges, there is a kernel of truth in Kray's work, especially in the attitudes it conveys. Ron and his twin Reg were born in October 1933, the same year as Derek Bentley, in Stene Street, Hoxton. Before the war began, the family moved to Vallance Road, Bethnal Green, around the corner from Sidney Street, where the police and the Army had had a shoot-out with anarchists twenty-odd years earlier. The house at No. 178 was not far from the Ripper's killing grounds in Whitechapel. Charlie Kray, the twins' dad, was a 'pesterer', 'recycling' gold, silver and clothing at a profit:

> There were quite a few scraps and the kids in our street used to have brick battles against gangs of kids from other streets. It was a tough area and they used to say if you came from the East End you finished up either a villain, a thief or a fighter.[15]

The Krays, of course, became all three.

The war had a huge effect on the Kray boys, six when it broke out. Their father was called up and ordered to report to the Tower. 'But our father wasn't having any of that,' so deserted and remained on the run for twelve years, hiding out with various friends all over London. The police came looking for Charlie Kray several times: 'I hated the police,' Ron remembered, 'and I hated Hitler and the Germans. They destroyed ten thousand houses in Bethnal Green alone and they killed and injured hundreds of innocent people.'[16]

For children of the Krays' age, despite the abject terror in which they sometimes found themselves, the war was one big adventure playground. The twins were thrown out of their beds when the nearby railway arch took a direct hit and Ron delighted in the searchlights, the explosions, the fires. He revelled in the warmth and camaraderie of the air raid shelters, with the music and the dancing, but he enjoyed the evacuee experience of rural Suffolk too, 'breathing in the air and seeing the animals'.[17]

A hatred of the police, a broken home, a family already on the edges of crime. It was so with hundreds of families, perhaps thousands. As the war ended, Reg Kray got into trouble with the law for the first time. His 'crime' was little more than youthful exuberance, but it involved a slug gun (air pistol) and the situation could have been serious. It was certainly serious years later when Ron found an arch-enemy, George Cornell, drinking in one of 'his' pubs, the Blind Beggar in Bethnal Green. He pulled out a revolver and shot the interloper above the right eye as he sat at the bar. When told of the killing, brother Reg shrugged. 'Ronnie does some funny things.' But no one apart from the Krays was laughing.

Edward Smithies[18] notes that the rate of juvenile crime varied hugely from town to town and from police authority to police authority. Glasgow was the 'worst' city in Britain in terms of gang warfare, violence, drunkenness and juvenile delinquency, but the formidable Percy Sillitoe, the Chief Constable, claimed a huge decrease in all of this by 1937. In an approach discussed elsewhere, and echoed today in David Cameron's silly sound-bite of 'hugging a hoodie',[19] the Chief Constable of Plymouth explained:

> My desire was to prevent, by friendly talk and advice [juveniles'] appearance in the Police Court. These talks were given in my office in the presence of parents and the results have been remarkably successful.[20]

Even so, this was pre-war and it is doubtful whether the Chief Constable – or the miscreant's parents – would have had time for such chats once war broke out.

A detailed crime survey conducted in Bath towards the end of the war threw the spotlight onto delinquent girls. The Georgian city, with its incomparable architecture, witnessed little of the worst aspects of the war, but under the Baedeker raid system, it was hit on two successive nights in 1942, resulting in 400 deaths. Exeter, Canterbury, Norwich and York were all pulverized that spring – cities that had minimal defences in terms of searchlights and ack-ack batteries. 'I saw Bath the next day,' wrote Mrs Paratoud, who would become a GI bride three years later,

> It was heartbreaking . . . I shall never forget the streets . . . all crunchy with broken glass and rubble. The shocked, tense faces of the people and this stiff upper lip thing that kept them from crying and raging over the loss and the desolation. Why didn't they weep and mourn and lament?[21]

What they did do, at least the teenaged girls among them, was to forget the horrors of the war by providing a service for several local American bases. Only 9.4 per cent of crime in Bath in 1944 was attributable to juvenile crime and much of that centred on prostitution. The local police closed five brothels in a twenty-two-month period but the authorities were equally worried about the class of casual 'good-time girl' we have met already. 'There are girls in Bath,' the *Weekly Chronicle and Herald* quoted a probation officer in October 1943,

> whose only ideas in life are men, lipstick and showing as much of their bodies as they can. Wartime conditions were having an appalling effect . . . children of school-age were becoming utterly spoilt . . . too much money and many soldiers with money to fling about were factors leading to their downfall.[22]

The (female) probation officer singled out a 'tremendous change for the worse in girls she knows since the raids . . . last April. Some girls were to be pitied. Some were undoubtedly suffering from sexual mania'. Do-gooders rallied to defend the ancient City's good name by holding meetings and drawing up petitions. The Bath Vigilance and Rescue Association no doubt meant well, but the more cynical could have seen in them a dim shadow of the sinister control methods in use in Nazi-occupied Europe. Smithies quotes the case of one girl, aged fifteen, who went to a Christmas Eve party at a local American base and spent the night in a railway station cloakroom (alone or with company is not recorded). Christmas Day was spent walking the streets of Bath until seven o'clock, when she had a meal with an American soldier. That night she slept in a barn and went to London the next day with another soldier, presumably on furlough. There she met a third soldier, went to the cinema with him and returned to Bath where, suitably dressed by a fourth soldier, went with him to a dance. From there she went to the camp, then to a pub with a soldier who was, in the still Victorian parlance of local papers, 'intimate with her'. The girl was pregnant, but since it is likely that at least six men had had sex with her in a three-day period, she could not say who the father was and ended in an approved school.

Smithies quotes five cases of delinquent girls in trouble in Bath between January 1944 and January 1945. This was a time when, in many ways, the physical condition of children was deteriorating, which in part prompted the National Health legislation of the post-war period. On the other hand, the rate of juvenile delinquency was actually falling. Two girls aged fifteen and sixteen were caught drinking beer outside a pub. They lied about their ages and were told not to visit public houses again, but to go to a youth club instead. Another girl of fifteen was placed under a supervision order having stayed out all night in the company of the black soldiers she preferred to white. 'It was amazing,' the court recorded, 'the self-assurance the girl had, and she seemed to know more about sexual matters than some women did at 40.'[23]

In October 1944, two teenagers were sent to approved school after their behaviour included being 'very fond of US soldiers' and smoking forty cigarettes a day – 'an absolute scandal,' said the magistrate, 'because it is a wicked waste of money and the mother has encouraged it.' Presumably, he was talking about the smoking.

Teenaged vice was not the creation of wartime. Superintendent Robert Fabian was concerned about it in 1920s London:

She was young, slender as a cornstalk and her hair as yellow. She used the railing as a footrest and adjusted the ankle-strap of her pencil-heel shoe. Her eyes watched me. Her leg would have looked better in school socks, I thought . . . 'Late for a kid like you – lurking about in a street like this, isn't it?'[24]

The girl was not, in fact, a prostitute, but a good-time girl nonetheless, paid by one of the 310 nightclubs of the West End, to lure punters in to spend money. When Fabian quizzed a barman in a dive above a shop in Curzon Street, his reply was:

Well, Mr Fabian – you know how it is with kids these days. Tougher'n we are, some of 'em. We get the zombies [police-women] around here with the Children's Waggon[25] pretty often – but it's easy to pick up another lot.[26]

Most of them were runaways from remand homes and recruitment to the clubs was by word of mouth. In a phrase full of foreboding for the drug culture that was to come, Fabian wrote:

The job [of the girls] is to empty that [punter's] wallet – whether they do it with pink champagne and satin-quilted walls; or by meths-and-ginger ale, marijuana cigarettes and dope-jumping teenage girls who, for £2, would cuddle a baboon.[27]

The drugs trade more properly belongs to the post-war era, but even pre-war, the more exotic foreign nightclubs of London offered: 'reefers, giggle-smoke, love-weed, bharg, ganji, Indian hay . . . It hangs in the air like the taste of sin.' And constantly, in clubs like this, the female companions of the African musicians and dancers were 'pitifully young girlfriends'.

The rather pompous Inspector Jack Henry devoted a short chapter to 'Crime and the Juvenile' in his autobiography and focuses on the thirties, with ominous rumblings of what lay ahead in the post-war years. He pours scorn on the old notion that scrumping apples was a schoolboy lark, a phase through which everybody went, and makes the fair point that theft is theft and may well gravitate to more serious and consistent adult crime. He places the onus squarely on parents, although makes the obvious comments about fathers missing in the Armed Forces and children running wild as a result:

> Both in the last war [1914–18] and the present one, juvenile delinquents assumed and are assuming staggering figures.[28]

As commander of V Division of the Metropolitan area, Henry was appalled by the stubbornness of some offenders and the craftiness of others. Unable by law to fingerprint anyone under sixteen, the police were not always able to prove cases of burglary, for example, and Henry cites the case of one lad, just before the war, who was sent to a remand home, from which he absconded. On his six-week escapade, the boy committed more than thirty cases of housebreaking. He also reached his sixteenth birthday, so Henry was able to tie him in with a whole string of other offences elsewhere.

Most of Henry's V Division experiences with juveniles related to theft. In one case, two young housebreakers operated through the mother of one of them, who was a 'fence', and Henry pontificates grimly on their home life: 'for rarely have they known anything but cuffs and kicks in squalid surroundings.'[29] He cites one instance of a boy who robbed at knifepoint, and of gangs having to be broken up by force, but interestingly, all this relates to *pre-war* levels of crime, away from the usual influences we have been discussing. A third of all crime in V Division was carried out by lads under seventeen.

Henry is kinder to girls. They did not commit crime as often or as seriously as boys and were usually lured into it by older females. He has an almost touching faith in the youth courts and female police officers in putting youthful offenders back on the straight and narrow.

Most child psychological studies today point to greater delinquency in dysfunctional families and broken homes. There is no doubt that the Second World War created just such conditions.

Future Moors Murderer, Ian Brady, was born the year before the war began and was brought up by his father in the gang-ridden Gorbals, the roughest area of Glasgow. His killing partner, Myra Hindley, was born in 1942 in Crumpsall, Manchester, and was the target of physical abuse by her paratrooper father. Fred West, one of the most prolific serial killers in British history, was born into rural poverty in 1941 in Much Marcle, Gloucestershire. He claimed his father committed incest with at least one of Fred's sisters.

The childhood experiences of the world's monsters are crucially important in explaining how they became demonized and clearly we cannot excuse the actions of arch-criminals by blaming the war. Life is infinitely more complex than that. Millions of people who were brought up in wartime went on to lead perfectly ordinary, honest lives. But the war created a breeding ground of inhospitality, a seething melting pot of anti-social behaviour, from which it was impossible for some children to step back.

CHAPTER SEVEN

'Be Good; We're Still Open'

In February 1942 Winston Churchill broadcast over the wireless a tribute to all branches of the Civil Defence. He singled out the police especially – they 'have been in it everywhere all the time. And, as a working woman wrote to me in a letter, "What gentlemen they are".'[1]

The wartime image of the police owes a great deal to nostalgia. To the professional underworld they were 'coppers', hard-nosed detectives you recognized instantly in pubs, and who you always addressed respectfully as 'Mister'. To the honest citizen who survived the war, they were the living, breathing embodiment of Lawson Wood's cartoon 'bobbies' of the twenties and thirties: over-weight, moustachioed, avuncular and none too bright. The pre-war generation remembered bobbies cuffing them round the ear for scrumping apples and frogmarching them home to dad for a bit more of the same. They remembered the 'White Horse' Wembley, the cup final of 1923, when PC George Scorey, riding a grey, accompanied by four other mounted policemen, had prevented a terrible disaster when crowds broke through wire fencing and invaded the pitch. And they remembered too the callous shooting of PC Gutteridge of the Essex constabulary in September 1927, when ex-cons Browne and Kennedy brought him down with gunfire, then shot out both his eyes.

The Second World War was undoubtedly the finest hour of the 183 police forces up and down the country. Stretched though the thin blue line undoubtedly was, the policemen and women rose to the huge demands made on them and somehow coped. The title of this chapter comes from a hand-painted sign hanging at a rakish angle outside a bombed police station in London – and it says it all.

Policing in its modern sense was still relatively new in Britain. When war broke out, the Metropolitan Police – the 'most public institution in the world' – was 110 years old. Other forces were newer. By a series of Parliamentary Acts in the nineteenth century, constabularies on the Metropolitan model had been set up in counties and boroughs, often to cope with the unruly behaviour of large-scale troublemakers like the Chartists and the railway navvies.[2] But it was only twenty years before Hitler invaded Poland that the police had notoriously gone on strike, largely over the injustices of pay and conditions arising out of the First World War. And it was less than twenty years since forces had been able to recruit women onto the payroll: in 1939 there were still only 282 of them.

With Chamberlain's government expecting saturation bombing from the first day of the war, the police strength throughout the country was increased by 50 per cent. With the centralist paranoia of the wartime government, chief constables and police authorities lost the *laissez-faire* control they had held in peacetime and everything became tightly co-ordinated from the Home Office. There were nearly 60,000 police in 1939 and even though some 9,000 of them were either Army reservists or, under twenty-five, liable for call-up, all were kept on the strength.

Clearly, no one could predict how long the war would last, but the farcical optimism of August 1914 – that it would 'all be over by Christmas' – was not repeated now. More policemen had to be found and they came from four sources. The First Police Reserve was a 10,000-strong body of ex-policemen who were paid a retaining fee. On the outbreak of war, they were instantly returned to police stations, although their numbers dropped alarmingly as the toll of stress and sheer physical exhaustion hit home. The Special Constabulary of 130,000 men was another level and most of these men spent the entire war as full-time constables. The Police War Reserve, set up by the Met in May 1938 as a precautionary measure, could supply several thousand more, all men over thirty. Most other forces followed the London lead once war began. Finally, after much campaigning, a fourth area of recruitment came from the Women's Auxiliary Police Corps, set up in the month before the war started. Their uniforms resembled those of auxiliary firewomen and their duties were at first confined to clerical work, answering phones and making the tea. Only as the government became more desperate were they allowed to join their male colleagues in the front line.

The Police and Firemen (War Service) Act of 1939 made it impossible for policemen to retire with a pension unless on genuine medical grounds and auxiliaries were prevented from doing so by the Defence Regulations. The War Reservists among the regular police were detached for other duties by Christmas, training Army recruits and acting as Military Policemen with their distinctive scarlet caps. By 1941 the total figure of all police in the country stood at 92,000 – an unprecedented situation.

Robert Fabian had joined the police twenty years earlier, in what was a far more leisurely time. 'A few days later, I received Form A1/R8 which told me I should be of British birth and pure British descent; over twenty but under twenty-seven; be 5 feet 9 inches tall in my bare feet; able to read and show reasonable proficiency in writing from dictation and simple arithmetic.'[3] A rigorous medical checked whether he had flat-feet, tumours or had ever been ruptured.

Murderer John Christie, joining as an emergency Reservist eighteen years later, presumably underwent the same tests, but now there was a war on and nobody even checked his criminal record. He signed the form:

I . . . do solemnly and sincerely declare and affirm that I will well and truly serve our Sovereign Lord the King in the office of Special Constable for the Metropolitan Police District without favour or affection, malice or ill will; and that I will, to the best of my power, cause the peace to be kept . . . [and to] discharge all the duties thereof faithfully according to the law.

The law, as far as the average constable understood it, was printed in *Police Law* by Cecil C H Moriarty, Chief Constable of Brighton.

Both Fabian and Christie would have carried in their pockets the sixth edition, produced in 1939. The book covers a vast range of criminal activity, some of which would have met a wartime policeman on an almost daily basis. Crime itself was defined, protocols of arrest, the procedures of magistrates' and crown courts and the nature of evidence. 'Offences against the person' were listed: assault, murder, rape, abduction, prostitution and indecency, with a separate section for child victims. Next came 'offences in connection with property': breaking and entering, larceny, malicious damage, coinage and forgery, as well as the old country pursuits like poaching. The section dealing with 'offences against the community in general' began with Treason. Looming large by the 1930s was 'Traffic Law'. The Highway Code was only eight years old and the list of vehicles still has a Dickensian feel to it: 'Carts and wagons, Hackney Carriages and Stage Coaches'. Only in Chapter Twenty-eight do we read about the *first* purpose of a police force – crime prevention. The section dealing with 'His Majesty's Forces' was concerned with the small, professional regular establishment of the Army, Navy and Air Force. It perhaps did not envisage a nation-in-arms along the lines of the Second World War. Other sections dealt with trade, pawnbroking, the use of explosives and firearms. Public entertainments were covered, as was public health, and there was a massive twenty-page section on the laws relating to the sale of liquor. Of the statutes still in existence on the outbreak of war, many were hopelessly obsolete. Among the crimes that have been rarely, if ever, encountered were Dangerous Performances by Juveniles[4] and failure to comply with the Chimney Sweepers' Acts (Repeal) Act 1938.

The average constable was, nevertheless, expected to be familiar with all this and to use his, sometimes split-second, judgement as to how to proceed. Above all there was a whole plethora of loopholes and case law for the unwary. For instance, the Children and Young Persons Act of 1933 made it an offence to sell tobacco to anyone under sixteen. It was not illegal, however, to sell to 'boy messengers in uniform in the course of their employment' or 'persons employed by tobacconists for the purpose of their business'.[5]

As police authority T A Critchley wrote: 'The police are always at war in fighting crime,'[6] but the Second World War changed their duties considerably. The bewildering range of Defence Regulations meant that every officer from the Commissioners at Scotland Yard to the bobby on the beat anywhere in the kingdom, had to learn many more Moriarty-type chapters. They had to know the law concerning the carrying of a camera and had to be aware of the blackout orders and what constituted an infringement of them. They had to be up to speed on the Aliens' legislation and to take seriously any whiff of possible espionage.

The conventional pattern of policing changed slightly as a result of the war. An uncertain number of potential criminals and a known number of recidivists was removed from the equation by conscription. Such men may have contrived to cause a headache for the Military Police wherever they were billeted, from Catterick to Cairo, but at least they were no longer a nuisance on the streets. Traffic problems lessened because the rationing of petrol reduced the use of casual motoring but accidents, even with fewer cars on the roads, increased because of the effects of the blackout. Juvenile delinquency increased, as we have seen. And with the Broadgate bomb in Coventry, no force could afford to ignore entirely the activities of the IRA.

As well as hunting the Fifth Column, the police had to guard 'vulnerable points'. This was the first time in history that policemen were issued with guns. A possible 15,000 men patrolled the docks, gasworks, railway stations, airfields, armaments factories, telephone exchanges, post offices and oil installations, day and night, in case of sabotage. This was tedious, unglamorous and usually thankless work, later taken over by the Home Guard.

The most obvious, dangerous and heartbreaking work of the police, the area that led to most deaths, injuries, stress and citations for gallantry, was their handling of air raids. It was the bobby who was often first on the scene of destruction. If bombs fell on his beat, the stately 2½ miles an hour at which he walked speeded to a run as he dodged falling masonry and flying glass. He may have to dig out survivors with his bare hands, comfort shocked and traumatized sufferers, patch up the wounded, hold the hands of the dying and carry out the dead. He may have to put out fires before the Fire

Brigade arrived, bandage a wound before the ambulance came, cordon off roads where an unexploded bomb might lie, hours before the Army's Bomb Disposal Unit arrived. Some men became specialists in these fields, known as 'incident officers' and they could be found in London, Coventry, Plymouth, Hull, Bristol, Sheffield, Manchester and Southampton – anywhere the Luftwaffe might strike in 1940–42 or the Doodlebugs rain down in 1944–45. In Hull alone, there were seventy-three night attacks, leaving over 1,000 dead and 100,000 without homes. The 'Baedecker' raids hit cathedral cities, the 600-year-old church of St George the Martyr in Canterbury crashing in ruins in 1942, never to be rebuilt. The shell of the great cathedral in Coventry still stands. An estimated 2,300 flying bombs fell on London, killing more than 5,000 and injuring 15,000 more. A further 7,600 were the casualties of the V2 rockets.

The original intention was for those members of the force who were struggling with all this on a nightly basis to be replaced by colleagues from other constabularies in rural areas. There were many such volunteers for action, but not a single policeman left London. In the Blitz proper, between September 1940 and July 1941, there were 1,000 alerts, 23,000 deaths and over 40,000 injuries. On 11 May 1941, Scotland Yard itself took a direct hit.

With so much enemy activity aimed on London, it was inevitable that the Met was under the greatest strain, although any city force found itself at times near to breaking point. On 12 August 1943 Sub-Divisional Inspector James Cole was called to an incident in Dulwich, where a madman with a shotgun was behaving in a dangerous manner in Barry Street. While the Home Guard and police distracted the lunatic, Cole crept in through a window and released a hostage before the gunman shot himself. Cole was the only Met officer to receive a bar to his King's Police Medal for gallantry as a result of this heroism under fire. In the first year of the war alone, ten officers won the Police Medal for bravery; Detective Sergeant Tom Bailey forced a getaway car to stop by jumping onto the running-board; Constable Matthew Busnall arrested a drunken gunman in Bayswater, despite having been shot by him; Constable Alexander Carmichael was hit in the leg by bullets chasing fugitives in Dollis Hill station; Frederick Champs, having lost his torch, walked a live railway line in the middle of the night to save a potential suicide from an oncoming train; Albert Cosham chased a gang of post office robbers for over 40 miles, despite attempts to force him off the road; off-duty policemen George Henley, Frederick Crouch, Cecil Rackham and Elliott Pillar overcame two armed deserters in Barking; and Arthur McKitterick went back again and again into a gas-filled house to rescue occupants.

The George Medal was instituted in 1940 for acts of bravery not quite on a par with those that won the George Cross, established in the same year. Eighty-two George Medals were awarded and a total of 276 commendations were given.

It was also a given that much work done by the police went unsung. The Home Secretary, Herbert Morrison, wrote: 'It is no exaggeration to say that the reputation of the British police for service to the community stands higher than ever before.'

Some of the institutions with which many of us grew up were still relatively new on the outbreak of war. The 'Mobile Patrol Experiment' of 1920 had developed into the fully-fledged Flying Squad four years before the invasion of Poland. Their brief was to combat the increasing use of cars for crime, especially armed robbery, and the Squad – known to the Underworld then as the 'Heavy Mob' – was equipped with black Railtons, capable of speeds in excess of 100 miles an hour. The famous 999 telephone number for emergency services was set up in London in 1936, after a serious fire in Wimpole Street left five people dead and a Scotland Yard switchboard jammed with calls. Whitehall 1212, the Yard's number, was the most famous in the country, but the technology could not cope with the 56,724 calls logged in the first half of that year. The new system, opened fully on 1 July 1937, received 1,336 calls in the first week, with the usual multi-claimants of those who swore they were the very first to dial the number.

Wartime emergencies undoubtedly gave the police force new directions of development and a new impetus. The Pig Club was a short-lived success story, when Sergeant Harry Baker began to keep pigs in Hyde Park in line with the encouragement of the Ministry of Food. Officers in Chelsea built four sties on a bomb-site next to the station and some 250 animals were reared by 1945 – five years' bacon ration for every man, woman and child in Chelsea!

Inevitably, the most high-profile policemen were the detectives, that small group of Yard men who became cult figures in the 1950s, with their trench coats, trilby hats, pipes and references to villains as 'chummy'. We have already met Fred Cherrill, Head of the Fingerprint Bureau between 1938 and 1953. Fascinated by prints, having seen his own in the dust of a flour mill as a small child, he could recognize recidivists' prints by sight; his work on the Cummins case was uncanny. But we have to be wary of the rash of autobiographies that appeared as these detectives retired in the 1950s and 1960s. It is likely that the Met and the Home Office took a dim view of men who blew their own trumpets and this may explain the rather humdrum way in which their stories are told.

Ex-Detective Chief Superintendent Edward Greeno was one of the 'Big Five'[7] who dominated the Yard in the war years. When he wrote his memoirs in 1959, the *News of the World* predicted a rush to the bookstalls by the Underworld – 'eager to know what "The Guv'nor" has to say'.[8] Molly Lefebure, Keith Simpson's secretary, met Ted Greeno in the spring of 1942:

> More than anything, he resembled a huge, steel-plated battle-cruiser, with his jaw thrust forward instead of a prow. He spoke little, noticed everything and was tough not in the Hollywood style, but genuinely, naturally, quietly, appallingly, so . . . The grim light of battle glimmered in his eyes and he started asking me questions in a rather rasping voice that sent shivers down my spine. He was on the warpath and I thought 'God help the poor fool he's after.'[9]

Today, Greeno would not be allowed to be a policeman. His autobiography reveals quite candidly that he bet heavily on the horses, doubling his detective's salary of £2,000 a year. It was at the races he got to know the faces of the thugs who comprised the racecourse gangs, a serious problem in the Britain of the twenties and thirties. He joined the Met in January 1921, did his ten weeks' basic training at Peel House in Pimlico, going through: 'all sorts of physical and mental hoops until I could wrestle with a drunk and grapple with the wording of a summons.'[10]

In H Division, Whitechapel, Greeno walked his beat for £3 5s a week: 'and if we had learned to sleep standing up we would have been more cosy than in our iron beds.'[11] The world that Greeno describes was destroyed by the Luftwaffe and the great social and economic upheaval that was the Second World War. He showed visitors the colourful East End. They 'loved Cable Street where the Negroes walked and the opium dens, rat-holes of dirty divans and sackcloth curtains, where the Chinese smoked.'[12] He remembered Wapping with its beautiful children in the Corpus Christi Day celebrations and their less than beautiful fathers knocking seven bells out of the police and each other on Corpus Christi Night.

When he joined the Flying Squad, he was chasing armed robbers and cracking down on the gangs. Darby Sabini was the godfather of his day and his boys were well armed – clubs, bottles, guns, iron bars, fence posts – anything, in fact, that would pass for a blunt instrument.

In the thirties, many of the crooks with whom Greeno dealt were aliens, mostly Eastern European, often Jewish, and many of them claiming they could not be deported because as former citizens of Tsarist Russia, their homeland had ceased to exist. It was an interesting point of international law. He was rarely involved with vice, but did close down a high-class brothel in Dover Street. When he entered the place, he found 'whips and racks and spiked girdles and the biggest bed in the world, currently occupied by the Misses May, June, Betty and Helen,' plus a man over fifty, a boy under twenty, and a 'glistening six-foot Negress in thigh boots and nothing else'. Everybody else was naked. When Greeno appeared in court, the elderly client who wrote the Negress 'incredibly filthy letters with "funny drawings"' complained because Greeno referred to him as 'this man' whereas, in fact, he was a solicitor!

Greeno makes no mention of the outbreak of war and the effect it had on the Met, but just over a year later he was with the 'Murder Squad' – as Press and public knew it – and seems to have been involved in several of the high-profile murder cases of the war. He claims twelve successes in his autobiography and we have already seen his involvement in some of them.[13] His first child murder was that of eleven-year-old Sheila Wilson, in the third summer of the war, and he gives us a clear glimpse of society at the time when he wrote:

> When a child doesn't come home in the country you go round asking at grandma's or auntie's, assuming everything will be all right. But when a child is missing in the city it pays to suspect the worst straightaway and act accordingly.[14]

Ironically, Sheila Wilson *should* have been in the country. She had been evacuated to Dorset two months earlier but had come back in May 1942, that euphoric lull between the two Blitzes on the capital. Sheila had been given twopence by a neighbour to buy a newspaper that Wednesday evening, 15 July, and had not come back. Her mother Edith contacted the police and the Divisional Inspector in Lewisham, Bill Chapman, sent for Greeno. Everyone in Leahurst Road was questioned, including 38-year-old Patrick Kingston,[15] a lodger with the Graham family at No. 19. Kingston worked at the local ARP station, unable to do much for the war effort because a bomb blast in November 1940 had permanently damaged his left leg and hand. The same blast had killed his six brothers and sisters. In fact, on the night that Sheila disappeared, Kingston had hurt his leg again, reopening the old wound.

The newspapers were given a description of the missing girl and because of her clothing, used the cliché title 'The Girl in Green Case'. And that became the 'Girl in Green Murder' when Sheila's body was found. The Lewisham police had knocked on doors, searched bomb-sites, dragged the River Quaggy. What they had not done, until Greeno suggested it, was search the tiny cellar at No. 19. It was only 3 feet deep, piled 2 feet high with rubble and a constable stood, reeling away, gagging. He had found the remains of Sheila Wilson. She had been strangled with window cord and, wrote Greeno grimly years later, 'there were other things too – the stamp of the sex killer'.[16]

In the meantime, Kingston had 'done a runner', but Greeno had a sixth sense that he would come back. He posted men in the house and the lodger was arrested days later, when he returned to repay, according to him, a £1 debt he owed to the landlord. 'I had been on the drink practically all the week,' Kingston said in his statement. 'When she came back and said what paper did I want, I said I didn't want a paper at all, I just wanted to kiss and cuddle her. She started to scream and I caught her by the arms to try and stop her screaming and I went mad.' It was during the hasty burial in the half-cellar that he hurt his leg and reopened the old wound: 'There are people who say,' wrote Greeno, 'a killer should never hang. There are others who say he always – or nearly always – should and I am one of them.'

Albert Pierrepoint hanged Patrick Kingston at Wandsworth on 14 September 1942.

'Whoever killed Mark Turner,' Greeno wrote, 'battering in his shiny, craggy skull nine times with a hammer, sat down afterwards in the same tiny room with his body and wolfed down the old man's rations – nine eggs, fried on the old man's stove. After his meal, he found a bottle of Scotch the old man had prized and he guzzled until he was sick. He rifled the old man's pockets for his wallet and for every copper coin. He changed into the old man's suit and stole a suitcase to pack more clothes. He took the old man's spectacles he could not wear and the rosary he surely could not respect.'[17]

Mark Turner was eighty-two, the oldest murder victim of the war and he had made the mistake of befriending Canadian Army deserter Mervin McEwen, who was living rough in a derelict Army hut in Savile Park, Halifax. The deserter's battledress and cap badge were found in the dead man's room.

McEwen could have been anywhere and Greeno put out a nationwide search, which in wartime was difficult. Even so, it yielded 'results' – McEwen was seen, all on the same night, in London, Glasgow, Liverpool and even Cyprus! Greeno even sent out radio messages to ships at sea. Eventually, the eagle-eyed Redcaps [military policemen] in a canteen in Piccadilly, Manchester, recognized the man the Yard and Halifax were looking for. The next day, McEwen, using Mark Turner as an alias, confessed to Greeno. He had broken into the old man's room and helped himself to cold meat and Scotch before the real Mark Turner woke up:

> There was a hammer on the table. I wanted to stop him shouting. I went towards him with the hammer and he sat up. I hit him with the hammer and I saw blood. He still kept shouting. I was so scared I hit him again and again with the hammer.[18]

Then he stabbed him with a knife.

McEwen was tried at Leeds, claimed diminished responsibility by virtue of being drunk and was found guilty in forty minutes. He was hanged by Thomas Pierrepoint on Thursday 3 February 1944.

It was Ted Greeno who took on what was probably the last murder committed in the Second World War. One of the problems with researching crime is that unless someone is convicted, those who write on a case are cagey about naming names. Greeno does not name names in the 'Blood on the Corn' case because the murderer's death sentence was commuted to life imprisonment.

A courting couple were out for a walk 'somewhere in Suffolk' on 8 July 1945. Germany had surrendered months before, but Japan remained stubbornly in the field and there were still some 300,000 British troops stationed in East Anglia under Eastern Command. The couple stumbled on fourteen-year-old Daphne Bacon, who was lying 'on her back with her knees flexed up, one eye black and closed and her brunette bob thick with blood. Her skull was fractured seven times'[19] but she was still conscious and told the pair that a soldier had attacked her and beaten her with a stick. She died in hospital the next night.

Greeno was called in and launched a huge enquiry, issuing a questionnaire to every member of the Armed Forces in the area. Bearing in mind the scale of this task and the fact that there was, after all, still a war on, it was a brilliant feat of organization and tenacity. 'The guv'nor' and his long-suffering number two, Fred Hodge, were sorting these questionnaires when they heard shouting in the street outside their hotel. Hodge went to investigate and returned

> with a grin that shifted his ears. 'Know what, guv'nor?' he said, 'the war's over.'
>
> 'Come on, Fred,' I said. 'Let's down tools for ten minutes. We must have a drink on this.'[20]

It was 15 August, VJ Day and Japan had finally succumbed. Greeno's personal war on crime, however, was not over. Every alibi had to be checked, especially with soldiers' penchants for covering each other's backs on barracks comings and goings. Men seen in the cornfield in question were eliminated forensically; local Italian prisoners-of-war were found to have cut their hands in the line of duty, as it were, taking down barbed wire, now that there was no longer a need for it. Greeno brought his wife and sons up to Great Yarmouth for a much-needed holiday and 'the guv'nor' hoped for some time off to get to the Newmarket races. One soldier whose alibi Greeno double-checked shot himself in the armoury. Why was never ascertained. He was in Lewisham at the time of Daphne Bacon's murder and that story checked out.

But there was one man whose story did not. A gunner in the Royal Artillery swore he had been playing cards all day in an Army hut with his mates. This was not quite true: he had absented himself for well over two hours and was over-vocal perhaps in his reaction to news of the murder – 'I'd like to get my hands on the dirty bastard, I'd strangle him, hanging's too good; he ought to suffer like that little girl.' The anonymous Gunner changed his story several times to Greeno, but his size eleven boots fitted exactly the prints found at the scene of the crime. Then

> his head hung limply and, looking at the floor he said 'I think I'd be much better if I tell you truth. It was a girl I hit . . . I left her in the cornfield.'[21]

This was one job Pierrepoint did not get because the sentence was commuted to life in prison.

George Hatherill was a surprisingly cosmopolitan policeman. For six years before the war he worked as liaison officer with the Belgian police, based in Brussels and Antwerp. This had come about because, having completed his training in February 1920, he was seconded to Special Branch largely because of his shorthand speed. Back in England by 1932, he was nevertheless constantly crossing the Channel in connection with European crimes. Molly Lefebure remembered the man's awesome reputation as a fluent speaker of several languages. The war found him investigating Black Market crime[22] but in 1943, he was a Detective Superintendent in charge of east and north-east London, effectively another of the 'big five'. In his autobiography[23] Hatherill allows himself the occasional aside on his job: 'There is no glamour in crime. Most of it is sordid and in many cases it is vicious, brutal or even bestial.'[24]

In the Berlin Olympics in 1936, Hatherill found himself in a special stand next to Hitler's enclosure. At the invitation of Heinrich Himmler, the most powerful policeman in the Third Reich, Hatherill was given a guided tour of Gestapo headquarters in Prinz Albrechtstrasse by Himmler's Number Two, the 'blond beast' Reinhard Heydrich. It was Heydrich who masterminded the forgery operation of printing Bank of England notes above the value of £5 to attempt to destabilize the British economy. By the middle of 1941, some 200,000 notes were printed each month at the camp at Sachsenhausen, near Berlin, and were used routinely in transactions with neutral countries. Three years later, one of the most brilliant forgers of the century, Solomon Smolianoff, was hired to work on the larger denominations, including dollar bills. The scam did little to affect Britain directly, but it probably saved the life of Smolianoff, who would otherwise have been one of the countless victims of the Nazis.

Even during a war, con artists continued to ply their trade. Harry Clapham was vicar of St Thomas's Lambeth and in the twenties began fund-raising for his church. By the late thirties however, his lifestyle had become extravagant. On an annual stipend of £400, he was spending months at a time travelling in Germany, Austria, America and the West Indies. By May 1942, fate caught up with Harry Clapham in the shape of Inspector Bray and his boss, George

Hatherill. The extent of the vicar's embezzlement and fraud was breathtaking. He had an army of staff, filing cabinets, typewriters, addressing machines and mailbags all stashed away in the basement of the vicarage. Hatherill estimated Clapham was sending out about a million begging letters a year and discovered he had ninety-one different bank accounts and owned property all over London worth an astonishing £117,576. Found guilty at the Bailey, he was sent to prison for three years.

Detective Superintendent Robert Higgins – as he became at the height of his fame – hailed from Oakham, in what was then the country's smallest county, Rutland (which had the lowest crime rate in Britain throughout the century). Barely getting into the police (a job his mother worried about) in terms of height and weight, he was posted to S Division of the Met, covering a large area of North London. Writing his autobiography in the late 1950s, he gives the lie to the peaceful twenties with his description of street fights and drunks being strapped into handcarts in Camden Town to be wheeled off to the 'nick' in Albany Street.

By September 1941 Higgins had gravitated from the Flying Squad to the rank of Inspector in C Division, Tottenham Court Road: 'Despite the dangers run in visiting the "target" capital,' he wrote years later, 'thousands of troops converged on London, many of them gaining acquaintance with the big city for the first time in their lives and they soon became easy prey to the vultures, both male and female, who lurked in the dark shadows.'[25] Higgins echoes the memories we have already heard from Molly Lefebure about the effect the war had on perpetrators and victims alike:

Perhaps it was the forced gaiety and the 'don't care' spirit, always a by-product of war . . . I am sure it made most of them behave more irresponsibly than they would have allowed themselves to do under normal conditions.[26]

Higgins had his hands full with professional burglars and amateur smash-and-grab raiders taking advantage of the blackout. The Tottenham Court area was the heart of the 'van-dragging industry'

– theft from unattended vehicles. Higgins and his Number Two, Detective Sergeant Saul, were working on the paperwork associated with just such a case when a V2 rocket scored a direct hit on the station. Windows blew in, glass flew everywhere, papers and documents fluttered into the London sky. In the crater outside lay the bomb-blasted body of a policewoman. 'Though death and horror were often all around us,' Higgins wrote, 'society had to be maintained and murderers and felons were still pursued relentlessly.'[27]

Of all the policemen's autobiographies I have read, the most smug is that of Divisional Detective Inspector Jack Henry. To be fair, his earlier book is better and he dedicates his *What Price Crime?* to his colleagues at the Yard. His high-handedness must have rankled with local forces:

> The small and petty crimes could be left safely in the hands of the [locals]. Scotland Yard undertook the detection and apprehension of the more skilful type of crook and scientific thug.[28]

As a young copper in the notorious Seven Dials district, Henry had his share of scrapes with the razor gangs of the capital in the thirties and records an incident which, sadly, would be alien to most policemen today. Tackling a razor-wielding thug at the Elephant and Castle, Henry was backed up by a soldier and a taxi-driver. 'The police,' he wrote at the end of the war, 'owe much to the members of the services who will invariably assist them when they run into a spot of uneven trouble.'[29]

By the time the war started, Henry had already resigned from the police on grounds of ill-health, but the Belsize Tavern in Hampstead he ran in his retirement became a temporary fire station during the Blitz and he had his work cut out in fire-fighting and rescue duties.

John du Rose, eventually Deputy Commander at Scotland Yard joined the Met at the age of twenty in May 1931. As Police Constable 254C, he walked his beat in Mayfair and Soho, then the haunt of 'prostitutes, high-class shoplifters, Greek pickpockets and ace "con" men'.[30] Like all bobbies in his day, du Rose patrolled with a partner and shared a grim section house. His was in Charing Cross Road and he had a bed and a locker. The toilet was a long walk and washing was carried out with cold water in leaden troughs. Food, pre-war, usually consisted of bacon, egg, tea and condensed milk. The station sergeant, always a martinet, collected rent and laundry dues. Du Rose's take-home pay was £3 a week in the thirties, cut to £2 in the interests of national economy. 'Thank goodness,' he wrote in his autobiography, 'those "good old days" have gone.'[31]

When he first became a detective, like all his colleagues, he became a winter patrol officer, patrolling with two colleagues between three in the afternoon and eleven at night. Because court appearances were added to this, his usual day was fourteen hours, with a short lunch break. In 1938 he was moved to Dartford and

new kinds of villains were bred during the war. Looting after air raids became prevalent and the old standards of honesty began to slip. We moved into the era of the spiv and the smart alec, the get-rich-quick types.[32]

The London docks, then still the largest in the world and a nightly target for the Luftwaffe in 1940–41 were a closed shop, no one was prepared to help the police with their enquiries, but the emergency situation of wartime London meant that few policemen stayed put for long. By 1943, as a detective sergeant, du Rose was in Bow Street with another 'clannish' and secretive population in Covent Garden.

It was while he was still on the Mayfair beat that he came across organized vice for the first time – an extremely lucrative trade that became even more so in the war years. The five Messina brothers, originally from Sicilian parentage, rented flats and houses that housed girls whose patch extended about 200 yards from their front doors. Everything was very businesslike with no nattering to other girls and a mere ten minutes allotted to each client. The girls had maids and lived in some style, with tailored clothes and fur coats. During the war, they could earn up to £50 a week 'pocket money' out of their considerable earnings, which they were allowed to keep. The Messinas themselves were called up, but using an army of front men and moving continually, they evaded the authorities, only to emerge as the war ended. Throughout these years, the high-class call-girl business had carried on as usual.

Former journalist Iain Adamson has thrown a welcome spotlight on Reginald Spooner, eventually, like du Rose, Deputy Commander at the Yard.[33] Spooner attended for interview in February 1924 with sixty other candidates and by the end of the day only nine remained who had passed the physical and answered the panel's questions satisfactorily. One of these became PC475 Reginald Spooner of J Division, Hackney, but three years later, the bright, ambitious young man applied for a transfer to the CID. He was actually much too conspicuous for plain-clothes work, standing 6 feet 5, but as a colleague remembered at interview:

> I don't know how Reg managed it. When he went into the office [for selection] he seemed about 3 inches shorter than usual, he was wearing wide trousers and he somehow bent his knees without showing it and hunched his shoulders.[34]

George Hatherill knew the man well:

> He had the ability to place himself in another person's mind and work out what he might have done. He had a very sardonic sense of humour, but at the same time was very human. During the air raids . . . my impression of him was of a man with terrific courage. And he never willingly did harm to anyone.[35]

Molly Lefebure remembered his charm and his 'very horn-rimmed glasses'. Spooner's rise was meteoric and he gained much experience quickly – Whitechapel with H Division; the Information Room, the power house of Scotland Yard; C Division in the West End. In 1938 he was in charge of policing the 'dirty book trade' centred on Soho. The area provided a very expensive 'library' service in which customers bought books and photographs and returned them to the shop to receive between a quarter and a third of their money back. He was commended in July for the number of prosecutions he had brought under the Obscene Publications Act.

Spooner was holidaying with his family in Sandown, Isle of Wight, when the war broke out. His initial idea was that his wife and daughter should spend the war there, at specially reduced boarding house rates, but this did not last and Spooner had a very matter-of-fact and businesslike arrangement keeping his nearest and dearest away from London, as the most dangerous city in the country. He was earning £11 a week on his detective's salary, but he was also a chain-smoker and a hard drinker and keeping his family elsewhere was expensive. Eventually they all moved in together in Palmers Green, North London. He was a workaholic, as most Yard men were, but he enjoyed the policeman's cliché of rose-growing and loved playing Lexicon with his daughter, who he always put first before his long-suffering wife.

The year 1940 found him working in the West London Aliens Tribunal, sorting out the various categories and generally working on the more complicated or higher profile cases. On the fall of France he was seconded to Wormwood Scrubs to work with MI5 as head of B57, an anti-espionage and anti-sabotage group. He caught Edward Coles sabotaging aircraft production in Bristol and George Crellin, a naval architect, who got fifteen months for offences under the Official Secrets Act. Much of Spooner's wartime work could not be reported at the time because the resulting trials were held in secret. He constantly travelled to Bristol, Glasgow and Barrow-in-Furness in search of saboteurs.

At the end of the war, Spooner was commissioned in the Intelligence Corps with a Captain's rank and wrote home to his wife:

> Paris is a wonderful city . . . the women also come up to one's expectations. How they have managed to keep their poise and smartness in dress I don't know . . . The food is almost over-powering . . . [36]

So much for five years of Nazi oppression! But he had had an extra-ordinarily busy war, saying ruefully to a colleague who had asked for time off to see his wife, 'I haven't seen my wife in daylight since 1939.'[37]

Looming larger than the detectives who ran cases and certainly than the largely anonymous uniformed men and women who were equally essential to them, the pathologists and police surgeons of wartime acquired a status that is awesome.

Bernard Spilsbury was already a legend long before the war began and his name attached to a case in the newspapers was bound to attract attention. Superintendent Robert Higgins wrote glowingly of him:

> he was the greatest detective of us all; the man who solved more cases than anyone the Yard has ever produced . . . His word was accepted by judges and juries throughout the country, more often than not without question.[38]

When war broke out, Spilsbury was working out of a small laboratory in University College in Gower Street. He had a smaller one still at his rooms in Verulam Buildings, until that took a direct bombing hit and he had to abandon it. A workaholic for whom the job was everything, Spilsbury produced thousands of cards in an index system detailing every case he was called to, performing, by the late thirties, over 1,000 post-mortems a year. When he could, he would spend time with his family of four children at their home in Marlborough Hill or a holiday retreat in the West Country.

On the day after Chamberlain's announcement of war to the nation, the 63-year-old Spilsbury was at Battersea Coroner's Court and the day after that carrying out a post-mortem at St Pancras. Shortly before Christmas he was giving evidence at the Old Bailey on the circumstances of the cut-throat of Arthur Haberfield. His murderer, Sidney Pitcher, was found guilty, but insane.

In May 1940 Bernard Spilsbury had a stroke, collapsing over a mortuary table. He was out of action for the minimum time, but those who knew him well were shocked by his next court appearance. The old man in a hurry suddenly seemed pale and slow. Spilsbury was a familiar figure to anyone in the Met throughout the forties. They routinely ignored his illegal parking of his Armstrong-Siddeley and the fact that he drove down one-way streets in the blackout.

On 7 September, St Thomas's Hospital, along with the Docks and Stepney were ablaze with incendiary bombs. Among the casualties was Peter Spilsbury, the pathologist's son who was a surgeon at the hospital. The elder Spilsbury was never the same again, withdrawn, aloof, throwing himself into work at a time when he should have been seriously considering retirement. 'To the public,' wrote his biographer, 'he was still the figure he had been for a generation – the incomparable witness and solver of mysteries, an outstanding personality in the criminal courts, a walking legend.'[39]

And his work rate was phenomenal. Soon after his stroke he was carrying out post-mortems on the shotgun-blasted bodies of Florence Ransom's victims in Kent. In October, he was at Ventnor, in the Isle of Wight, investigating the shooting of Frank Cave by Mabel Attrill. In December he was back in London giving evidence in the trial for murder of Lance Corporal James McCallum of the Canadian Military Police, who had shot a man named Sholman.

In the next year, a dozen murder cases claimed his attention. William Flack, a psychopath serving with the Royal Corps of Signals drove his lorry over the head of Lilian Welch of the ATS in Chichester. Antonio Mancini went to the gallows after a jury decided Spilsbury's testimony was compelling in the gangland killing of Harry Distleman. Lionel Watson, bored by the family he had acquired bigamously, poisoned Phyllis Crocker and her eighteen-month-old daughter Eileen using prussic acid. Not even Spilsbury's prowess, however, could solve the murder of Maple Church, when her body was found in a bombed building in Hampstead Road. Wartime produced its own peculiarities. Deprived of food because of rationing, two cases of asphyxia in 1942 were caused by gorging. In one, a mass of meat 5 inches long was removed by Spilsbury from the dead man's larynx. Another died by swallowing a rasher of bacon whole. Meanwhile, suicides were on the increase.

In March 1941, Spilsbury moved into a hotel in Frognal, Hampstead, where, apart from his daily trips to work, he was a recluse. Staff and students had long ago been evacuated from University College and Spilsbury was often the only inhabitant of the building. He ate at the United Universities Club and spent his evenings in his hotel room, writing up notes. When the air raid sirens wailed, he would troop down with the other guests to a back room at ground level and just carry on with his work. By 1943, most of his cases were confined to St Pancras, where his friend, the coroner William Bentley Purchase, kept the pathologist busy so he would not have to travel so far.

In the spring of 1945, as the Allied armies closed on Berlin, Spilsbury was told that he may have to help identify the Führer's body. In the event, the Russians stole what was left of it after Hitler's aides had botched his last orders by setting the body alight with insufficient kerosene. Three pieces of leather sent to Spilsbury from Buchenwald, one a knife-sheath, another heavily tattooed and a third part of a lampshade, were all made from human skin.

If Spilsbury's star was falling by the middle of the forties, there were any number eager to take his place. First among them was Keith Simpson, whose opinion differed from Spilsbury's in the John Barleycorn murder in Portsmouth in November 1944:

> 'I find it difficult to separate fact and opinion in your report,' Spilsbury had told Simpson, who believed Harold Loughans was responsible for strangling Rose Robinson. When Simpson attempted to justify his findings, an irritable Spilsbury cut him short. '"No, don't bother me now. I'm involved." . . . I was dismissed; the "headmaster" had finished with me.'[40]

Spilsbury never got round to writing a book on forensic medicine he had planned all his life; Simpson rattled off five, all landmarks of the skills involved in catching criminals, plus a series of novels under the pseudonym Guy (Guy's was Simpson's teaching hospital) Bailey (the courtroom where he made some spectacular appearances).

Simpson's career is fascinating in that it was shadowed by the books written by his first secretary, Molly Lefebure, so that we have the pathologist's and the laywoman's versions of the same events. Together with Francis Camps and Donald Teare, Simpson soon made his mark in the solving of crime. Camps was based in Chelmsford as a GP and Teare was a pathologist at St George's Hospital in London. Simpson's book exudes a cold detestation of

Spilsbury, which was probably mutual. Just as the clash of barristers in a criminal court makes the whole process adversarial, so does the clash of medico-legal experts. Simpson, Camps and Teare – 'the three musketeers' as the police called them – were much more impressed by Sydney Smith, in the Chair of Forensic Medicine at Edinburgh University.

When Simpson set up shop in the London of the thirties, forensic science was still in its infancy. It was only some thirty-five years since the Fingerprint Bureau was set up at Scotland Yard and only twenty-five since fingerprint evidence had been conclusive in solving a case.[41] Lord Trenchard, Commissioner at the Met, was establishing the country's first Police Laboratory in an attempt to make the all-important forensic science less amateur. The gun expert to whom the Met turned time and again, Robert Churchill, was, after all, a gunsmith with no scientific training at all. Roche Lynch was a chemist at St Mary's, Paddington, completely untutored in the analysis of dust, blood groups, glass and hair-fibres he was now asked to undertake. J J Mitchell was the graphologist, expounding a science in which nobody had any faith and John Ryffel, at sixty, was referred to as Junior Home Office Analyst. This ramshackle group, more amateur and ad hoc than the government department they served or the police with whom they worked, were going through their respective paces when war broke out.

At Guy's, Simpson's wartime work was hectic, driving around bomb craters, taking detours because whole streets had disappeared, hiding under mortuary slabs as the building shook and the glass flew. For relaxation, he would meet with Camps and Teare, and occasionally Eric Gardner, the Surrey pathologist, to dine at L'Etoile in Charlotte Street, where the four of them were still able to 'muddle through', despite rationing and wartime restrictions. The 'maitre d', Nino, served a powerful substitute for dry Martini and Pernod, which he called ARP – absinthe, rum and paregoric.[42] They would then go on to the Euston Hotel, especially when Dr Grace, the Chester and Liverpool pathologist joined them, since it was from that station that he caught his train home. It was here, in the summer of 1941 that Simpson and Gardner got into a debate over whether self-strangulation (i.e. suicide) was possible. A woman named

Marjorie Fellowes had been found dead in bed by her husband and Gardner's post-mortem found that the cause was asphyxia occasioned by a ligature wound and knotted twice around her neck. The pathologists went into the hotel toilets, so as not to attract attention, and Simpson wound a ligature round his neck à la Mrs Fellowes.

'Quick tightening of the hand or a ligature round the neck can kill like a karate chop,' Simpson had the good fortune to ponder later. And he envisaged the next day's headlines had things gone wrong: 'Keith Simpson found strangled in hotel toilets; noted pathologist held on suspicion.'[43] As it was, all was well, and the coroner's jury on Marjorie Fellowes returned a verdict of suicide.

But war did for Simpson what the inter-war years had done for Spilsbury; it made him famous. Using Pearson's Formulae and Rollet's tables, he was able to identify the body of Rachel Dobkin, found under the vestry floor of a bombed Baptist church in Vauxhall Road in July 1942. The fibroid growths he found in her uterus were remembered by Dr Marie Watson of the Mildmay Mission Hospital, Bethnal Green. Her dental work was that of Barnett Kopkin, who 'blurted out excitedly "That's my patient! Those are my fillings!"'[44] as soon as he saw the dead woman's reassembled skull on Simpson's laboratory bench at Guy's. The result was the death by judicial hanging of Harry Dobkin, who had been the fire-watcher at the church in Vauxhall Road.

In November 1942, Simpson received a visit from the fifth of Scotland Yard's 'Big Five', Chief Inspector Chapman, known to the underworld as 'The Cherub'. A naked woman had been found tied up in four potato sacks on the banks of the River Lea at Luton, Bedfordshire. There were no identifying marks on the body, but she was in her thirties, with dark, bobbed hair and was 5 feet 3 inches tall. She had had her appendix removed years before and was five months pregnant; neither would this have been her first child. She had been half-strangled, then the left side of her face and head had been demolished by a blunt instrument. It speaks volumes for the effects of war that Chapman's team traced or eliminated from their inquiries no less than 404 missing women. Some 681 addresses of women were obtained through *postes restantes* or undelivered mail.

And since so many people went to the 'pictures' as a means of escape, Chapman brought the horrors of murder home to them by having the relatively undamaged side of the dead woman's face shown in cinemas in the Luton area. In the end, it was laboratory work that identified her. A laundry tag from a coat rescued from rubbish bins led to her name: she was Rene Manton, of Regent Street, Luton. As was so often the case in wartime murder – as at any other time – this was a 'domestic'. Her husband Bertie had quarrelled with Rene. He dumped her body in the cellar while giving his children their tea, then sent them to the cinema while, under cover of darkness, he tied his wife up in sacks and laid her across the handlebars of his bike before wheeling her to the river's edge and leaving her: 'I then rode home and got the children's supper ready,' he told Chapman. 'They never suspected anything.'[45]

Molly Lefebure had different memories of the same experiences. Simpson remembered her with admiration and affection, because hers was certainly an unsuitable job for a woman:

> Young, blonde, lively and amusing, she was with me for most of the war and never seemed to have time for reflection on the disadvantages of working for a man who always seemed to have got his hands on some malodorous body in a mortuary, who never seemed to notice the time, who was mad at secretaries who got colds and who didn't on the whole agree with 'time off'.[46]

Molly Lefebure was a journalist covering crime and news for a London paper and as such had more than her fair share of Blitz experience before she went to work for Simpson, when life became

> a non-stop round of post-mortems, investigating murders, suicides, manslaughters, infanticides, accidents, criminal abortions . . . [47]

She carried a notepad and envelopes for the collection of crime scene clues – hairs, fibres, buttons, cigarette ends. Her girlfriends were fascinated by her work, demanding to hear all the gory details, but some boyfriends found it off-putting. She walked on average 12 miles a day, up and down staircases at the huge complex of Guy's Hospital, in and out of tube stations, across bomb-cratered London and through the soggy undergrowth of some murder site in Surrey, or Kent or Cambridgeshire. She worked twelve hours a day, seven days a week and Simpson paid her £1 a week.

Molly Lefebure's first post-mortem took place in Southwark mortuary on the site of what was once the Marshalsea Prison:

> There was a mingled odour of bodies and disinfectant [she remembered] to which I gradually became acclimatized. The thing about post-mortems which I most disliked in those early days was the sound of a saw raspingly opening a skull.[48]

She typed up Simpson's notes, perched on a stool in mortuaries across London and elsewhere, sharing the peculiar life of the pathologist and his assistant S F Ireland. At one point, to prove the cleanliness of another assistant, West, Molly saw Simpson pick up a sandwich from the floor and eat it!

Dead bodies did not bother her, either recently found *in situ* or on Simpson's slab, but there was one exception. The upper storeys at Guy's, where Simpson had his laboratory, was new and largely glass and as it was impossible to black it out according to wartime regulations, the electricity on the upper floors was switched off promptly at four o'clock, leaving Molly in an eerie twilight. Lying inches from her desk were the remains of Rachel Dobkin, and although the body did not frighten her, Molly always expected to see the hanged shade of her killer husband, Harry, staring in through the window in lieu of her own reflection. On those afternoons, she *ran* to join 'CKS' for tea in the hospital canteen.

Naturally, in her line of work, 'Miss Molly' met any number of policemen, mostly from the Met. They found her invaluable when making inventories of dead women's clothing: 'Miss Lefebure – what's this?' one of them asked, while stripping a corpse. 'A camisole,' I replied, after a moment's staring. 'Never seen one of them before,' was the rejoinder.[49]

Among the weird trophies Simpson and his team acquired in the war years were a number of fingers they bequeathed to Fred Cherrill for his fingerprint research, and a very heavy metal weight attached to a rope and a suicide note which read: 'I expect you will find me over Battersea Bridge – if you are interested.'

With her journalistic, even literary, bent, it was natural that Molly would ponder the realities of wartime murder:

> The English are a great race for detective fiction and they enjoy murder on the radio, television,[50] the films. Nearly all the people interviewed by the detectives must have had at least one murder thriller tucked away on a bookshelf, they must have switched on the wireless at night to listen to a murder play, or trotted round to the cinema to see a film with corpses, cops, killer and witnesses complete. But when a policeman arrived on their doorstep, showing a photo of a murdered woman . . . the crime-fiction addicts found it impossible to grasp the situation . . . Murder is something you read about . . . but you never came across it in your own life.[51]

Of course, Molly Lefebure did. She came across mortuary keepers, immensely proud of their calling, coppers who always looked on the bright side: 'Keep your pecker up, Miss Molly,' PC Doughty of Shoreditch beamed at her one morning when her spirits were low, 'and I'll see you get a blood-orange at Christmas.'[52] And coppers who would have lost their jobs if it had not been for wartime: Constable Goodwin thought he was being so helpful in tidying up a crime scene in which a homicidal husband had butchered his wife with a Samurai sword.

Molly had all the prejudices of her day, of her sex and of her class. When she took notes in Wanstead mortuary, as Simpson carried out a post-mortem on a soldier who had taken cyanide rather than face the choppy Channel crossing on 6 June, D-Day:

> we all stared at the body in silence. Without putting it into words, we all felt he was a blot upon our escutcheon. Nevertheless, being mere civilians, we had a delicacy about saying so.[53]

She also sums up wartime murder better than anyone:

> Sordid details, dirty scraps of newspapers and torn odds and
> ends, a drain to be delved into, a patch of wasteland to be
> searched again and again under a gruelling sun, much ques-
> tioning, the wearisome taking of repetitive statements, discreet
> enquiries from all and sundry, more searching of the waste-
> land, more enquiries, a long and patient watch kept on a
> suspect, finally the closing of the trap, painful scenes, tears,
> admission.[54]

And Molly Lefebure should know. She had seen all this, while still
in her twenties, countless times, as when she accompanied Simpson
to the inaptly named Little Heaven in Brixton to the scene of the
killing of a former West End prostitute:

> ' . . . thought she'd like to spread her wings,' PC Griffin had
> said drily, 'and try the other Heaven for a change.'[55]

When the forensic team arrived:

> The bed was tossed, disordered and sodden with blood. Lying
> obliquely across it on her left side lay Maisie Rose, clad in a
> blue satin nightgown, her bloodstained hands raised to her
> breast and a cloth placed over her head. This was exactly how
> the charlady had found her, so the murderer must have put the
> cloth there; perhaps he didn't like to see what he had done.[56]

The woman had been battered to death with an old shillelagh she
kept, ironically, for self-defence:

> 'Although she lived in a clean little flat and had dressed so
> neatly and smartly,' Molly wrote, 'she concealed behind this
> façade an active gonorrhoea and old syphilis (I suppose one
> might refer to them in her case as mere occupational
> diseases).'[57]

In the event, the two American servicemen probably responsible for her death never faced justice: 'Perhaps,' Molly pondered, 'they met their just deserts in the form of German bullets. Maybe they were lucky and finally returned home as two worthy American veterans, to be welcomed royally and proudly toasted by some small town. Nobody will ever know.'[58]

Post-mortem rooms were Molly Lefebure's second home for four years. The mortuary in Poplar, just down the road from Chinatown, had a viewing room for the Jews, whose custom it is to watch the dead, day and night until burial:

> These watchers [Molly wrote] are often extraordinarily ancient women, either very stout or very skinny, dressed in a collection of shabby garments apparently collected over the course of years . . . they sit in their little rooms in the mortuaries . . . through the long and weary hours when everything in the mortuary is dark and silent and still.[59]

Twelve hundred miles away, the watchers' counterparts in Auschwitz-Birkenau were themselves dying, in their hundreds of thousands.

Mortuary keepers never failed to fascinate. At Poplar, Molly gave the man the nickname 'You Are My Sunshine' after the song he habitually crooned. PC Hyde, the coroner's officer, was a country lad from Bedfordshire who had served for thirty years in the Met. His oppo, PC West, was a Londoner who was resigned to his fate: 'Hitler'll get me. Of course he'll get me. I'm one of his targets.'[60]

What strikes us today about dying in wartime Britain is the sense of a passing era. A murder (again by American servicemen) in the legendary Charley's Bar in Chinatown led Molly Lefebure to describe a part of London that was all but gone in the rubble of the Blitz and the Doodlebugs. PC Hyde reminisced about the 'good (bad) old days' when Chinatown:

> had been a jamboree of foreign sailors, strange tongues, loud-mouthed brawls, knifings and beatings up, stuffed alligators, little live bears on chains, cussing parrots, wonderful oriental

carpets, joss sticks, Samurai swords, Japanese lanterns, brass gongs, sharks' teeth . . . [61]

When the various inspectors of constabulary produced a report at the end of the war, they wrote:

The public appreciation of the police has never been greater. The confidence that is placed in the police has never been higher and the relationship between the public and police service was never better.[62]

Herbert Morrison, the Home Secretary, was correct in his praise of his policemen and women. Their duties, he said: 'were sometimes unspectacular, often dangerous and always of the greatest importance to the Home Front . . . It is no exaggeration to say that the reputation of the British police for service to the community stands higher than ever before.'[63]

CHAPTER EIGHT

Judgement Day

A hundred years before the outbreak of the Second World War, Charles Dickens' Mr Bumble delivered his famous dictum on the law. On being told that the law supposes that he directs his wife in all things, he explodes, 'if the law supposes that . . . the law is a ass – an idiot.'[1] The playwright/poet George Chapman, friend of Marlowe and Shakespeare, was saying exactly the same thing three centuries earlier. And the raft of preposterous legislation brought in by Chamberlain's and Churchill's government meant that the idiocy continued for six years of war.

We have to remember that the whole panoply of the law, from the bewigged and robed Lord Chief Justice to the lowliest lay magistrate, reflected the laws themselves enacted by Parliament. We have already seen that some of these laws – notably on treason and serious crimes like murder and armed robbery – were framed years or even centuries earlier and were woefully out of date. Others were brought in quickly, in a sense of panic and crisis management by a government faced with a wholly unprecedented kind of war.

In 1939 came the Defence Regulations, subtly different from Defence (General) Regulations, followed three years later by Defence Regulation 42 CA. The Emergency Powers (Defence) Act of 1939 was followed by another the next year. The outbreak of war also saw the Motor Fuel Rationing Order, the National Registration Act, the National Service (Armed Forces) Act, the Prevention of Violence (Temporary Provisions) Act, the Prices of Goods Bill and the Eire: Offences Against the State Act. The year 1940 saw the Lighting (Restrictions) Order, the Limitation of Supplies Order, the Maximum Prices Order, the Sugar (Control) Order and the Treachery Act. In the relatively legislation-free 1941 came the Acquisition of Food (Excessive Quantities) Order, the Clothes Rationing Order and the Making of Civilian Clothing (Restrictions) Order. The year 1942 saw the Paper Order, the Soap Rationing Order and the United States of America (Visiting Forces) Act. In the following year (1943), Parliament found it necessary to produce the Toilet Preparations Order and the Transportation of Flowers Order. All was quiet in 1944 with the government presumably preoccupied with Doodlebug raids, the build-up to D-Day, the passing of the Butler Act for education and the implications of the Beveridge Report. In the last year of the war (1945) there was the Supplies and Services (Transitional Powers) Act and yet another Treason Act, the last one having been passed in totally different circumstances in 1697.

If you were bored by reading the last paragraph, you belong to a very large club! I was bored by writing it, but the point at issue is that every judge and magistrate in the land had to be familiar with all this, as well as the everyday law of the (peacetime) land. The police, as we have seen, had to be aware too. And, most bizarrely of all, the public were supposed to be aware of it and to read every piece of literature provided by the Ministry of Information.

The passage of various Acts relating to crime is very telling. The composition of Lords and Commons was more seriously out of step with actual representation than it is today. There were no women in the Cabinet, and only five female MPs in the Commons. The vast majority of MPs were white (inevitably, when the ethnic mix was so limited), public school and University educated, which incidentally was even more true of judges throughout the land. Their appreciation of what they called 'the criminal classes' was limited, confined to the hearsay of their constituencies or influenced by reports from Chief Constables and the social services.

One of the very first Parliamentary Acts of the war, the Emergency Powers (Defence) Act, passed by 457 votes to 11 in the Commons, meant that Parliament was actually giving up the sovereignty it had held since 1689. All legislation now was to be controlled by the Prime Minister, Cabinet departments and civil servants. The long-cherished safeguards like *habeas corpus* could be swept away in the arbitrary regime now set up. It could confiscate property, search premises, suspend or amend existing law. In an extraordinary reversal of the whole presumption of English law – that a man is deemed innocent until proven guilty – a Mr Oliver was sentenced to three years' imprisonment and fined a staggering £8,500 (in today's money) for supplying sugar without a licence, contrary to the Sugar (Control) Order of 1940. When Oliver appealed, he was told that the burden of proof did not lie with the prosecution. In other words, it was up to him to prove his innocence, not the other way round.

Many 'crimes' were strict liability offences, giving judges and magistrates no leeway at all. Some of them showed their disapproval of arbitrary government tactics by imposing the lightest fines possible. When Henry Sitwell, an Aldershot grocer, found himself in court in April 1940 for selling butter without coupons: it transpired that he had been persuaded to do it by an undercover Food Office minion who promptly reported him to the authorities. In peacetime this would have been entrapment and the case thrown out. As it was, the magistrate ordered a £2 fine on the grocer to show his disgust.

Petty regulations abounded in the 1940s. Anyone visiting an exclusion zone that ran 20 miles inland from the Kent or Sussex coast was fined or imprisoned. There were ten o'clock curfews imposed in resorts along the south coast and constant security checks on inhabitants in those areas deemed most at risk of invasion, or later part of the build-up to D-Day.

The use of 'Gestapo tactics', such as those listed above, were raised in Parliament, but by definition, there was a limit to the amount of objecting a man – even an MP – could do before finding himself in court or behind bars. To the majority of people – especially as the threat of invasion faded and the police and magistracy seemed all too keen to use ever more draconian powers – the government appeared as arbitrary and tyrannical as the one they were fighting across the Channel.

Those 'in the know' were depressed by Parliament and its proceedings. The government was national, that is cross-party, and if Churchill's War Cabinet – the inner sanctum of men he trusted – were largely Conservative, to dissent, even over minor matters, was regarded as a mild form of treason. George Orwell complained that you couldn't tell one party from another: 'It is just a collection of mediocre-looking men in dingy, dark suits, nearly all speaking in the same accent and laughing at the same jokes.'[2]

Democracy in Britain was limited in all sorts of ways during the Second World War. Apart from the arbitrary powers the government had assumed, actual voting was a peacetime luxury. At a by-election in Acton in 1943, only 16 per cent of the electorate turned out. Apathy and the general war-weariness were to blame. Given this lethargy and the sense that somehow, a lid had to be kept firmly on the potential cauldron of revolt and/or collapse of society, most people gave in to a judiciary that was seen as autocratic and out of touch, carrying out the whims of a government that may have the best interests of the country at heart, but whose authority could not be challenged in any serious way.[3]

F T Giles was Chief Clerk of Clerkenwell Magistrates' Court throughout the war. In 1954 he wrote a book[4] that encapsulates in many ways the law and the judiciary as it stood in those years. Not surprisingly, he was a staunch supporter, his opening sentence being: 'English law will probably be regarded as the greatest system of law the world has ever known.' Importantly, in British government, the judiciary has been independent of the legislature and executive for several centuries. In the reign of James I, judges were 'lions under the throne', expected to support a king who was (albeit before James' time) the font of all law-giving. The rule of the Stuarts had changed all that and the judiciary operated under the joint principles of precedence and justice, with the laws obviously passed by Parliament. But the asinine aspects of the law to which Chapman and Dickens referred included its creaking slowness and its hideous expense.

In 1873 the courts that Dickens knew – Chancery, King's Bench, Common Pleas and Exchequer, along with the minor ones of Doctors' Commons, Probate, Divorce and Admiralty – were swept away by Gladstone's government to create the system that Giles was

writing about. The High Court now had three divisions amal-
gamating most of the above and its judges now had powers to hear
any case. In terms of criminal law, the King's Bench handled these
cases. Here sat the Lord Chief Justice – for most of the war Thomas
Inskip, Viscount Caldecote – and seventeen other judges, their
heavily sandbagged headquarters the Royal Courts of Justice in the
Strand.

The mechanics of arrest and trial are not the remit of this book,
but as the wording of the key stages have now changed, it is useful
to remind ourselves of them. A policeman carrying out arrest might
well, in the heat of the moment (then, as now) tell a miscreant that
he is 'nicked', but the law demanded he say: 'You are not obliged to
say anything unless you wish to do so, but whatever you say will be
taken down in writing and may be given in evidence.' Failure to do
this might see an entire case thrown out, although the perfect world
of the law as described by F T Giles was, as we have seen, not exactly
what went on in wartime.

In fact, there was a great deal of latitude given to judges in their
interpretation of the law and a powerful judge with plenty of
experience could easily cow a less experienced barrister and
certainly a jury. In one case after the war,[5] such was the bigotry of
the judge in a murder trial that it took nearly fifty years to undo the
harm he had done.

Inevitably, the cases that made the headlines in the war years were
the murder trials that involved a matter of life and death of the
defendant. Pre-eminently the Central Criminal Court of the Old
Bailey was at the heart of this, in fact and fiction. Built on the site
of Newgate Prison, the Bailey was the theatre of innumerable
dramas, in which the judge, counsel for the prosecution and defence,
ushers and all the other participants acted out scenarios in the
attempt to find the truth. Inspector Jack Henry, in *What Price
Crime?* wrote:

I have seen and played an important part in these real-life
dramas, often as the principal witness. Never have I witnessed
one that was not scrupulously fair and just from every view-
point . . . The scene is most impressive. The robed judge, stern

and yet with an air of benevolence, set high above the well of the court, where bewigged and gowned counsel concentrate on their briefs, never missing a word or a sign that might aid their case. These in turn are ringed by the Press tables where reporters write furiously, setting down every phrase. Then the jury box, lined with twelve citizens on whom the fate of the prisoner must depend. They are just ordinary, unimportant folk, deeply moved by the sense of their responsibility . . . Then, there is the dock where the spotlight – if there was one – would be turned. Over all, there is a tense hush that can almost be felt.[6]

Two such trials, six months apart, will shed light on the operation of the law at the extreme end of serious crime.

Harry Dobkin, as we know, was accused of murdering his wife and hiding her body under the floor of the Baptist church in Vauxhall, where he was a fire-watcher. His trial opened at the Bailey on 17 November 1942. Because of the shortage of personnel in wartime, all cases not involving the death penalty had juries cut to seven. In capital cases like Dobkin's, however, the usual 'twelve men and true' were sworn. The judge was Mr Justice Wrottesley, who had been called to the Bar in 1907 and was appointed to the King's Bench thirty years later. At the time of Dobkin's trial, he was sixty-two and descended from a very distinguished family. For the prosecution appeared L A Byrne, who had recently been appointed chief prosecuting counsel for the Crown and was Recorder of Rochester. His number two was Gerald Howard, Recorder of Bury St Edmunds. 'Harry Dobkin,' said the Clerk of the Court, 'you are charged with the murder of Rachel Dobkin on the 11th day of April 1941. Are you guilty or not guilty?'[7] The answer, of course, was 'Not guilty' and the jury were sworn:

> Members of the Jury, the prisoner at the bar, Harry Dobkin, is charged with the murder of Rachel Dobkin on the 11th day of April 1941. To this indictment he has pleaded 'Not guilty' and it is your charge to say, having heard the evidence, whether he be guilty or not.

It is one of the most important elements of British justice that the jury remain anonymous. They are simply twelve citizens who were Dobkin's peers, but although this anonymity is right and proper, it poses huge questions for the historian of crime. We do not know how many women, if any, were on the jury, or what the precise backgrounds of the chosen twelve were. Jury selection is an important process in itself. A female juror might identify with the dead Mrs Dobkin. A fire-watcher on the jury might feel empathy for Dobkin himself. A Baptist may have been outraged by the desecration of his church. Above all, there was and is, no intelligence test for juries, and in long, technical and complex cases, this could cause endless difficulties.[8]

Byrne, for the prosecution, outlined the main facts of the case, then called a succession of witnesses over the next two days. Constable William Slater of M Division produced a detailed plan of the murder site and the judge put a couple of questions to him to clarify the situation for the benefit of the jury. When Mr Lawton, cross-examining for the defence, asked for a further description of the chapel area, the judge was equally careful to make sure he was being clear. The most ordinary slip can give a totally false impression to a jury. Detective Sergeant George Salter produced a series of photographs of the site and again he was examined and cross-examined on them. Polly Dubinski was Rachel Dobkin's sister. She not only explained the poor relationship between the dead woman and Dobkin, but testified to her height (a vital element in the prosecution's case, because of Keith Simpson's measurements of the body). Lawton, in cross-examination, was unable to shake her on this point – Dobkin was already halfway to the gallows.

At the end of the first day, the jury were allowed home, warned by the judge not to discuss the proceedings with anyone.

On the second day, Lawton objected to a line of evidence offered by Divisional Detective Inspector Frederick Hatton. Since this was a technical matter and the court would have to hear Dobkin's statement to Hatton given soon after the discovery of the body to decide it, the jury were sent out while Wrottesley made his deliberations. The Judges' Rules, by which evidence was admitted to court, specified that a caution had to be given (by Hatton to Dobkin) and that this had not taken place. Howard for the prosecution was able to cite a precedent – Rex v. Voisin 1918 – in which this was made a matter for the judge to decide. Wrottesley decided in Howard's favour and the trial resumed. Inevitably, Lawton gave Hatton a grilling in cross-examination, but his case was falling apart around him.

Worse was to come when the medical experts held forth. John Ryffel, the Home Office analyst, Keith Simpson, the pathologist, Mary Newman of the photographic department of Guy's Hospital, and above all, Barnett Kopkin, Mrs Dobkin's dentist, who recognized his bridgework: all effectively condemned Dobkin to death. Simpson got the grilling of his life. His testimony, in examination and cross, runs to eighteen and a half pages in the trial transcript.

On the third day, Lawton called Harry Dobkin himself. Defendants were not allowed to speak on their own behalf until 1898 and it was always a risk when they did. A short-tempered or stupid person could easily be goaded or caught out under cross-examination. On the other hand, if the defendant did well, he/she might appeal to the jury as a wronged party justifiably protesting innocence. Dobkin's testimony barely took ten minutes and he did himself no favours. Under Byrne's quiet, implacable assault, he dodged questions, did U-turns and finally, as the last point the jury heard on the fourth day, claimed that he had been threatened with death by the police unless he confessed to the murder: 'And you ask the jury to believe that, do you?' was the withering scorn in the prosecution's last question. Outraged, Dobkin asserted, 'I certainly do.'

Annoyingly for the historian, neither Byrne's nor Lawton's summations have survived intact. Part of Lawton's was printed in the *Hackney Gazette*, but the original transcript is now lost to time. The judge's, however, we have, and he delivered it on the fifth day of the trial, Monday 23 November. Wrottesley reminded the jury that the decision of guilt or innocence was now theirs. It was up to the prosecution to have proved guilt and if they had not done so, then Dobkin must be acquitted. They had to be sure of their verdict, in the immortal phrase, 'beyond a reasonable doubt'. He then proceeded to remind them of all they had heard in the cut and thrust of adversarial law over the last few days. In the trial transcript, the judge's summing up runs to thirteen closely typed pages.

The jury were only out for twenty minutes and at 12.45 p.m. filed back into court to deliver the verdict:

> 'Do you find the prisoner, Harry Dobkin, guilty or not guilty of murder?'
> 'Guilty, my lord.'
> 'You find him guilty and that is the verdict of you all?'
> 'That is the verdict of us all.'

As was customary, the Clerk of the Court then asked Dobkin if he had anything to say. The purpose of this is now lost to time. The sentence had been given and it is unlikely that a few words from a man facing the death penalty is going to make any difference to the situation. In fact, nobody in that courtroom had any power to affect what was going to happen. The jury had made no recommendation to mercy, because all the evidence pointed to Dobkin's cold and callous guilt. The judge was duty-bound to pass the sentence of death. Only the Home Secretary, Herbert Morrison, had the power, on behalf of the Crown, to commute the sentence: he did not. Dobkin made a short speech, still accusing the police of brutality and coercion: 'I hope I have not said too much.' He hadn't. Wrottesley had the black cap placed on his bewigged head by the Clerk of the Court and delivered the dread words, now vanished from British courts:

> The sentence of the court upon you is, that you be taken from this place to a lawful prison and there to a place of execution, and that you be there hanged by the neck until you be dead; and that your body be afterwards buried within the precincts of the prison in which you shall have been confined before your execution. And may the Lord have mercy on your soul.

One figure common to the Dobkin case and that which took place six months later, was Keith Simpson. On Wednesday, 24 February in the Surrey Winter Assizes at Kingston, August Sangret, a private serving in the 5th Regina Rifles, was accused of the murder of Joan Pearl Wolfe, 'on a day unknown in the month of September 1942'.

This time the judge was Mr Justice Macnaghten, like Wrottesley, an 'Oxbridge' man with impeccable credentials and a courteous and humane reputation. Eric Neve, for the prosecution, was one of the new brand of lawyers with a grammar school rather than public school background. He had served in the Middle East in the Great War and was fifty-six at the time of Sangret's trial. His number two was Geoffrey Laurence, a talented musician as well as lawyer, whose voice was so melodic, it was said that he could make the pattern on a carpet sound interesting!

Linton Thorpe KC defended the Canadian. He was a product of Manchester Grammar School and had risen to the rank of major in the 1914–18 conflict. He was the last British judge of the Supreme Court at Constantinople (Istanbul) and a leading light in the Conservative Party's Carlton Club. He was assisted by Laurence Vine, an ex-London journalist now operating on the south-eastern circuit. Neve, in his opening statement, defined murder for the jury's benefit: 'the taking by one person of another person's life with malice aforethought'. That meant intent, but not necessarily premeditation, and this was an important point in his case. Sangret came across as a surly individual with a chip on his shoulder. He was slow to anger, but once crossed, had a vicious temper. This was the scenario, Neve contended, that led to Joan Wolfe's death.

He called seventeen witnesses on the first day: photographic experts, police constables, serving soldiers who were Sangret's comrades at the vast Witley Camp near Thursley. The following day came the Canadian Military Police and locals, including three children, who had seen the deceased in the company of Joan Wolfe in the days before her disappearance. Keith Simpson's evidence we have noted already, the firm, confident and brilliant findings of the pathologist, which resulted in Joan's skull – riveted together for the purpose – being shown in open court. Doctors Eric Gardner and Roche Lynch both offered testimony on the state of the corpse, the likelihood of Sangret's damaged knife as the potential murder weapon, and the existence of bloodstains on Sangret's battledress and blanket. The senior policemen in the case were headed by

Greeno from the Yard and Thorpe's cross-examination made no indentation whatsoever in his armour-plating.

Macnaghten delivered his summing up on the fifth day, Tuesday 2 March, honing the problem for the jury perfectly: 'The only question you have to determine is: Have the Crown satisfied you beyond all real doubt that the prisoner, August Sangret, is the man who murdered [Joan Wolfe]?' Nearly two hours later the jury decided that they had, and Sangret was found guilty. Before hearing the death sentence passed – the jury made a recommendation to mercy, which the Home Office duly ignored – Sangret's last words were: 'I am not guilty, sir. I never killed that girl.'

But Keith Simpson was not the only figure common to the Dobkin and Sangret cases. The other was Albert Pierrepoint, the executioner. Judicial hanging had come a long way from the dark days of the Bloody Code, when hangmen like William Marwood had so bungled his killings that he was known to jump up and drag at a victim's kicking legs to attempt to end his suffering. Hanging, in public until 1868, was a slow, ghastly torture, in which the victim could convulse at the end of a rope for twenty minutes, to the roar and delight of the crowd.[9] From the far more humane James Berry in the 1880s, through the Billingtons and John Ellis, hanging by the 1940s was scientific, merciful and above all, quick.

Albert Pierrepoint became an executioner, eventually 'Number One' by 1943 because it was his father's trade and his uncle's. In what may have been the most peculiar post in the country, the Pierrepoints carried on routine day jobs in various Yorkshire towns, being summoned away by the Home Office to attend places of execution as the courts proscribed. Harry Pierrepoint, Albert's father, took to drink – as many executioners did – but kept a careful record of the age, height, weight and physical appearance of his victims. In a rather bizarre and unorthodox quirk, Harry placed the noose over the neck *before* the white hood, almost certainly adding to the distress of the moment. His brother Thomas was altogether steadier and less inclined to discuss his work. He ran a shop and was a 'bookie' when not helping the Home Office. When he took over as 'Number One' from Harry, the execution sheds around the country came to be known as 'Uncle Tom's Cabin'.

Having assisted his uncle several times, Albert took the top job as independent executioner shortly after Dunkirk. He continued to work with Thomas, but his usual assistant was fellow Yorkshireman Stephen Wade. His fees went up from three guineas to £15, but that was paid in two halves – £7 10s on the day of the hanging and the balance two weeks later, only if the job was wholly satisfactory. In his autobiography, Pierrepoint wrote of his journeys:

> to prisons around the country, in blacked-out trains with criss-cross tape gummed on the windows and interminable delays, and with the young men who were to do the work and the dying standing in the corridors in rough serge and hard boots, hearteningly cheerful, unconquerably patient.[10]

Pierrepoint was a perfectionist, checking and double-checking the details of the prisoner's height and weight given to him in writing by the prison authorities. He also watched them through the 'judas-hole' in the condemned cell, noting their muscle-tone and especially the thickness of their necks. The length of the drop would vary depending on all this and he became extremely proficient at the deadly routine of 'cap, noose, pin, push, drop':[11]

> The swift but measured course of events [Pierrepoint wrote] which leads to the humane killing of a man demands rehearsed competence and unquavering confidence from all concerned. From my experience I must include in this company the condemned man. In his mind he has rehearsed this brief last act many times. I believe that frequently he is strongly moved to perform that exit with dignity and stride rather than shuffle. In this determination, I, as executioner, have always tried to support him.[12]

Particularly chirpy was Antonio (Babe) Mancini who, dressed immaculately in a suit (albeit minus tie and shoelaces), smiled cheerfully as he followed Pierrepoint from the condemned cell to the execution shed (in practice only a few steps through a sliding metal wall) and onto the platform. This was Pierrepoint's first job as

Number One and the mobster whispered 'Cheerio' under the hood just before the executioner pulled the lever. When it was all over: 'There was a snap as the falling doors were bitten and held by the rubber clips and the rope stood straight and still.' The prison governor shook Pierrepoint's hand: 'I have seen your uncle work on many occasions,' he said, 'he is a very good man indeed. Never has he been any quicker than you have been this morning.'[13]

In a curious blend of modesty and bombast, Pierrepoint's autobiography names some names and not others. So he is quite happy to mention Neville Heath, John Haigh and John Christie (all hanged by him after the war) but makes no mention of Mancini, Sangret or Dobkin, nor even the man for whom no one has any sympathy, Frederick Cummins. Pierrepoint listened without intervening in railway carriage conversations in which the participants *knew for a fact* that all spies were shot in the Tower, whereas he himself hanged fifteen of them at various places around the country. The only one who gave him any trouble was Karel Richter, who, for some reason, he calls Otto Schmidt. We have come across this case in Chapter Two, but Richter in the death cell had no intention of going quietly. He was facing Pierrepoint as he entered the cell at Wandsworth on the morning of Wednesday 10 December 1941 (it was usually arranged that the condemned man had his back to the door that the hangman entered) and he head-butted the wall before fighting with prison guards and the executioner. There were at one point five men, including a Judo expert, holding him down while Pierrepoint tightened the straps around the man's wrists. Even then, Richter was able to break free and on the trap, the spy jumped a split-second before Pierrepoint hit the lever. It could have gone horribly wrong, with either a Marwood-style strangulation or decapitation being the result. In the event, Richter died as the others did – the spinal cord snapping between the second and third vertebrae.

More ghastly for Pierrepoint – and even worse for his victim – was the American system at Shepton Mallet. With efficiency and humanity in mind, Pierrepoint reckoned to carry out his work between eight and twenty seconds from his entering the condemned cell. Under the American system, the prisoner, already pinioned and standing with his feet on the trap, had to stand for upwards of six minutes while the charge and sentence were read out and he was asked if he had anything to say.

Towards the summer of 1946, the modest little man with the trilby hat and herringbone coat, so proud of his craft and his light baritone voice, was despatched to Berlin to deal with some *real* war criminals – the defendants of Nuremberg.

Not every High Court judge sat on capital cases continually. F T Giles does his best to explain to laymen who have never had the experience how the criminal law works. Proceedings began either with summons by warrant or by arrest without summons or warrant. Crimes were divided into three classes: treasons, felonies and misdemeanours.

Treasons were offences against the state, the sovereign, his consort and heir. We have seen these in action in Chapter Two. Felonies, says Giles, 'are still definitely upper class in the sociology of crime'. They include murder, manslaughter, rape, burglary and theft. Everything else counts as a misdemeanour – the minor offences dealt with summarily in magistrates' courts. They nevertheless included serious crimes like perjury, forgery, fraud and malicious wounding. Even misdemeanours, however, could involve serious crimes such as evasion of Purchase Tax by the furniture firm of Harris and Sons of Bethnal Green. John Harris, company director, was sentenced to six months' imprisonment and a fine of £150.[14] As we have seen, wartime legislation added enormously to the work of these courts.

Some magistrates were professional and salaried. There were twenty-five to thirty of these in the Metropolitan area. And there were lay magistrates, advised by a solicitor or barrister, operating elsewhere and especially in the juvenile courts. Certain crimes could be handled by a single magistrate, others required a panel. One of the 'worst' crimes that magistrates faced – and which they often passed to the Assize courts – was looting. On 5 March 1941 Mr Justice Charles, at Lewes, made a pronouncement that probably spoke for everyone:

The task of guarding shattered houses from prowling thieves, especially during the blackout, is obviously beyond the capacity of any police force. In view of the fact and having regard to the cowardly, abominable nature of the crime . . . the Legislature has provided that those found guilty of looting from premises damaged or vacated by reason of attacks by the enemy are on conviction liable to suffer death or penal servitude for life. Thus the law puts looters into the category of murderers and the day may well be approaching when they will be treated as such.[15]

In fact, although no one was punished as severely as this, (the maximum penalty seems to have been fourteen years' imprisonment) the crime itself left a very nasty taste in the mouth and is still regarded as one of the most obscene forms of war-profiteering. More than that, it smacked of lawless anarchy, in which survival of the fittest became the only norm – hence the government's and the judiciary's attitude. It was a particular problem because not only were culprits committing spur-of-the-moment, spontaneous crime, but the organized underworld of pickpockets and racetrack gangs were bringing their skills and expertise to this new enterprise. There were 390 cases of looting in London in the first two months of the Blitz. Of the fifty cases heard at the Bailey on 9 November, twenty involved looting and half of these were perpetrated by the Auxiliary Fire Service! But society, via the magistracy, was particularly appalled when soldiers became involved in crime:

Even in the midst of war [Mr Justice Charles said at Lewes on 1 December 1941] one has to do something to keep law and order in the country. With the exception of about five cases, every one in this calendar is a soldier – bigamy, housebreaking, rape – and I shall be told in every case that he is an excellent soldier and that the Army cannot afford to lose him. That doesn't affect my mind in the least.

We have seen already that all sorts of social delinquents put on the king's uniform by reason of conscription, but somehow it seemed incongruous that a man prepared to put his life on the line for king and country, should also be prepared to steal from, con, and otherwise swindle that country should the opportunity present itself. At a case heard at the Bailey in February 1941, thirty-three members of the Royal Engineers appeared charged with stealing lead from the roofs of bombed buildings. There were so many squeezed into the dock – all in khaki of course – that they had to wear numbers pinned to their battledress blouses. The following year, a number of soldier-looters received between five and eight years' hard labour. Hardliners made the point that these men got off lightly – in Germany looters were executed as a matter of course.

Such was the rampancy of looting by the summer of 1941 that some MPs demanded that Herbert Morrison appoint a Director of Anti-Looting on the grounds that there had been 4,584 cases in London alone the previous year. Morrison refused and of course, with the end of the Blitz, the problem lessened severely, only to re-emerge in the Doodlebug years.

Some of the cases that came before the magistracy and judiciary were bizarre in the extreme. In Edinburgh, the manager of the crematorium and an undertaker were charged with stealing 1,044 coffin lids, seven coffins and a huge number of shrouds. These items were sold, to be turned into utility furniture at a time of national shortage, and the courtroom itself was filled with the paraphernalia of death, as Lord Chief Justice Clerk struggled to try the case.

Although we have looked at the huge industry of Black Market crime elsewhere, the attitude of the magistrates was very different from most of the public. Pilfering was seen by many as a perk, at a time when there were precious few perks available. When a magistrate handed out prison sentences on six women from South London in 1942, however, he called this sort of thing 'a form of petty treason in wartime', appalled that Britons could behave in this way.

In all phases of history, some crimes are fashionable and fads come and go. The war was no exception. The bomb lark was a crafty con in which people claimed to have been bombed out in order to claim compensation. With so much devastation, especially in the major cities, it was not always possible for the authorities to check. The billeting lark was another, in which unscrupulous landladies drew allowances for putting up soldiers who had long moved on.[16] By 1942, vice in London and elsewhere focused on illegal gaming and betting. Defence Regulation 42CA was introduced in March, designed to put a stop to this. Exactly how entertainment could constitute a threat to the realm is difficult to explain, and although large fines were imposed on various clubs, the government was here taking on very powerful elements of its own establishment. Gentlemen's clubs like White's, Brookes' and Crockford's had many MPs and members of the Lords on their books. They simply paid their fines and carried on as before.

Although crime statistics are notoriously difficult to interpret, there is no doubt that the courts were having to cope with a marked increase in crime at all levels as the war went on, though not perhaps to the extent that pessimists feared. In the higher courts, involving serious crime, the numbers found guilty nearly doubled, from 8,612 in 1939 to 15,848 in 1945. If we divide the convicted into the under twenty-one and over twenty-one age bracket, it is noticeable that the younger offenders were treated more harshly in terms of sentencing, perhaps to act as a deterrent in the years to come.

We have already looked in detail at the punishment meted out to those guilty of capital cases. What of lesser crimes? The ever-optimistic Jack Henry of Scotland Yard referred to juvenile courts:

> Cases are tried in special courts, in camera, away from the prying eyes of the public. These places are as unlike courts of law as they can be and no officer appears in uniform . . . From start to finish, cases are conducted in an atmosphere of kindness and sympathy, as a first step towards winning confidence, for the young offender will react more readily to gentle firmness than to forceful correctives. In extreme cases, juveniles are sent to approved schools and sometimes to Borstal. Here, the treatment – it is treatment, not punishment – is psychologically sound and they are taught trades and all the rules of good citizenship. A very high percentage master their weaknesses, make good and give no further trouble.[17]

The Borstal institution had been set up at the old convict prison of the same name near Chatham, following the passing of the

Criminal Justice Act in 1908. It was specifically designed for juvenile-adult offenders aged sixteen to twenty-one. The emphasis was on training, evening classes, all based on progressive trust involving personal responsibility and self-control.

The grim Victorian prisons like Pentonville, Wormwood Scrubs and Wandsworth in London, Barlinnie in Glasgow and Strangeways in Manchester, stood in the Second World War as they do today. We know a great deal about them in the 1940s because of a detailed report drawn up twenty years earlier by Stephen Hobhouse and Fenner Brockway. These men were prison reformers, so perhaps their findings were a little suspect. They disapproved of much that was still Victorian and forbidding, and Brockway himself had 'done time' for conscientious objection during the Great War. *English Prisons Today* published in 1922 stated that

> the principle of the English system is to deter by an exact though not a severe discipline, inculcating habits of obedience and order and at the same time to reform by labour, education and religious ministration.[18]

The problem, as always and particularly with the recidivist, the professional criminal, was that he usually possessed no work ethic, had given up on education a long time before and religion merely offered little more than the opportunity of helping himself from the church plate or the lead from the roof.

The prisons that Hobhouse and Brockway describe had cells for single inmates (their original purpose) measuring an average of 11½ feet by 7 and 9 feet high. Windows were usually 18 inches by 4 and only some panes could be opened. There were bars on the outside and cell temperatures in the winter were only 50 degrees Fahrenheit at best. Floors were cold stone. As Brockway and Hobhouse learned from the ex-prisoners and prison officials they interviewed: 'the only reform to which the buildings can be usefully subjected is dynamite'.[19]

An inmate sentenced for any crime in the forties would have arrived at a prison little different from this. He would be made to strip and bath in a regulation 9 inches of warm water and given a shapeless, collarless tunic that fitted him nowhere. He was given a Bible, a Prayer Book, a brush and comb and a towel. In his cell, he found a wooden table, a stool and a bed, made of planks and measuring 6 feet long by 30 inches. Privileges such as books or more letters from the outside had to be earned by good behaviour. Visits took place once a month, lasted for half an hour, and no physical contact was allowed. The prisoner rose to a bell at 6.30 a.m., slopped out his cell (the toilet was still, in the more basic prisons, a bucket) and carried out menial tasks for the war effort. His breakfast, at 7.30 a.m., was porridge (hence the slang for a prison stretch) and bread. In the twenties there was still a daily religious service at 9 a.m. and there was to be no talking throughout this ceremony, on the way there or on the way back. There was limited exercise, usually walking in the prison yard, a meal at midday and a forty-minute break, followed by more menial work and a last meal, of cocoa, bread and pickle at 4.15 p.m. The cell doors were then locked and lights went out at nine.

By 1934, a prisoner's diet was to include 1lb of bread a day and water if he was in the punishment cells, but in other respects, the recommendations of Hobhouse and Brockway had some effect. Some prisons allowed restricted smoking; others let their inmates make tea. The shaving of heads and the broad government arrow clothing beloved of cartoonists had gone by the early thirties. But in September 1943, prison reformer Mrs R Lonsdale visited Holloway and found that the inmates had no nail brushes, hair brushes or combs, a towel had to last nearly four weeks and there was no change of pillow slip. There was only one pen and a bottle of diluted ink for each landing.[20]

Prison populations fluctuated enormously. As Home Secretary before the Great War, on a wave of liberal reform, Winston Churchill introduced fines and a probation service that reduced the numbers going into the cells. For the first full year of the war (1940–41) there were 9,377 people in prison in England and Wales (easily the lowest in the entire century) and ten years later, a staggering 20,474, higher than any previous number. The difficulty in wartime was twofold. First, the prison authorities were stretched, as were the police, and for the same reason: some officers volunteered for the Armed Forces. Second, prisoners-of-war arriving in the country had – by the terms of the Geneva Convention – to be housed somewhere. Special barracks were built in some places, like 'The Farm' near Bridgend in South Wales, where *Feldmarschal* von Runstedt was held, but in other cases, existing prisons had to accommodate POWs. The result was that judges and magistrates tried to avoid prison sentences where possible and professional criminals were well aware of this.

Some prisons assumed specialist roles during the war. Brixton, under Regulation 18B, held those suspected of sympathy with the enemy. Oswald Mosley was there briefly before joining his wife in Holloway, and the spy Josef Jakobi was placed in solitary confinement in Brixton before his execution.

There were plans to close Pentonville on the eve of the war, but the events of the summer of 1939 put that, like much else, on hold and the closure never happened. Wandsworth saw the arrival of the *Abwehr*-cum-MI5 agent Arthur Owens two days after the outbreak of war. He reported to the police on 4 September, offering to transmit messages by wireless to Germany. From his prison cell, he tapped out the message: 'Must meet you in Holland at once. Bring weather code. Radio, town and hotel Wales ready.' The implication that a disheartened Wales contained spies ready to work on behalf of the Third Reich seems to have been taken seriously by at least some of those who received the message in Hamburg. This was the birth of the Double-Cross system based at Latchmere House (see Chapter Two).

Holloway was emptied of its female prisoners within days of the outbreak of hostilities. Short-term prisoners were discharged and long-serving offenders transferred to Aylesbury in Buckinghamshire. The building itself was due to undergo a transformation under Sir Samuel Hoare, the great-nephew of one of the greatest of all prison reformers, Elizabeth Fry, but again, war stopped developments. This was another specialist holding pen under 18B, where potential Fifth Columnists and aliens were interned. By 1942 however, as the Fifth Column and alien threat proved illusory and the Blitz died away, the original inmates were returned. Holloway scored a first in the last year of the war when the country's first female governor, Dr Charity Taylor, was appointed.

Wormwood Scrubs underwent a total transformation ten days before war was declared. The Borstal trainees or 'star' prisoners were moved to Feltham and as we have seen already, MI5 took over part of the building, much to the ribald amusement of the local bus service. The heavy water needed for atomic research was smuggled out of collapsing France and lodged in twenty-six cans in the Scrubs before being transferred piecemeal to the custody of the librarian at Windsor Castle! In 1942, 324 prisoners were returned and the hospital wing served as a holding unit for condemned men who would be hanged at Wandsworth and Pentonville.

On the outbreak of war, the *Daily Mirror* reported the release of 1,000 short-term prisoners in Wandsworth, Pentonville and the Scrubs. In a chilling single-line paragraph, the *Mirror* wrote: 'No one sentenced for IRA outrages is to be freed',[21] which spoke volumes for the relationship between Britain and the Republic of Eire.

Outside London, various specialisms were allotted to other prisons too. Dartmoor, the grim convict prison in the West Country, accommodated in one of its sprawling wings military prisoners who were being punished by courts martial. At the end of the war it briefly became a Borstal institution before reverting to its convict role.

Outside capital punishment and prison sentences, other punishments remained. The barbaric stocks, pillory, branding and maiming of earlier centuries had long gone by the war years but, curiously, flogging remained. The public hated it, but the authorities were unhappy to let it go, especially in cases of juvenile delinquency. In one of those odd footnotes to penal history, flogging in the Army was abolished in 1877. It survived, at least in the form of the cane, in schools long into the twentieth century. When Leo Page wrote *Crime and the Community* in 1937, he found that birching and use of the cat o' nine tails was mostly used for cases of robbery with violence. Other crimes for which this punishment was meted out included indecent exposure, male soliciting, living on the earnings of a prostitute and malicious damage, arson and larceny by teenaged boys. Unlike most people who wrote on the subject, Page wanted flogging to be increased as a deterrent to would-be lawbreakers, hence its unbridled use on the young. Birching was usually delivered on bare buttocks with a thin cane, often in a police station or court building. Canes had different lengths and widths and certain types were to be used on the under-tens, over-tens and adults.

The tendency of the courts, as the war progressed, was to punish more harshly than in the early years and we have the chicken-and-egg conundrum: was crime increasing in 1944–45 and the law merely responding? Or were the courts meting out punishments that criminalized people who would earlier have been let off with a caution? There is no satisfactory answer to this.

One thing was certain. The great days of advocacy were over. Whereas the police and the forensic field were producing giants whose fame would long outlive their careers, there was no one of the stature of Edward Marshall Hall now to speak for their clients in courtrooms. But one other thing stood out: the need for law and order and the rule of law itself in a world changed forever by the circumstances of the People's War.

CHAPTER NINE

What Crime Did You Commit in the War, Daddy?

Today, as we celebrate victory, I send this personal message to you and all other boys and girls at school. For you have shared in the hardships and dangers of a total war and you have shared no less in the triumph of the Allied Nations.

I know you will always feel proud to belong to a country which was capable of such supreme effort; proud, too, of parents and elder brothers and sisters who by their courage, endurance and enterprise brought victory. May these qualities be yours as you grow up and join in the common effort to establish among the nations of the world unity and peace.

*– George VI's message to schoolchildren
8 June 1946*

In phased sequences early in May 1945, Germany surrendered to the Allied forces in Europe and the whole war effort was transferred to beating Japan. The last V2 rocket had fallen in England in March and VE Day – Victory in Europe – was announced on Tuesday the 8th. That day and the next were declared public holidays. A 23-year-old clerk in the ATS remembered London that day:

> In Piccadilly Circus, the crowds are fairly dense and also down Coventry Street. We exclaim at a neon sign in Leicester Square and at the lighted revolving dome of the Coliseum – sights forgotten in these six years.

On Sunday:

> My father came home from Liverpool and we stayed in listening to the radio . . . In the centre of the table was a dish of canned pineapple, which Mother had saved through all the long years for this day . . . Russia is the great query of the moment.[1]

Indeed it was. The government that was so paranoid about giving away secrets to the Nazis five years earlier was now equally obsessed with giving nothing away to the Communists. In June 1946, the newspapers were reporting the imminent trial of Professor Raymond Boyer on a charge of revealing information about the atom bomb to Russia. Even though the case was Canadian, it made it perfectly clear that the Cold War had already been declared.[2]

A 34-year-old teacher wrote on 10 May:

> We *could* make the future different if only we widened our interests. Why can't we act together as we do in wartime? . . . Will there be more food and clothing soon?[3]

And hostel worker Muriel Green wrote:

> I wonder if the world has learned the lesson of war this time. Will my unborn children know the horrors that my generation

has known in the same way that our parents knew before us? [. . .] The slightest thing makes me jump lately. I feel a bundle of nerves. Lots of staff are on sick leave, I suppose the war and food has got most of us down.[4]

It was not until 15 August that Britain could celebrate VJ Day, a week after the *Enola Gay* dropped its deadly atomic payload on Hiroshima. But the 'lovely day tomorrow' promised by the song-smiths of the time somehow never arrived and the world would never, after all, be free.

Casualties of war were replaced by the casualties of peace. First, Winston Churchill, whose reputation has led him to become 'the man of the Millennium', fell at the polls. 'If the soldiers don't want me,' he said, no doubt in the grip of his famous 'black dog' melancholy, 'I will go.' They didn't. And he did.

Which left the brave new world to Clement Attlee, Aneurin Bevan and the Socialists, determined not to repeat the fiasco of 1918, in which returning heroes from the trenches got nothing but nasty little council houses. The Welfare State, begun by the Liberals before the Great War, was completed on the basis of Beveridge's determination to destroy the social evils of the inter-war years. Butler's Education Act and Bevan's Health Service would put all this into practice. The political right complained at the time and have complained ever since that the nationalization and government control of these years which have led to our 'nanny' state, was the result of enforced socialism. There is of course an element of that, but Attlee's swingeing reforms could not have happened without the overbearing authoritarianism of the wartime government. The Ministries of Information and Food might be dismantled, but the bossiness of Westminster has never gone away; the 'nanny' state was a creation of the Second World War and the claustrophobic paranoia of wartime government has not disappeared either. In 2005 Tony Blair's government passed, seven years after it said it would, a Freedom of Information Act. The cheers of those who support civil liberties were strangely muted, however, because the exceptions and exemptions of the Act are huge. For example, certain files on the flight of Rudolf Hess in 1941 were made available to the public; others, in the Swiss section of the Foreign Office, were not.

The second great casualty of the post-war period was the pathologist Bernard Spilsbury. Already by September 1945 the police were failing to ignore his transgressions. He was fined £10 with £2 19s 8d costs at Odiham, Hampshire, for dangerous driving. On 17 December, Spilsbury performed his last post-mortem, dined at his club and handed his keys to the porter, saying he would not need them again. Then he went back to his laboratory and killed himself with carbon monoxide. He was seventy. Despite the glowing obituaries that appeared and the eulogies of men like Higgins, Spilsbury in a way stood for the certainty and granite resolution of the British establishment, rather in the way that Churchill did. And today, we know that both men's reputations were shaky indeed. 'Winnie' constantly bullied and overrode his generals and admirals, on the rather flimsy ground that he was briefly a soldier himself. Spilsbury, as his latest biographer makes clear, undoubtedly condemned innocent men to death.[5]

But if Churchill and Spilsbury represented what was already a different era, men suddenly and swiftly out of joint with the times, a new man emerged to hold the line steady. He was Rayner Goddard who replaced Lord Caldecote as Lord Chief Justice. Goddard was a throw-back, a defender (as was Spilsbury) of the death penalty at a time when many others had joined Mrs Van Der Elst in demanding its abolition. He insisted that women wore hats in his court and fully approved of birching. Like Churchill and Spilsbury, he was a Victorian, ignoring the views of psychiatrists and social workers whose evidence came before him. He was more tolerant of criminal lawyers, however: in March 1948 he overturned a case in which a client was not only an MP but a barrister, on the grounds that he should have been indicted on one charge of conspiracy, not three![6] In what was a highly prophetic article, Captain Raymond Blackburn, prospective Labour candidate for King's Norton, Birmingham and himself a lawyer, foresaw the dangers of a world run by lawyers: 'There is as much a vested interest in law as in trade and industry and it will need a political upheaval to change that too.'[7]

The brave new world of Attlee and Co. was actually a rather miserable one. It was the age of austerity, with rationing still in full swing, deprivation everywhere, bomb-damaged cities, a chronic housing shortage and, after the first flush of victory euphoria, the dislocation that always results in a return to peace. With his tongue firmly in his cheek, the famous homosexual civil servant Quentin Crisp lamented the departure of American soldiers: 'Oh, the horrors of peace!'

But crime was old, and if defeatism and switching on lights and criticizing the government were no longer offences, much else was. The war years had seen an increase of 69 per cent in all reported crime. The only area in which there was a decline (down 18 per cent) was fraud and false pretences, probably because wartime Britain was registered, numbered and watched as never before. The leaving behind of stamped articles at scenes of crime that had hanged men like Cummins and Hill were tangible examples of how much under Big Brother's thumb everyone was. If today we are alarmed at the crippling weight of bureaucracy, especially associated with the European Union, we only have to look at the 1940s to see how it all began. And that at a time when we were desperate to stay out of Europe.

Elsewhere, crime was rampant. Larceny, always the largest offence in war as peacetime, had risen by 62 per cent. As we have seen the war provided opportunities aplenty for theft, from pilfering in the workplace to looting after air raids. Breaking and entering had gone up by a staggering 120 per cent, made all the easier because of the half-demolished premises of the two Blitz periods. Sexual offences had risen by 70 per cent and violent crime by 74 per cent. Crime causation is a complex subject. The political right has always attributed it to the flaws in human nature; the political left to society's injustices. There is no doubt that the war had taught society that life was cheap and the arrival of the Americans with their relaxed views to authority had had the tendency to erode moral attitudes, especially among the young.

The plain fact was that there was no return to pre-war patterns of behaviour. Nothing would be the same again. Such was the enormity of Nazi aggression everywhere in Europe that standards of decency took a serious blow, from which they have never recovered. Most glaringly, the leading Nazis put on trial at

[187]

Nuremberg were not accorded the theoretical fairness of British justice.[8] No one cared because these men's war crimes were so appalling that the consensus was they should be allowed no defence. In his closing remarks at the end of the Craig and Bentley trial for the murder of a policeman in November 1952, Lord Goddard's nod in the direction of Derek Bentley's defence ran to a mere two lines out of a total summation running to five pages. In the process of the trial, he had interrupted 104 times, in all but two instances to bolster up the case for the prosecution. The last thing the jury saw before they left the court to make their decision was the Lord Chief Justice of England and Wales brandishing a knuckleduster – 'Did you ever see such a horrible weapon?' – which had no bearing on the case whatever.

It was juvenile crime that worried the authorities most. The Craig and Bentley case, billed as the 'trial of the century' and dogged by a huge press coverage not available in wartime, highlighted what was seen as a growing crime wave. Even though statistics showed that violent crime was actually *falling* by 1952, the public refused to believe it. The age of the 'cosh boy' had arrived – vicious young thugs like Christopher Craig swaggered around in ludicrous trench coats imitating their silver screen heroes James Cagney and Humphrey Bogart. Craig, at 16, owned seven guns, one of which he used to kill PC Sidney Miles on a Croydon rooftop in the course of a failed robbery. Thousands of guns, many of them brought back as souvenirs by returning servicemen, were delivered up in an amnesty in 1947; clearly Craig's were not among them. Within months of the hanging of Derek Bentley, the first 'Teddy Boy' killing took place in South London and this, in turn, would evolve into the running battles between Mods and Rockers in the early sixties. We cannot attribute all the nation's juvenile criminality to the war years, but the 'Teds' of the fifties were the littlest gang members of the war years left to roam at will without school influences or parental control. The child psychiatrist Frederic Wertham was convinced that American children were being seduced into violence, especially against women, by the suggestive and pernicious comic literature they read (Christopher Craig was said to be addicted to these) and if our young generations are more influenced by mind-numbing video games and the overt violence of the 'video nasty', it does not detract from the impact of comics at the time.

Among other attitudes that had a bearing on post-war crime was the apathy and indifference of adults. 'War-weariness' should have ended in 1945, but today we realize that such emotional pressure can last for years – in some cases for the rest of people's lives. There were at least 18,000 deserters from the Armed Forces in the summer of 1945 and a further 50,000 who had faced courts martial or were held on various charges, from murder to insubordination and Black Marketeering. Although it would be totally wrong to ascribe criminal tendencies to all these men, what they did have in common was a contempt for authority and the rule of law. This they happily passed on to their descendants. 'Make do and mend' became 'Bugger you, Jack – I'm all right' as the much-remembered camaraderie of wartime, always nebulous, disappeared in so much smoke.

And, perhaps with hindsight, the 1950s seem the age of classic murder. John Christie, his sadistic appetite whetted during the war, continued his collection of corpses with a series of murders at 10 Rillington Place. He swore away the life of his lodger Timothy Evans for the murders of Evans' wife and baby before Christie's other victims were found concealed in cupboards, his wife under the floorboards and the wartime victims in the back garden. John George Haigh continued his murderous spree by dissolving Olivia Durand-Deacon in a drum of acid in his workshop. In a last gasp attempt to claim insanity and avoid Mr Pierrepoint, he sensationally claimed that he had drunk his victims' blood in a vampiristic orgy. It didn't work. The executioner used a special calf-leather strap on certain of his 'subjects'. It was a personal quirk of his and he noted its use in red ink in his diary. Pierrepoint does not specify the significance of this, but it seems to be linked to the 'worst' offenders. In the months ahead, people would queue up to shake Pierrepoint's hand and thank him for a job well done.

The new killer on the block in the summer of 1946 was Neville George Clevelly Heath, a Borstal boy with three wartime courts martial against his name. Posing as a group captain in the RAF, Heath tortured and killed Margery Gardener in the Pembridge Hotel, Notting Hill. She had been lashed with a whip, her vagina lacerated and her nipples all but chewed off. Three weeks later, Heath committed similar atrocities on Doreen Marshall, leaving her mutilated body in a bush-covered chine at Bournemouth. The jury decided that Heath was a pervert and sadist, but he was not insane and he asked for a double scotch before taking a short walk with Pierrepoint at Pentonville on 16 October.

When the executioner wrote his autobiography in 1974, he outraged the hanging-and-flogging brigade by saying:

> The fruit of my experience has this bitter aftertaste; that I do not believe that any one of the hundreds of executions I carried out has in any way acted as a deterrent against future murder. Capital punishment, in my view, achieved nothing except revenge.[9]

If it is not actually possible to ascribe the behaviour of Christie, Haigh and Heath to the pressures of wartime, the lingering existence of the Black Market certainly had an ongoing effect. The years 1946–48 saw an even greater rise in this sort of crime than in the war years. Receiving had increased by 195 per cent (the biggest increase of all crime) between 1938 and 1945 and the pattern continued. What probably contributed to it was the fact that rationing could no longer be placed at the door of wartime restrictions. Now it was the 'dollar gap' and the crippling debt that the country faced at the very time it was trying to rebuild. As long as rationing remained – it was Churchill's 1951 government that finally removed it, along with identity cards – so the Spiv and the Black Market enjoyed an Indian Summer.

The jury is still out on whether we live in a more dangerous age today than at various times in the past. Government statistics do not tell the story, for anyone who is the victim of crime will not see things in a balanced, rational way. That there has been a decline in the legitimacy of authority since 1945 cannot seriously be denied. A whole raft of Criminal Justice Acts and Human Rights Acts since 1948 have created greater rights for the criminal at the expense of his victim. At the same time, it cannot be denied that it was not until the fifties that society took seriously the high-handed and often illegal treatment routinely doled out to suspects by the police during questioning. When a 6 foot 2, 17-stone detective like Ted Greeno wrote in his memoirs of a suspect – 'he soon cracked' – people from the liberal, chattering classes began to ask exactly what that meant. In a tiny five-line article in the *Scottish Daily Express*, as Germany collapsed in chaotic defeat, the newspaper reported that Herbert Morrison denied in the Commons that a special department had been set up at Scotland Yard to keep watch on police officers suspected of offences.

By contrast, in the world of fiction, both Robert Fabian and Jack Henry became 'B' feature film and television personalities, appearing, trilby-hatted, pipe-smoking and lantern-jawed, as old-fashioned bastions of honesty, beacons in a lawless world. Towering over them all, Jack Warner starred in a long-running series *Dixon of Dock Green*, his character taken from a London copper shot by murderous 'cosh-boy' Dirk Bogarde in *The Blue Lamp* in 1950.

Today, traditionalists lament the fact that the schools no longer exert the control and discipline they did; the Church's influence has gone. Sloppy border control has allowed the world's criminals into the country fuelled by drugs and anti-social attitudes; we stare a terrifying new crime wave in the face.

Historians think differently. If we could transport ourselves back to the nineteenth century we would be appalled by the squalor, the grinding poverty and the lawlessness of the period. What is actually an aberration no one has fully explained, is the relative law-abiding character of the inter-war period despite the slight trend towards juvenile delinquency. I have no doubt that aberration, whatever its causes, came to a sudden end as a result of the Second World War. For the briefest of times, dinosaurs like Lord Goddard tried to hold back the tide, but it couldn't work for ever. In June 1940, a defendant referred to as 'Algernon' apologized in court for an altercation he had outside a tube station. He used an offensive word, which he described as, 'a Bernard Shaw expression'. When Mr Broderick, the magistrate, asked what the expression was

Algernon timidly uttered Eliza Doolittle's adjective, the substantive being 'swine'. 'Yes, I've heard that,' said Mr

Broderick, unmoved. He hears much worse language in the course of a week.[10]

It would no doubt be worse still after the war!

If we look at the flavour of crime today, we find it all already there in the forties. Edward Greeno spoke of the scourge of prostitution in London's West End, of the drug dealing among the tiny Chinese and West Indian populations and of the organized mayhem of the protection rackets. Although never a serious problem in this country, the Hell's Angels chapters wrought havoc in various American states with motorcyclists terrorizing townsfolk and each other. Their origins lie in the demobilized pilots of the American Air Force, whose thrill-filled lives were suddenly, oddly, empty. Their skull insignia and flaming ball motif is a direct legacy of the 85th Fighter Squadron and the 552nd Bomber Squadron, both based in Britain.

Those who point to the 1960s as the cause of all our criminal woes, with its accent on anarchy, drugs, sex, and rock 'n' roll – with just a hint of flower power – ignore the stark fact that the teenagers of that decade were born to the children of the war, the most delinquent generation ever recorded in Britain.

Nazi Germany was responsible for more than the thousands of deaths of British servicemen and women and their civilian counterparts, for the destruction of millions of pounds worth of property. It was also responsible for a change in the nation's criminality, when, for all the guts and determination of the war years, and all the hope and optimism that followed, the darker side of men's lives not only survived but was nurtured in a set of circumstances that is totally unique in British History.

'What crime did you commit in the war daddy?' was probably not a question on many children's lips in the post-war period. But it was a rare man indeed who could answer – none at all. Most would admit to one or two. And some would answer: 'Every one in the book.'

Notes

Chapter One

1. Technically, this was the world's *second* taste. The phrase had been coined by the military theorist von Clausewitz to explain the dazzling speed of Napoleon Bonaparte's tactics in the early nineteenth century.
2. Unnamed reporter, quoted in *Chronicle of the 20th Century*, Longman, London 1988.
3. Hansard, 26.9.1939.
4. Quoted in Briggs, p. 88.
5. *Under My Helmet*, the ARP and AFS Magazine, 1940.
6. *Daily Mail*, 8 December 1941.
7. Quoted in Briggs, p. 107.
8. *Picture Post*, 1939.
9. Quoted in Briggs, p. 51.
10. Norman Shelley.
11. US Forces Literature, 1942.
12. Such was the stranglehold of the government at the time that an old man who was an ARP warden in Ryde, Isle of Wight, on lending me one of his leaflets, was concerned in case he might get into trouble. That was in 2005.
13. *New Statesman*, September 1940.
14. Molly Lefebure, *War on the Home Front*, p. 103.
15. US Forces Literature, 1942.
16. Crime statistics are notoriously difficult to trust. First, not all crime is reported, so how accurate are the figures anyway? And second, governments and police forces have a habit of massaging them to make better reading.
17. Simpson, *Forty Years of Murder*, p. 34.

18. *Evening Standard*, 4 November 1940.
19. *Reynolds' News*, January 1940.

Chapter Two

1. The *Luton News*, 27 June 1940.
2. Quoted in Iain Anderson *The Great Detective*, p. 127.
3. Speech made by Tavistock at Kingsley Hall, London, 3 April 1940.
4. Quoted in the *Hackney Gazette*, September 1939.
5. Quoted in *Chronicle of the 20th Century*, Longman, London.
6. As a result of the Evian Conference, for example, in June 1939, Britain agreed to take in an additional 40,000 Jews. The United States, whose President, F D Roosevelt, had called the Conference, took none.
7. Not the privation it would be today. Maps and road signs became a thing of the past anyway, to obstruct the invader as much as possible, should he come. Most people could not afford a car until long after the war.
8. Speech on Dunkirk, Hansard, May 1940.
9. *Daily Mail*, 14 June 1940.
10. *Picture Post*, April 1940.
11. The Deputy Führer's flight to Scotland is still a matter of intense debate. What is odd is that Churchill made no propaganda capital out of it. Was he protecting right-wing members of the aristocracy and even royalty? See *Hess: the British Conspiracy*, John Harris and M J Trow, Deutsch, London 1999.
12. Quoted in James Hayward, *Myths and Legends of the Second World War*, Sutton, 2006, p. 26.
13. Harold Nicholson, *Diaries and Letters 1930–64*, Collins, London 1980, quoted in Hayward 2006, p. 21.
14. Quoted in Hayward, p. 57. As I write, the Press is full of angst over some of the recently released Marine hostages captured by the Iranians, who were brazenly selling their stories. Those who bemoan the moral collapse of our Armed Forces should look to Dunkirk for a humiliating precedent.

15. *Kensington Post*, 8 November 1941.
16. Quoted in Iain Anderson, p. 127.
17. The excellent research by Goldhagen in *Hitler's Willing Executioners*, 1998, makes it plain that everyone except Jews and undesirables still had a choice in Nazi Germany.
18. *Daily Sketch*, 11 June 1940.
19. Quoted in Calder, 1992, p. 495.
20. There was one exception. Seventy-two-year-old Jane Yorke of Forest Gate, London, was tried at the Old Bailey on four charges 'of pretending to exercise or use a kind of conjuration contrary to the witchcraft act of 1735'. Reported in the *Daily Mail*, 3 August 1944.
21. *Leicester Advertiser*, 3 June 1944.
22. *Birkenhead Advertiser*, 11 August 1943.
23. *Daily Sketch*, 10 April 1940.

Chapter Three

1. Article in the *Sunday Pictorial*, 1953.
2. Ludovic Kennedy, *10 Rillington Place*, Panther Books, London 1971, p. 50.
3. Quoted in Kennedy, 1971, p. 53.
4. Quoted in Murder Casebook, Vol. 4.
5. Robert Higgins, *In The Name of the Law*, London John Lang, 1958, p. 62.
6. Cherrill of the Yard.
7. Ibid.
8. Ibid.
9. Ibid.
10. Ibid.
11. All quotations regarding Greeno are from his autobiography, *War on the Underworld*, Digit Books, London 1959.
12. Quoted in Greeno, pp. 103–4.
13. Cherrill.
14. Cherrill.
15. Greeno, p. 107.

16. Higgins, p. 62.
17. Less was known about sex crimes in the 1940s than today. For some killers, the thrill is achieved by the act of killing; actual sex is irrelevant. Hatherill and Spilsbury both noted that the girls' underwear had not been interfered with.
18. For the work of the hangmen, see Chapter Seven.
19. Greeno, p. 141.
20. Quoted in Gordon Honeycombe, *More Murders of the Black Museum*, London, Random House 1993, pp. 193–4.
21. Honeycombe, 1993, p. 195.
22. All quotations by Fabian are from *Fabian of the Yard*, Norwich, Jarrold and Sons, 1955.
23. It was almost certainly this laxity that allowed Aircraftsman Arthur Heys, engaged on remand in agricultural work, to post his infamous letter claiming his innocence (see p. 60).
24. See Chapter Two.

Chapter Four

1. *Sunday Pictorial*, 25 July 1943.
2. Between 1938 and 1944 the cost of living rose by 50 per cent. Wages rose by over 80 per cent.
3. Smithies, p. 78.
4. 'The Miners' Response', D S MacColl, 1915. From *Up the Line to Death*, ed. Brian Gardener, London, Methuen 1964.
5. *Hackney Gazette*, 18 January 1943.
6. Greeno, p. 133.
7. To the extent that, behind his back, Britain's only Jewish Prime Minister, Benjamin Disraeli, was known as 'Old Clo' from the street cries of the Jewish tailors.
8. Harrogate Magistrates' Court records, 20 February 1946.
9. The period from 1653 to 1660, when Britain was, in effect, under a military despotism spearheaded by Oliver Cromwell. The backlash of the restoration of Charles II was perhaps both inevitable and long overdue.
10. Central Criminal Court records, July 1942.

11. Quoted in A Noyes Thomas, *Calling Scotland Yard*, London 1954, pp. 139–40.
12. *Willesden Chronicle*, July 1944.
13. *Evening Standard*, 4 January 1945.
14. *ITMA*.
15. Calder, p. 407.
16. Quoted in Calder, p. 255.

Chapter Five

1. Quoted in Juliet Gardiner, *Over Here: the GIs in Wartime Britain*, London, Collins and Brown, 1992.
2. Slang for the typical American infantryman. It stands for 'Government Issue', which was stencilled and stamped all over American equipment.
3. Eric Knight, *A Short Guide to Great Britain*, Washington, War and Navy Dept., 1941.
4. Knight. A 'panty-waist' was a 'big girl's blouse' in English parlance.
5. The colour is usually described as 'pink' but that gives a false impression. 'Aurore' (the dawn's glow) was a colour adopted by some troops under Napoleon I and it comes closest to an accurate description of USAAF netherwear.
6. Supposedly a deliberate choice after the War of Independence (1775–83).
7. John Keegan, *Six Armies in Normandy*, London, 1982.
8. Keegan.
9. Lefebure, p. 101.
10. Edward Greeno, *War on the Underworld*, London, Brown, Watson Ltd., 1959.
11. Quoted in Gardiner, p. 149. The Purple Heart was Congress's highest award for death or injury in action. The menial tasks of the Second World War black soldier completely undermined the excellent fighting work of America's first black infantry unit, the 54th Massachusetts Volunteers, in the Civil War.
12. *Sunday Pictorial*, 6 September 1942.

13. Tickets allowing soldiers leave from their camps for one or two days.
14. Home Office Circular, 1942.
15. Quoted in Gardiner, p. 152.
16. Quoted in Gardiner, p. 154.
17. Quoted in Gardiner, p. 156.
18. Donald Thomas, in *An Underworld at War*, claims there were eight. The discrepancy, I believe, comes from the fact that the actual crime for which the five hangings took place was murder and rape was merely a preliminary.
19. Quoted in Gardiner, p. 119.
20. Robert Fabian, *London After Dark*.
21. Quoted in Gardiner, p. 119.
22. On the other hand, the introduction of double summertime to maximize war production, led to light late nights. As the US forces magazine, *Stars and Stripes*, put it: 'This British time/Is an awful crime./ What good is a park,/ If it ain't dark?' Quoted in Gardiner, p. 118.
23. Quoted in Gardiner, p. 122.
24. The working-class radical, Francis Place, was obsessed with prostitution and kept careful records of numbers along the Haymarket in the 1820s. They considerably outnumbered the girls seen by Sharpe.
25. In 1938 over 3,000 arrests; 1939, 1,865; 1940, 1,505. Figures quoted in Edmund Smithies, *Crime in Wartime*, London, Allen and Unwin, 1982.
26. And at least the bomber crews had a chance of coming back. Their fighter pilot counterparts among the Kamikaze units of the Japanese Air Force were allowed female companionship only on the night before their final mission.
27. She wrote her autobiography, *The Men in My Life*, in 1960.
28. Fabian, p. 21.
29. Figures quoted from various sources by Smithies, p. 145.
30. G B Shaw, letter to *The Times*, quoted in the foreword to C E Bechhofer-Roberts, *The Trial of Jones and Hulten*, London, 1945, p. 22.
31. The era of bootleggers and John Dillinger had only recently

come to an end in the States. Al Capone himself was in prison in 1944 on charges of tax evasion, the only crime the Federal government could pin on him.

32. Cavy means 'on guard'. From the Latin *cave*, beware.
33. *The Trial of Jones and Hulten*, The Old Bailey Trial Series, p. 165.
34. From testimony at the Old Bailey trial.
35. From testimony at the Old Bailey trial, p. 8.
36. From testimony at the Old Bailey trial, p. 11.
37. From testimony at the Old Bailey trial, p. 12.
38. *The Times*, 5 March 1945.
39. T-4 was named after No. 4, Tiergartenstrasse, Berlin, where the first examples of euthanasia – the removal of 'life unworthy of life' – were carried out.
40. George Orwell, quoted in *Murder Casebook No. 72*, London, Marshall Cavendish, 1991.
41. Charles Gattey, *The Incredible Mrs Van Der Elst*, London, Leslie Frewin, 1972, p. 192.

Chapter Six

1. *Sunday Pictorial*, 6 September 1942.
2. The myth remains among the Republican Left, even today, that this was merely royalist propaganda, that the King and Queen remained safely out of London throughout the war.
3. Quoted in Edward Smithies, *Crime in Wartime*, London, George Allen and Unwin, 1982, pp. 166–7.
4. *Hackney Gazette*, August 1945.
5. *Hackney Gazette*, 30 June 1944.
6. *Bath Weekly Chronicle and Herald*, 31 March 1945.
7. *Daily Mail*, 14 June 1940.
8. For centuries, children had been vital in collecting in the harvest 'ere the winter storms begin'. As a child in the 1950s, I loved 'helping in the fields' at harvest time and rounding up abandoned lambs in the spring.
9. Letter from Sackville-West to Harold Nicholson, taken from

the *Nicholson Diaries 1939–45*, London, Weidenfeld & Nicolson, p. 167.

10. Quoted in Philip Ziegler, *London at War*, London BCA, 1995, p. 148.

11. Angus Calder, *The People's War*, p. 225.

12. Ziegler, p. 139.

13. 'Pour encourager les autres' as Voltaire said in *Candide*, to explain why the British executed Admiral Byng in 1759.

14. R M Titmuss, *Problems of Social Policy*, London HMSO, 1950, p. 86.

15. Ron Kray with Fred Dineage, *My Story*, London, Sidgewick and Jackson, 1993, p. 9.

16. Kray and Dineage, 1993, p. 11.

17. Kray and Dineage, 1993, p. 11.

18. *Crime in Wartime*, London, George Allen and Unwin, 1982.

19. Anyone wearing a hood in the 1940s would have been laughed to scorn.

20. Quoted in Smithies, p. 182.

21. Mrs Paratoud, quoted in Felicity Goodall, *Voices from the Home Front*, David and Charles, 2006, p. 123.

22. Quoted in Smithies, p. 183.

23. Quoted in Smithies, p. 184.

24. Robert Fabian, *London After Dark*, p. 20.

25. The slang term for the blue police tender, which patrolled the major London parks each night to round up underage girls.

26. Fabian, p. 23.

27. Fabian, p. 21.

28. Henry, p. 74.

29. Henry, p. 76.

Chapter Seven

1. Quoted in H M Howgrove-Graham, *The Metropolitan Police at War*, London, 1947.

2. Chartism (1836–50) was a socio-political pressure group bent on key constitutional reforms. In the north, in particular, the

Chartists posed a potentially violent threat. But at their last major rally, in 1848, there were more policemen in attendance than Chartists! The navvies, largely Irishmen, Scots and Welsh, were notorious for their brawling and drunken behaviour wherever lines were being built.

3. Robert Fabian, *Fabian of the Yard*, p. 11.
4. Today's politically correct lobby would have apoplexy at the idea of child acrobats, sword-swallowers and fire-eaters.
5. C C H Moriarty, *Police Law Part II Chap XII*, p. 102.
6. T A Critchley, *A History of the Police in England and Wales 1900–1966*, Constable, London, 1967, p. 231.
7. Never an official title. The original 'Big Four' (a journalist's phrase) were: Fred Wensley, Arthur Hawkins, Arthur Neil and Francis Carlin, who, in 1921, were given command of a quarter of the Met area each as their 'patch'.
8. Jacket blurb, *War on the Underworld*, Edward Greeno, Digit Books, London, 1959.
9. Molly Lefebure, *Murder on the Home Front*, p. 54.
10. Greeno, p. 13.
11. Greeno, p. 13.
12. Greeno, p. 15.
13. The one with which I cannot agree is the guilt of the Canadian soldier, August Sangret, for the murder of Joan Wolfe in 1943. The case was a triumph of forensic deduction and an example of the sheer doggedness of the police, but Sangret was hanged on circumstantial evidence and I doubt Greeno's assertion that the Canadian Meti (half Cree Indian) confessed on the night before his execution.
14. Greeno, p. 107.
15. Greeno, working from memory seventeen years later calls him Edward.
16. Greeno, p. 111.
17. Greeno, p. 126.
18. Greeno, p. 129.
19. Greeno, p. 148.
20. Greeno, p. 149.
21. Greeno, p. 152.

22. See Chapter Four.

23. George Hatherill, *A Detective's Story*, Deutsch, London, 1971.

24. Hatherill, p. 35.

25. Robert Higgins, *In the Name of the Law*, p. 71.

26. Higgins, p. 72.

27. Higgins, p. 74.

28. Jack Henry, *What Price Crime?*, London, Hutchinson, 1945, p. 8.

29. Henry, p. 11.

30. Du Rose, *Murder Was My Business*, London, W H Allen, 1971, p. 15.

31. Du Rose, p. 16.

32. Du Rose, p. 22.

33. Ian Adamson, *The Great Detective*, London, Frederick Muller, 1966.

34. Adamson, p. 37.

35. Adamson, p. 47.

36. Quoted in Adamson, p. 123.

37. Adamson, p. 202.

38. Higgins, *In the Name of the Law*, p. 201.

39. Boone and Tullett, *Bernard Spilsbury, His Life and Cases*, London, Harrap, 1951, p. 390.

40. Keith Simpson, *Forty Years of Murder*, St Albans, Granada, 1978.

41. That of the Stratton brothers for armed robbery in 1905. Both men were hanged.

42. Since paregoric is a compound of morphine, benzoic acid and camphor, it was actually *far* more lethal (and habit-forming) than Martini, however dry!

43. Simpson, p. 55.

44. Simpson, p. 61.

45. Simpson, *Forty Years of Murder*, p. 104.

46. Simpson, p. 50.

47. Molly Lefebure, *Murder on the Home Front*, London, Grafton, 1990 [first published as *Evidence for the Crown*, London, Heinemann, 1954], p. 9.

48. Lefebure, 1954, p. 17.

49. Lefebure, p. 124.

50. This, I suspect, was added for the 1990 rewrite. Very few tele-visions were available in 1954 and not even Dixon of Dock Green had started then!

51. Lefebure, p. 155.

52. Quoted in Lefebure, p. 181.

53. Lefebure, p. 183.

54. Lefebure, p. 210.

55. Lefebure, p. 238.

56. Lefebure, pp. 244–5.

57. Lefebure, p. 245.

58. Lefebure, p. 247.

59. Lefebure, p. 251.

60. Lefebure, pp. 253–4.

61. Lefebure, p. 254.

62. Report of H M Inspector of Constabulary 1940–45, quoted in T A Critchley, p. 236.

63. Quoted in Critchley, p. 236.

Chapter Eight

1. Charles Dickens, *Oliver Twist*, 1838–9.

2. George Orwell, quoted in Philip Zeigler, *London at War*, London BCA, 1995.

3. It was partly this attitude that led to Winston Churchill's surprise electoral defeat in 1945.

4. F T Giles, *The Criminal Law*, London, Penguin, 1954 (1961 edition).

5. That of Regina v. Craig and Bentley – see Chapter Nine.

6. Jack Henry, p. 15.

7. In a story currently in the Press (2007) a case was thrown out after it was discovered that a juror was absent-mindedly doodling on a pad of paper when he should have been listening intently to evidence.

8. All quotations are from *Rex v Dobkin; The Old Bailey Trial Series*, ed. C E Beechofer Roberts, 1944.

9. When Charles Dickens attended the hanging of the Mannings in 1849, he was appalled, not by the hanging itself, but by the bestiality of the crowd that looked on.
10. Pierrepoint, p. 121.
11. The white cap pulled over the head, the rope placed around the neck, the safety pin removed, the lever pushed in, the thud as the trapdoors crash back and the body tumbles into space. This was the business of judicial execution as described by Albert Pierrepoint in *Executioner: Pierrepoint*, Harrap, London, 1974.
12. Pierrepoint, p. 125.
13. Pierrepoint, p. 129.
14. *News Chronicle*, 28 May 1941.
15. Mr Justice Charles, Lewes Assize 5 March 1941, quoted in Thomas, pp. 76–7.
16. This was a very old scam. John Churchill, the Duke of Marlborough, was put on trial for falsifying troop numbers. He was claiming pay for men who did not exist.
17. Henry, p. 75.
18. Quoted in Peter Hitchens, *A Brief History of Crime*, London, Atlantic Books, 2003, pp. 126–7.
19. Quoted in Hitchens, 2003, p. 128.
20. *Sunday Express*, 3 September 1943.
21. *Daily Mirror*, 4 September 1939.

Chapter Nine

1. Quoted in *Wartime Women*, pp. 230–4.
2. *Sunday Despatch*, 9 June 1946.
3. Quoted in *Wartime Women*, p. 243.
4. Quoted in *Wartime Women*, pp. 245–6.
5. Andrew Rose, *Lethal Witness*, Stroud, Sutton, 2007.
6. Detractors of men like Spilsbury and Goddard always go too far. There was a rumour that so isolated and depressed had the pathologist become by 1946 that he attempted sex with a corpse in his laboratory. And Goddard was said to have a spare

pair of trousers in capital trials in case he ejaculated with the sadistic excitement of passing the death sentence.

7. *Sunday Pictorial*, 11 March 1945.

8. It is generally held that had the conventional rules of evidence been used, Adolf Hitler could not have been found guilty of crimes against humanity – there is no paper trail of evidence.

9. Pierrepoint, 1974, p. 10.

10. *Evening Standard*, 17 June 1940.

Bibliography

ADAMSON, Iain, *The Great Detective*, London, Frederick Muller, 1966

ARMY AND NAVY STORES LTD, *Price List*, London, Trident Press, 1999

BAILEY, Brian, *Hangmen of England*, London, W H Allen, 1989

BECHHOFER-ROBERTS, C E (ed), *The Trial of Harry Dobkin*, London, Jarrolds, 1944

BECHHOFER-ROBERTS, C E (ed), *The Trial of Jones and Hulten*, London, Jarrolds, 1945

BEGG, Paul & SKINNER, Keith, *The Scotland Yard Files*, London, Hodder Headline, 1992

BENNETT, Alan, *Forty Years On* London, Faber and Faber, 1969

BRIGGS, Susan, *Keep Smiling Through*, London, Weidenfeld & Nicholson, 1975

BROWNE & TUCKETT, *Bernard Spilsbury: His Life and Cases*, London, George Harrap, 1951

BROWNE Douglas G & BROCK Alan, *Fingerprints*, London, George Harrap, 1953

BYRNE, Richard, *Prisons and Punishments of London*, London, Grafton, 1992

CALDER, Angus, *The People's War* London, Pimlico, (reprint) 2000

CAMERON, James, *Memory Lane 1930–53* London, J M Dent, 1980

COLEY, Joyce, *Bella: an Unsolved Murder*, Studley, H I P, 2007

CRITCHLEY, McDonald (ed), *The Trial of August Sangret*, London, William Hodge, 1959

CRITCHLEY, McDonald (ed), *Trial of Neville Heath*, London, William Hodge, 1951

CRITCHLEY T A, *A History of the Police*, London, Constable, 1967

DARBYSHIRE, Neil & HILLYARD, Brian, *The Flying Squad*, London, Headline, 1993

Du ROSE, John, *Murder Was My Business*, St Albans, Mayflower, 1973

EDDLETON, John J, *The Encyclopaedia of Executions*, London, John Blake, 2002

FABIAN, Robert, *Fabian of the Yard*, Norwich, Heirloom, 1955

FABIAN, Robert, *London After Dark*, London, Naldrett Press, 1954

FIDO, Martin, *Murder Guide to London*, London, Grafton, 1987

FIDO, Martin & SKINNER, Keith, *The Official Encyclopaedia of Scotland Yard*, London, Virgin, 1999

GARDINER, Juliet, *Over Here: The GIs in Wartime Britain*, London, Collis & Brown, 1992

GATTEY Charles, *The Incredible Mrs Van Der Elst*, London, Frewin, 1972

GILES F T, *The Criminal Law*, London, Pelican, 1961

GOODALL, Felicity, *Voices from the Home Front*, Cincinnati, OH, David & Charles, 2006

GREENO, Edward, *War on the Underworld* London, Brown, Watson, 1959

HATHERILL, George, *A Detective's Story*, London, Andre Deutsch, 1971

HAYWARD, James, *Myths and Legends of the Second World War*, Stroud, Sutton, 2003

HENRY Jack, *What Price Crime?*, London, Hutchinson, 1945

HIGGINS, Robert, *In the Name of the Law*, London, John Long, 1958

HITCHENS, Peter, *A Brief History of Crime* London, Atlantic, 2003

KENNEDY, Ludovic, *10 Rillington Place*, London, Granada, 1971

KRAY, Ron (with DINEAGE, Fred), *My Story*, London, Sidgwick & Jackson, 1993

LEFEBURE, Molly, *Murder on the Home Front*, London, Grafton, 1990

LINNANE, Fergus, *London's Underworld*, London, Robson, 2004

Marshall Cavendish Murder Casebook Series 1990–91: 'Blackout Killers'; 'Ritual Killings'; 'Three Crimes of Sadism'; 'The Acid Bath Murders', 'The Rillington Place Murders'; 'Deadly Delusions'

McCORMICK, Donald, *Murder by Witchcraft*, London, John Long, 1968

MORIARTY, C C H, *Police Law*, London, Butterworth & Co., 1939

MORRIS, Terence, *Crime and Criminal Justice Since 1945*, London, Bluebell, 1989

OHMS, *Front Line 1940–41*, London, 1942

PIERREPOINT, Albert, *Executioner: Pierrepoint*, London, Hodder and Stoughton, 1974

PONTING, Clive, *1940: Myth and Reality*, London, Hamish Hamilton, 1990

SCOTT, Harold, *Scotland Yard* London, Andre Deutsch, 1954

SHERIDAN, Dorothy (ed), *Wartime Women*, London, Phoenix Press, 2000

SIMPSON, Keith, *Forty Years of Murder* London, Granada, 1982

SMITHIES, Edward, *Crime in Wartime*, London, George Allen & Unwin, 1982

THOMAS, Donald, *An Underworld at War*, London, John Murray, 2003

TROW, M J, *The Wigwam Murder*, London, Constable, 1994

TULLETT, Tom, *Murder Squad*, London, Grafton, 1985

WERTHAM, Fredric, *Seduction of the Innocent*, London, Museum Press, 1955

WILSON, Colin, *The Mammoth Book of Murders*, London, Constable, 2000

ZIEGLER, Philip, *London at War*, London BCA, 1995

Index